Doing Research in Special Education

Doing Research in Special Education

Ideas into practice

Edited by
Richard Rose
and Ian Grosvenor

David Fulton Publishers
London

David Fulton Publishers Ltd
Ormond House, 26–27 Boswell Street, London WC1N 3JZ

www.fultonpublishers.co.uk

First published in Great Britain by David Fulton Publishers 2001

Note: The rights of Richard Rose and Ian Grosvenor to be identified as the editors of this work has been asserted by them in accordance with the Copyright, Designs and Patents Act 1988.

British Library Cataloguing in Publication Data
A catalogue record for this book is available from the British Library

ISBN 1–85346–735–9

The publishers would like to thank John Cox for copy-editing and Sophie Cox for proofreading this book.

Typeset by Elite Typesetting Techniques, Eastleigh, Hampshire
Printed in Great Britain by The Cromwell Press Ltd, Trowbridge, Wilts.

Contents

Acknowledgements

The editors are indebted to the many students and colleagues who have engaged in discussion and whose ideas, interests and enthusiasm have informed and inspired the production of this book. In particular, students on the MA in Professional Studies in Education at University College Northampton, and the many teachers who work in close partnership with the Centre for Special Needs Education and Research (CeSNER) at that institution, have been a regular source of support for which we are most grateful.

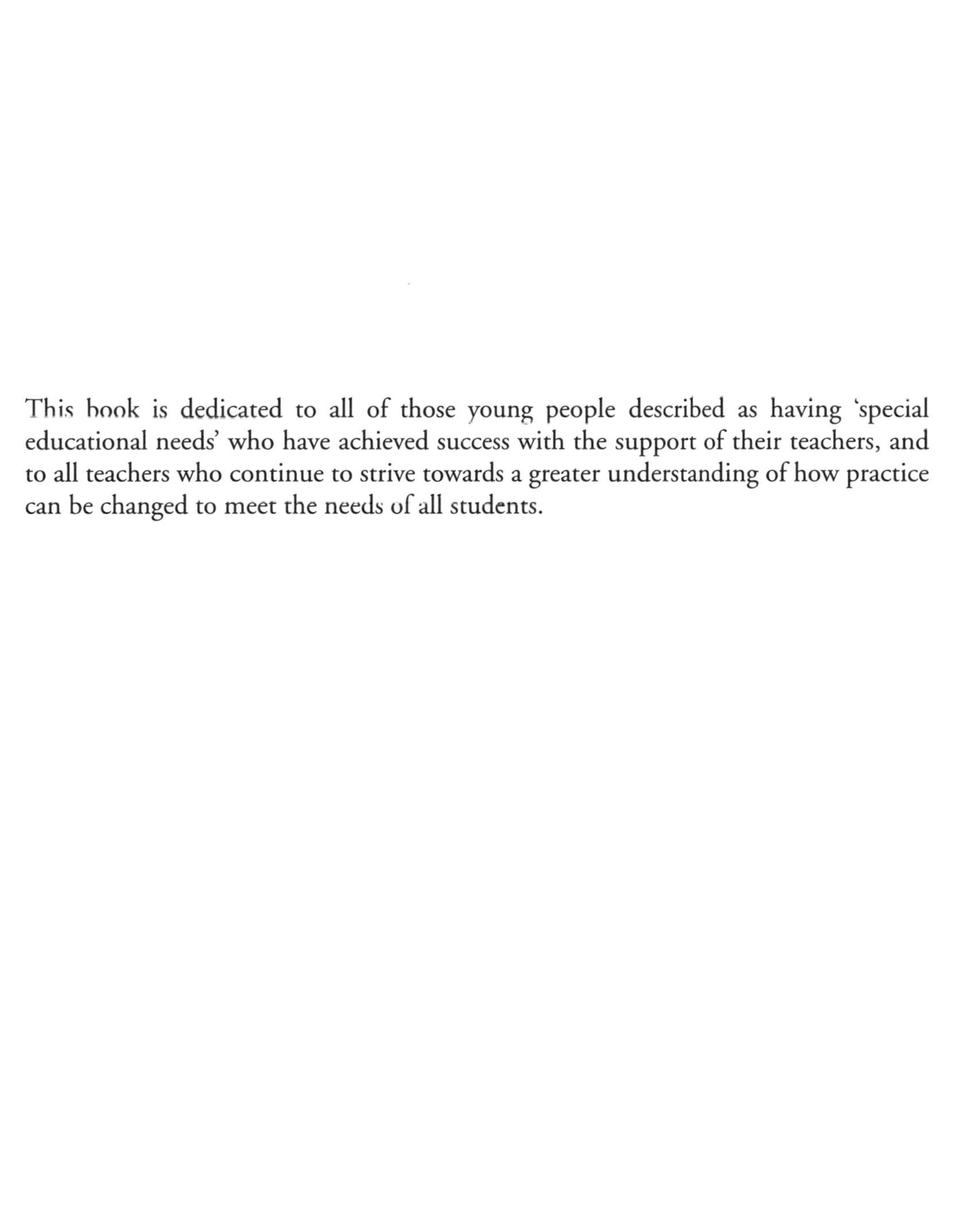

This book is dedicated to all of those young people described as having 'special educational needs' who have achieved success with the support of their teachers, and to all teachers who continue to strive towards a greater understanding of how practice can be changed to meet the needs of all students.

Contributors

Trudy Duffield is Deputy Head Teacher at St George's School, Peterborough. She has experience of working in special schools and as an LEA information technology advisor. Trudy has several years' experience of supporting families with children with special educational needs through a home education service.

Ann Fergusson is Lecturer in Special Education at the Centre for Special Needs Education and Research at University College Northampton. She has previously held posts as Deputy Head Teacher and as teacher in a number of special schools. Ann has contributed to numerous books and journals and was joint author of *Implementing the Whole Curriculum for Pupils with Learning Difficulties* published by David Fulton.

Will Fletcher is Deputy Head Teacher at Watling View School in St Albans. He has taught in several special schools in Hertfordshire, and was a member of the National Curriculum Development Team (severe learning difficulties) based at the University of Cambridge Institute of Education. Will has a particular interest in the development of personal and social skills in pupils with special needs.

Lani Florian teaches at Cambridge University Department of Education. She has a wide range of teaching experience in schools and higher education and has published widely. Lani was Legislative Assistant to the US Senate Subcommittee on the Handicapped during the 9th Congress and had responsibility for the development of Public Law 99-457. She is editor of the *Journal of Research in Special Educational Needs* and was joint editor of *Promoting Inclusive Practice*, which won the TES/NASEN Academic Book Award in 1999.

Pat Gilbert is Head Teacher of a primary school for pupils with learning difficulties, including provision for pupils with autistic spectrum disorders. She has taught in a range of special needs provision, and has a strong commitment to working in partnership with parents at all levels of education.

Ian Grosvenor is Senior Lecturer in the School of Education, University of Birmingham, having previously been Research Coordinator in the School of Education at University College Northampton. He has taught in primary, secondary and special schools, worked on Local Education Authority anti-racist initiatives, and worked in equal opportunities programmes. His current research interests are in the areas of new methodologies in the history of education and the cultural history of schooling.

Marie Howley is Senior Lecturer in Special Education at the Centre for Special Needs Education and Research, University College Northampton. She has previously taught in a number of schools and was teacher in charge of autism provision in a Northamptonshire special school. She is currently working on several research projects with a focus upon children with autistic spectrum disorders and is co-writing a book on the National Curriculum and Autistic Pupils with Garry Mesibov from the University of North Carolina.

Phyllis Jones is Senior Lecturer in Special Educational Needs at the School of Education, University of Northumbria in Newcastle. She has held a number of teaching and management posts in schools for pupils with learning difficulties. Phyllis has a commitment to collaborative research with teacher colleagues and parents and her recent published work has included a study of perspectives of annual review procedures.

Richard Rose is Head of the Centre for Special Needs Education and Research at University College Northampton, having previously been Inspector for Special and Primary Education, Head teacher of a special school, and held teaching posts in several parts of England. He has published several books on aspects of special education and contributed papers to a number of journals. His current research interests are in the areas of inclusive education and pupil involvement in the management of their own learning processes.

Martyn Rouse teaches in the Department of Education at Cambridge University. He has a wide range of teaching experience in schools and in higher education and has conducted research into many aspects of special education, including assessment and inclusion. Martyn's work has been published widely and he was joint editor with Margaret McLaughlin from the University of Maryland of *Special Education and School Reform in the United States and Britain.*

Christina Tilstone is Senior Lecturer in Special Education and programme of study tutor for the distance education course for teachers of pupils with learning difficulties (severe and moderate) at The University of Birmingham. She has taught pupils with severe learning difficulties in a number of settings and has worked in teacher education both in the UK and abroad. For several years Tina was editor of the *British Journal of Special Education.* She has published extensively, including her books *Observing Teaching and Learning,* and *Promoting Inclusive Practice.*

Liz Waine is Senior Lecturer in Special Education at the Centre for Special Needs Education and Research at University College Northampton. She has been a Local Education Authority Advisor and has taught in primary schools in Northamptonshire and London. Liz is currently conducting research into the management of pupils with dyslexia in mainstream primary schools, and into the student teachers who are diagnosed as dyslexic.

CHAPTER 1

Educational research – influence or irrelevance?

Ian Grosvenor and Richard Rose

Educational research, like all research, is fundamentally concerned with making a contribution to knowledge. This imperative informed Lawrence Stenhouse's definition of research as any 'systematic, critical and self-critical enquiry which aims to contribute to the advancement of knowledge' (Stenhouse 1975:156). However, in recent years educational researchers in the UK have been severely criticised for failing to fulfil this duty. In 1996 David Hargreaves, formerly Professor of Education at Cambridge University and currently Chief Executive of the Qualifications and Curriculum Authority, argued in his Teacher Training Agency (TTA) Annual Lecture that 'educational research is not in a healthy state' and there was too much:

> second-rate educational research which does not make a serious contribution to fundamental theory or knowledge; which is irrelevant to practice; which is uncoordinated with any preceding or follow-up research; and which clutters up academic journals that virtually nobody reads. (Hargreaves 1996a)

In particular, he singled out the 'gap between researchers and practitioners' as a 'fatal flaw in educational research'. Hargreaves' critique provoked quite heated debate in the press and academic journals (Bassey 1996, Budge 1996, Hargreaves 1996b, Gray *et al.* 1997). In 1997 the TTA issued its own fourfold criticism of current educational research:

1. Too few research projects focus on classroom teaching ... ;
2. Too much research stops short of working out the meaning of research findings for day to day practice;
3. Traditional research vehicles for reporting findings are not geared sufficiently to the needs of practitioners – findings of research tend to be disseminated to other researchers rather than to classroom teachers and when new findings are disseminated, they are not disseminated in a way that encourages teachers to consider the implications for their own practice; and

4. Too few research projects are used to inform the policy making process – research is not sufficiently focused on areas where action can be taken and findings are not made available to policy makers in an accessible way. (*Teaching Matters*, Autumn 1997:14)

The following year, the then Chief Inspector of Schools, Chris Woodhead, entered the debate and caustically asserted:

> Life is too short. There is too much to do in the real world with real teachers in real schools to worry about methodological quarrels or to waste time decoding unintelligible prose to reach (if one is lucky) a conclusion often so transparently partisan as to be worthless. (Woodhead 1998)

OFSTED also commissioned James Tooley and Doug Darby to subject educational research published in journals to scrutiny in the context of Hargreaves' earlier criticisms. Their report concluded that there was sufficient evidence to vindicate Hargreaves' critique: the majority of articles were not concerned with raising standards or improving classroom practice, employed 'sloppy methodology' and were partisan (Tooley and Darby 1998:79). In 1998 Hargreaves returned to the debate: appealing to the model of medical research and evidence-based clinical practice, he criticised the failure of educational research to investigate 'the symptoms and causes' of classroom problems and to develop 'therapeutic interventions' (Hargreaves 1998:2). In the following year he berated educational researchers for withdrawing 'from the messy world of short-term practical problems into intellectual obscurities masquerading as profundities whilst dreaming of ultimate recognition' (Hargreaves 1999:243). David Blunkett, Secretary of State for Education and Employment, in an address entitled 'Influence or Irrelevance: Can Social Science Improve Government?' expressed his frustration with the tendency for research to 'address issues other than those which are central and directly relevant ... to policy debate', to be 'driven by ideology paraded as intellectual inquiry or critique' and to 'fail to take into account the reality of many people's lives' (Blunkett 2000:12–13).

The new researcher, as Seamus Hegarty sagely observed, 'could be forgiven for thinking that research is a blight on the education landscape and should be eliminated forthwith' (Hegarty 1998b:21). In short, educational research in the UK at the end of the twentieth century was examined and found wanting: it failed to answer the questions which policy-makers wanted answered, it offered little or no help to practitioners in the classroom, it was fragmented, it lacked rigour and it was too often partisan. Such criticisms, it should be said, were not unique to the UK, in the USA disdain for educational research has been equally trenchant as John Goodlad observed:

> Criticism of educational research and statements regarding its unworthiness are commonplace in the halls of power and commerce, in the public market place,

> and even among large numbers of educators who work in our schools. Indeed, there is considerable advocacy for the elimination of the locus of most educational research – namely, schools, colleges and departments of education. (Berliner *et al.* 1997:13)

The diagnosis of 'unworthiness' has also been accompanied in the UK by a series of prescriptions for improving the health of the ailing body of educational research.

Hargreaves in the TTA lecture stated that educational research should seek to produce findings that offered 'conclusive demonstrations' that changing from one teaching approach to another would lead to 'a significant and enduring improvement in teaching and learning'. He advocated the establishment of a National Educational Research Forum whose function would be to sustain 'a continuing dialogue between all the stakeholders and to shape the agenda of educational research and its policy implications and applications' (Hargreaves:1996a). The DfEE established the Forum in 2000 with a remit to 'develop a strategy for educational research, shape its direction, guide the co-ordination of its support and conduct, and promote its practical application' (NERF 2001: Annex A). The TTA, in turn, developed a research strategy based on a greater role for users in determining and conducting educational research. Practice was to be informed by research evidence. The volume of 'relevant classroom-based pedagogic research' was to increase, 'teacher effectiveness' was to be examined 'in the light of evidence about pupil learning gain', 'rigorously evaluated digests' of research into teaching and learning were to be published and funding bodies were to be encouraged 'to pay more attention to how useful educational research is to headteachers, teachers and policy makers' (TTA 1997). Woodhead, in a little noticed observation, advocated in 1998 'a third way' for educational research:

> This is to recognise that the future lies, if it lies anywhere, in rediscovering the importance of historical perspective; in the patient application of disciplines such as economics and philosophy to the understanding of our education system; in suspending political and professional prejudice; and above all, in a return to what was once the classical terrain: issues, that is, concerning social class and educability and schools as social systems. (Woodhead 1998)

In the same year officials at the DfEE stated that the Government wanted research that improved 'classroom practice and policy development', that was geared to benefiting pupils, that was effectively disseminated to national policy-makers, local decision-makers and teachers, and teachers had to be trained to engage both with research findings and the research process themselves (Gold 1998, Budge 1998). More recently, Blunkett, at a meeting convened by the Economic and Social Research Council, defined the goal of educational research instrumentally:

> 'We need to be able to rely on social science and social scientists to tell us what works and why and what types of policy initiatives are likely to be most effective. And we need better ways of ensuring that those who want this information can get it easily and quickly.'

Blunkett ended his speech by commending to the research community this 'vision' and inviting researchers 'to work with us to achieve it' (Blunkett 2000:21).

Educational research: thinking about context and the authorial voice

Engaging in research 'is not something that can be done by slavishly following a set of edicts about what is right and wrong' (Denscombe 1998:3). That said, 'good' research always involves an act of location. The first part of this chapter has been concerned with identifying the perceived limitations of educational research in the UK. It has also identified some of the proposed solutions. Taken together these two elements provide the context in which to locate this text: educational research today constitutes both a politicised and contested space. This book is intended to fill a gap in the current literature relating to educational research and special needs education. It is aimed at practitioners in the classroom. However, before explaining in more detail the purpose and structure of this text it is necessary – again as in 'good' research – to locate the position and voice of the authors. Our position, by this we mean our understanding of, and response to, the criticisms and solutions associated with the critiques of educational research in the UK, has determined the process by which this book has been constructed. To this end, we have chosen to make four observations; given more space there would be others.

First, for some protagonists in the debate over the quality and 'relevance' of educational research criticisms are linked to broader political agendas. This point can be seen clearly in Woodhead's forward to *Educational Research. A critique* (Tooley and Darby 1998:1):

> To a significant extent teachers' effectiveness depends ... upon their intellectual command of the subject discipline(s) they teach and ultimately their personality. The training they receive as student teachers and teachers in service can, however, have a profound influence on their beliefs about the nature of the educational enterprise and the appropriateness and effectiveness of different teaching methods. The findings of educational research are important because for better or for worse they shape these influences and, in doing so, help to define the intellectual context within which all involved in education work.

Woodhead's attitude towards educational research should not be separated from OFSTED's declared distrust of the influence of university-based Initial Teacher

Training (ITT). The questioning of the value of academic research in education has been paralleled by a series of government initiatives aimed at ITT and couched in terms of 'quality' and 'accountability' which have questioned the quality of existing ITT provision and seriously eroded professional and academic autonomy.

Secondly, this unprecedented increase in central control over the content and delivery of teacher training has been accompanied by a concerted effort to establish teaching as an evidence-based profession. Sir Stewart Sutherland in his report on teacher education to the 1997 Dearing Inquiry into the future of Higher Education stated:

> the professional teacher should be one who has been trained and educated against a background of relevant and systematic research and has developed the critical capacities to use research findings as a basis for improving practice. (Sutherland 1997:5)

Student teachers as part of the requirements for Qualified Teacher Status have since 1998 been required to demonstrate that they 'understand the need to take responsibility for their own professional development and to keep up to date with research and developments in pedagogy' (DfEE 1998). The same year also witnessed the TTA in its Corporate Plan for 1998–2001 including among its strategic objectives: 'To help secure teaching as an evidence- and research-based profession' (TTA 1998). An 'evidence- and researched-based profession' requires educational research of a particular nature, research which is directly linked to 'teachers' effectiveness' in terms of practice. This leads to our third observation.

Classroom focused research is important, but it is not the only locus for research. As Hegarty has written:

> Classrooms and the students in them do not exist in isolation from the rest of the world. Educational research must therefore look at the classroom in context. It must take account of the multiple environments – family, cultural, socio-economic, media – within which young people learn. It must investigate the many policies and structures which have an impact on schooling. And it must have regard for theory, since otherwise research risks producing a jumble of unrelated facts. (Hegarty 1998a)

Further, credibility for researchers is not dependent upon providing answers to 'what works and why' and 'what is likely to be most effective'. Educational research can be concerned with improving our understanding of processes, practices and organisations associated with teaching and learning without requiring a rush to judgement, without needing to provide an answer. Educational researchers have a capacity and a responsibility to develop knowledge. This creative role can involve them in unsettling certainties, in being troublesome, in challenging the 'what works' philosophy and the single-vantage point, single-track model of education. Research independence is a necessary condition for advancing knowledge. Noam Chomsky's assertion of the mid 1960s still rings true – it is the duty of the academic researcher 'to speak the truth and to expose lies' (Chomsky 1966).

Our final observation relates to the increasing importance centred by government offices on the role of the practitioner as researcher. We fully endorse this principle in educational research – after all it is this recommendation that is at the centre of this book and gives meaning to the text. However, the idea of the teacher as researcher is not new.

Teachers as researchers

As early as 1977 Edwards and Furlong made the case for more classroom research to be undertaken by teachers and a few years later Stenhouse (1981) argued that teachers should be at the heart of educational research, if only because of the fact that they were surrounded by rich research opportunities. In 1989 *Research and the Teacher* was the title of a substantial text by Hitchcock and Hughes which aimed at enabling teachers 'to design, conduct and evaluate small-scale research into teaching and learning' (Hitchcock and Hughes 1995 (2nd edn):3). Critical engagement with the research process among special needs teachers has also been advocated. Writing in the early 1990s, Vulliamy and Webb suggested that those trained in psychology had dominated research in special education, and that much of this research emphasised a methodology grounded in positivism. They acknowledged the value of such enquiry, but also proposed that traditional models of research in special education could be associated with two particular problems. First, an inability of large-scale research to relate to the pragmatics of classroom practice or to provide the teacher with advice related to her own perception of her day to day work. Second, a failure of such enquiry to have an impact upon practice and to appear to be too far removed from the realities of school life. As a consequence they called for a 'broadening of traditional approaches to special needs research' to promote the involvement of teachers in smaller scale qualitative studies which considered intervention approaches, studies of influences upon pupil performance and a greater analysis of classroom structures and their potential impact upon learning (Vulliamy and Webb 1992:3). More recently, Ainscow (1998) has endorsed many of the concerns voiced by Vulliamy and Webb with regards to positivist approaches and has added further weight to the idea of the teacher researcher in the special needs classroom. For Ainscow an improved understanding of how educational contexts can be further enhanced to support the needs of all pupils is most likely to be achieved through the development of research which directly involves teachers working alongside experienced researchers.

However, it is one thing to advocate a research role for teachers; it is another matter to translate that idea into reality. Schiller and Malouf writing about the USA state that:

> For teachers, research is a small and indistinct voice in a very crowded and noisy arena. They have limited flexibility or motivation to use research-based innovations because of demands arising from externally imposed curricula, heightened accountability, and increasing student diversity; as well as such constraints as relative isolation, heavy work loads, inadequate pre-service and in-service training and insufficient resources. (Schiller and Malouf 2000:253–4)

The obstacles identified by Schiller and Malouf are also present in the UK. Apart from teachers engaged with research as part of Continuing Professional Development programmes or funded through government small-scale research initiatives (the TTA's 'Teacher Research Grant Scheme' and the DfEE funded 'Best Practice Research Grants') the number of teachers engaged in systematic educational research remains small. The perception of research held by many teachers is still that it is a process beyond their remit and their energy. Research remains within the realm of the academy.

All of the constraints put forward by Schiller and Malouf can act as an inhibitor of further progress in developing teachers as researchers or, by contrast, they could provide a catalyst for the more radical engagement of teachers within the research process. So, for example, there is evidence that teachers working in special education have been at the forefront of criticism of the nature and content of an imposed National Curriculum. Indeed, the innovations of some teachers working within special education have been instrumental in bringing about positive change to ensure that pupils' entitlement to a relevant and balanced curriculum has been achieved (Byers and Rose 1996, Carpenter, Ashdown and Bovair 1996). Such change would never have been brought about without research into classroom practices which identified challenges and offered potential solutions. Similarly, research which has focused upon student diversity and has striven to identify teaching approaches which promote inclusion and access has enabled some pupils to receive a better quality of education than had previously been possible (Zarkowska and Clements 1992, Nind and Hewett 1994). Such research has been important in enabling teachers to develop ideas and to put them in to practice, yet there remains an urgent need to develop a more clearly defined empirical base.

Professional educational practice and academic educational research are, as Brown and Dowling argue, 'distinct fields of activity'. Researching and teaching as distinct social practices each operate respective 'interrogative gazes' through which meaning is given. The two fields of activity 'stand in dialogic relation to each other'. Research may be plundered for techniques which will promote the genesis of a research-based teaching profession but this will fail to fully develop the potential of the teacher as a researcher. The teacher researcher needs to acquire the 'principles' not just the 'techniques' of research practice. Failure to recognise the distinctive nature of the two fields 'will result in the one being unduly subordinated to the principles of the other' (Brown and Dowling 1998:164–5).

Thinking about ethical issues

Ethics is a central principle of research practice. Representing others through educational research is not a neutral activity; it involves relations of power (Denscombe and Aubrook 1992). Simply stated, research ethics are about being clear about the nature of the agreement the researcher establishes with research participants. There are various sets of ethical guidelines issued by professional bodies, such as the British Educational Research Association (BERA)[1] and its US counterpart the American Educational Research Association (AERA), and a steadily growing body of literature on ethical issues in educational research which the new researcher can consult (Cohen and Manion 1994, Lindsay 2000, Simons and Usher 2000). That said, many ethical dilemmas remain. For example, there is still very little guidance in the research literature on interviewing people with learning disabilities and obtaining informed consent as opposed to obtaining evidence of consent or on proceeding with research if informed consent cannot be obtained (Homan 1991, McCarthy 1998). Informed consent is also an issue for the image-based educational researcher. Participants photographed in the research process see themselves and are seen by others (Prosser 2000). Also, an explicit consideration of ethical issues in conducting and reporting quantitative research in education is significantly absent from research texts (Jones 2000).

Being aware of the guidelines and the literature is not a sufficient basis upon which to undertake research. Ethical considerations must inform research practice. Contemporary feminist and post-modern thinking coupled with an increasing awareness among researchers of the complexities of the educational environment have challenged the traditional idea that ethics is a set of principles uniformly and validly applied to all situations. Feminist approaches, for example, have demonstrated that concepts such as reason and objectivity which are associated with ethical practice are not neutral but are coded by masculine assumptions (Simons and Usher 2000). Research often takes place within a context in which 'background assumptions' are taken for granted and certain interests and values predominate (Gouldner 1962). Values are related to both professional background and gender. Individual values can be a reflection of self-interest. Teachers as researchers will necessarily display a tendency to make assumptions about how a school works, the role of the teacher and so on, and also be possessed of views about what constitutes a 'good' education. Such assumptions and values need to be examined as part of the research practice itself. Every research context is unique. Universal statements of ethical principles are important and helpful, but the socio-cultural and political contexts of research will mediate ethical practice. Thus, operating in what are increasingly recognised as complex environments, the researcher has to be clear both about personal motivation and values and how he or she can interact with both the research process and the researched. Reflexivity is a principle of research practice.

[1] The BERA research ethical guidelines can be obtained from the BERA website at www.bera.ac.uk

The research process

What can be known? What are the proper objects of research? What counts as a contribution to knowledge? How can research be advanced? What are the methodologies and techniques available to the researcher? What are the ethical issues? What are the constraints in terms of context, resources, time and support? All these questions need to be addressed in any educational research project. Guidance on identifying a research question, undertaking a literature review or constructing a position statement; selecting a methodology, gathering data, data analysis, writing up and disseminating findings can be found in a large number of general texts on 'doing' social/educational research (see, for example, Brown and Dowling 1998, Blaxter *et al.* 1996, Burgess 1984, 1985, Cohen and Manion 1994, Denscombe 1998, Griffiths 1998, Hammersley 1986, Hitchcock and Hughes 1995, May 1998, Walford 1991). The aim of this book is to bring together research on special education with a commentary on research method. It has been written to help the teacher new to research to think about possible research topics in special education and how they might be conducted.

How the book is organised

Each chapter offers a brief but critical overview of a particular research method and a detailed account of a research practice utilising the method. Each account has seven elements:

- a research question linked to special education;
- contextual framework;
- research method, including rationale;
- ethical dilemmas;
- research findings;
- research findings and the classroom teacher;
- guide to further reading: research area and method.

In presenting detailed accounts of how researchers actually engaged with the research process this collection offers a different perspective from that generally presented in the research methods literature.

Each of the contributors has used research as a form of enquiry to affect change within their own practice or to assess the effectiveness of already introduced procedures. The scale of the projects outlined vary from the very small single school study, to the larger analysis intended to give a broader, whole LEA view of an important issue. Of course, where research is focused upon a single institution or specific population its findings may not be generalised beyond the confines imposed upon the study. However, an equally important feature of classroom research must be its ability to provoke discussion, generate ideas and provide a possible basis for further enquiry which may be conducted in other situations. While none of the writers within this book would suggest that they have discovered any form of immutable truth, all have conducted studies which provide valuable insights into the workings of schools, the deployment of approaches or the analysis of procedures which can be used to inform practice or support change. Other researchers reading these studies are provided with important discussion points based upon the findings of the research and may also be assisted in constructing a framework for further investigation. In the nature of much educational research the individual projects have probably raised as many questions as answers and careful consideration needs to be given to the ways in which the findings are used.

Endnote

The aim of research, its context and the constraints operating will determine the method or combination of methods used in educational research. Its successful execution depends, in the end, to a large degree on the skills of the researcher. Doing research is not a smooth linear journey from beginning to end. It is often difficult and frustrating, absorbing a lot of time and energy, but it is a journey which is rewarding. Educational research does matter and we believe, to adapt an old adage, that in research practice 'teachers *as researchers* can make a difference'.

References and further reading

Ainscow, M. (1998) 'Would it work in theory? Arguments for practitioner research and theorising in the special needs field', in Clark, C., Dyson, A. and Millward, A. (eds) *Theorising Special Education*. London: Routledge.

Bassey, M. (1996) 'We are specialists at pursuing the truth', *TES*, 22 November.

Berliner, D. C., Resnick, L.b., Cuban L., Cole, N., Popham, W. and Goodlad, J.I. (1997) 'The Vision Thing: Educational Research and AERA in the 21st Century, Part 2: competing Visions for Enhancing the Impact of Educational Research', *Educational Researcher*, June–July, 12–18, 27.

Blaxter, L., Hughes, C. and Tight, M. (1996) *How to research*. Buckingham: Open University Press.

Blunkett, D. (2000) 'Influence or Irrelevance: Can Social Science Improve Government?' *Research Intelligence*, 71, 12–21.

Brown, A. and Dowling, P. (1998) *Doing Research/Reading Research*. London: Falmer Press.

Budge, D. (1996) 'A cosy world of trivial pursuits?', *TES*, 28 June.

Budge, D. (1998) 'Shake-up on the way as research is scrutinised', *TES*, 20 February.

Burgess, R. G. (ed.) (1984) *The Research Process in Educational Settings: Ten Case Studies*. Lewes: Falmer Press.

Burgess, R. G. (ed.) (1985) *Issues in Educational Research: Qualitative Methods*. Lewes: Falmer Press.

Byers, R. and Rose, R. (1996) *Planning the Curriculum for Pupils with Special Educational Needs*. London: David Fulton Publishers.

Carpenter, B., Ashdown, R. and Bovair, K. (eds) (1996) *Enabling Access*. London: David Fulton Publishers.

Chomsky, N. (1966) 'The responsibility of intellectuals', in Chomsky, N. *American Power and the New Mandarins*. Harmondsworth: Penguin.

Cohen, L. and Manion, L. (1994) *Research Methods in Education*, 4th edn. London: Routledge.

Denscombe, M. (1998) *The Good Research Guide*. Buckingham: Open University Press.

Denscombe, M. and Aubrook, L. (1992) '"It's just another piece of school work": the ethics of questionnaire research on pupils in schools', *British Educational Research Journal* **18**(2), 113–21.

Department for Education and Employment (DfEE) (1998) Teaching: High Status, High Standards: Requirements for Initial Teacher Training (Circular 4/98). London: DfEE.

Edwards, T. and Furlong, J. (1977) 'Time to go inside?', *TES*, 3 June.

Gold, K. (1998) 'Pleased as Punch with Judy', *THES*, 1 May.

Gouldner, A. (1962) 'Anti-Minotaur: the myth of a value-free sociology', *Social Problems* **9**(3), 199–213.

Gray, J., Goldstein, H. and Kay, W. (1997) 'Educational research and evidence-based practice: the debate continues', *Research Intelligence* **59**, 18–20 February.

Griffiths, M. (1998) *Educational Research for Social Justice*. Buckingham: Open University Press.

Hammersley, M. (ed.) (1986) *Case Studies in Classroom Research*. Milton Keynes: Open University Press.

Hargreaves, D. (1996a) 'Teaching as a research based profession: possibilities and prospects', TTA Annual Lecture, April 1996.

Hargreaves, D. (1996b) 'Educational research and evidence-based educational research: a response to critics', *Research Intelligence* **58**, 12–16.

Hargreaves, D. (1998) *The production, mediation and use of professional knowledge among teachers and doctors: a comparative analysis*. Paris: OECD Centre for Educational Research and Innovation.

Hargreaves, D. (1999) 'Revitalising educational research: lessons from the past and proposals for the future', *Cambridge Journal of Education* **29**, 239–49.

Hegarty, S. (1998a) 'On the purposes of research', *Research Intelligence* **63**(5).

Hegarty, S. (1998b) 'Orchard with too little fruit', *Guardian*, 28 July.

Hitchcock, G. and Hughes, D. (1995) *Research and the Teacher: A Qualitative Introduction to School-Based Research*, 2nd edn. London: Routledge.

Homan, R. (1991) *The Ethics of Doing Social Research*. New York: Longman.

Jones, K. (2000) 'A regrettable oversight or a significant omission? Ethical considerations in quantitative research in education', in Simons, H. and Usher, R. (eds) *Situated Ethics in Educational Research,* 147–61. London: Routledge.

Lindsay, G. (2000) 'Researching children's perspectives: ethical issues', in Lewis, A. and Lindsay, G. (eds) *Researching Children's Perspectives*. Buckingham: Open University Press.

May, T. (1998) *Social Research. Issues, Methods and Process*, 2nd edn. Buckingham: Open University Press.

McCarthy, M. (1998) 'Interviewing people with learning disabilities about sensitive topics: a discussion of ethical issues', *British Journal of Learning Disabilities* **26**, 140–5.

National Education Research Forum (NERF) (2000) *Research and Development in Education. Consultation Document*. London: NERF.

Nind, M. and Hewett, D. (1994) *Access to Communication*. London: David Fulton Publishers.

Prosser, J. (2000) 'The moral maze of image ethics', in Simons, H. and Usher, R. (eds) *Situated Ethics in Educational Research*, 116–32. London: Routledge.

Schiller, E. P. and Malouf, D. B. (2000) 'Research syntheses: implications for research and practice' ,in Gersten, R., Schiller, E. P. and Vaughn, S. (eds) *Contemporary Special Education Research*. Mahwah, New Jersey: Lawrence Erlbaum Associates.

Simons, H. and Usher R. (eds) (2000) *Situated Ethics in Educational Research*. London: Routledge.

Stenhouse, L. (1975) *An Introduction to curriculum research and development*. London: Heiemann Eductional.

Stenhouse, L. (1981) 'What counts as research?', *British Journal of Educational Studies* **29**(2), 103–14.

Sutherland, Sir S. (1997) *Teacher Education and Training: A Study*. London: The National Committee of Inquiry into Higher Education.

Teacher Training Agency (1997) *Teaching Matters*, 1. London: TTA.

Teacher Training Agency (1998) *Corporate Plan for 1998–2001*. London: TTA.

Tooley, J. and Darby, D. (1998) *Educational Research. A critique*. London: OFSTED.

Vulliamy, G. and Webb, R. (1992) *Teacher Research and Special Educational Needs*. London: David Fulton Publishers.

Walford, G. (ed.) (1991) *Doing Educational Research*. London: Routledge.

Woodhead, C. (1998) 'Too much research, or not enough?', *The Independent*, 9 April.

Zarkowska, E. and Clements, J. (1992) *Problem Behaviour and People with Severe Learning Disabilities*. London: Chapman and Hall.

CHAPTER 2

Action research

Vulliamy and Webb (1992) suggest that 'pedagogic' research has as its main purpose the improvement of classroom practice and that while it may contribute to an increase in theoretical knowledge, its main thrust is in assisting teachers to become more focused and to tackle difficulties in their own teaching situation. This being the case, it can be seen that working within an action research model is likely to have advantages for many school based researchers. Action research has found favour within many schools because of the ability which it provides for the researchers to be able to focus upon specific institutional issues. Cohen and Manion (1994) describe action research as being a process which deals with problems located in an immediate situation and which through a systematic approach monitors progress towards solving the problem over time. It is this concentration upon solving a problem or improving existing practices which suggests that action research may be a valid approach for schools which are concerned to examine current practices and to engage with issues of school improvement. Kemmis and McTaggart (1982) emphasised that:

> The linking of the terms action and research highlights the essential feature of the method: trying out ideas and practice as a means of improvement and as a means of increasing knowledge. (Kemmis and McTaggart 1982)

McNiff, Lomax and Whitehead (1996) suggest that it is this stress upon action which motivates the researcher precisely because of the anticipation that action may have an impact upon practice and be an effective agent for change. However, they also recognise that even in the best ordered action research projects there are sometimes difficulties in interpreting the overall impact, which the project itself may have had upon change. This should not discourage teachers and researchers from working together using this approach. Teachers who have been involved in action research projects often report that it has enabled them to reflect upon their practice and to consider in more detail the challenges of their everyday working situation.

The model normally adopted for action research is one of self reflection which follows a set pattern of planning, actions, observations and modifications. Hutchinson (1998) writes about the empowering nature of research which adopts this model. He suggests that empowerment comes about through a process which enables staff to take greater critical control over themselves and their working context. An action research approach encourages teachers to question existing practices and also enables them to take ownership of the approaches adopted to find solutions. From Hutchinson's perspective, action research can play a valuable role effecting school change by recognising that management is concerned with 'interactively developing the understandings and improving the practices of school staff' (Hutchinson 1998:381). This is achieved by emphasising the role of teachers or practitioners as located at the centre of the research and thus enabling them to see the direct relevance of the project to their own situation. Early developments of this approach were based upon the work of Lewin (1946). Illustrations of the action research model can be found in a number of texts (McNiff 1988, Robson 1993, Kemmis and Wilkinson 1998) and can be simplified into the flow chart shown in Figure 2.1.

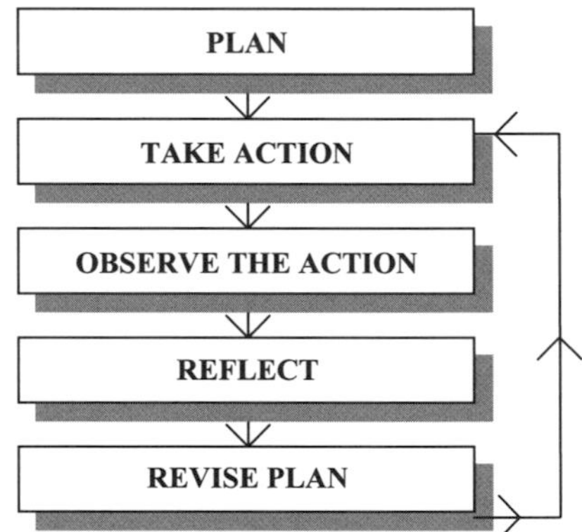

Figure 2.1 Action research model

An important factor within action research is the time spent ensuring that each stage of this model is undertaken systematically in order to provide a logical sequence of actions which remain focused upon the original problem or issue. Many action research projects take a considerable time to reach completion, as was the case in the work described by Fletcher (see Chapter 3). It is not always easy to anticipate how many times the cycle will need to be followed until a satisfactory outcome is achieved. Patience is an important element of action research projects and some flounder either because of the inability to maintain enthusiasm or because other priorities take over. Action research projects demand good leadership and effective organisation skills in order to see them through to completion.

An advantage of action research is its ability to incorporate a number of methodologies for data collection. In the case of Fletcher's project described in this book, interviews, observation and document scrutiny were combined to provide a triangulated picture of the changing situation in target setting. As the action research cycle unfolds it is sometimes possible, and even desirable, to introduce new approaches to data collection. From the point of view of the researcher it is important to keep all parties informed of progress, to take account of opinions and to ensure consistency of interpretation of the research tools being used. Good action research projects begin by ensuring a consensus and understanding of the issue to be researched. Elliot (1985) has discussed the issue of ownership in action research projects. In asking the question 'who defines the focus of the research?' he recognises that a conflict can occur where the core of the research activities may not find ownership by all parties involved. Indeed, some institutions may not lend themselves readily to this form of enquiry. Time spent on this, and in making sure that everyone is working to the same definitions and has a clear understanding of expectations with regards to their own actions and the data collection methods to be used, usually pays dividends.

Critics of action research point to a lack of scientific rigour within the approach as a possible concern. However, its proponents would suggest that action research as the antithesis of a scientific approach, gathers strength from its focus upon specific situations and events, and its ability to examine the atypical and unrepresentative occurrences which are present in an individual institution. By working within a restricted sample the action researcher has little control over variables, and can seldom expect to achieve results which are easily generalisable. However, well organised action research can effect change within the institution through the development of a project which looks in detail at an identified issue, and can more clearly address the needs of the subjects under scrutiny.

The use of action research

Project described by Will Fletcher

The action research project described by Fletcher tackles an important and complex issue which is of current interest to all teachers. The role of the pupil within the learning process has been discussed and debated over a number of years and it is generally accepted that the encouragement of pupils to take some responsibility for their own learning can have major benefits (Griffiths and Davies 1995, Gersch 1996). Pupils need to have an understanding about intended learning outcomes and through greater involvement in discussing these are enabled to retain a focus upon teacher intentions. Pupils with special educational needs, and in particular those who have difficulties as complex as those discussed by Fletcher, present a major challenge to the teacher in terms of the encouragement of pupil involvement. Yet within existing legislation there is an intention that all pupils, regardless of needs or abilities, should be involved in decision-making which affects any major aspect of their lives. The Children Act (DoH 1989) and the *Code of Practice on the Identification and Assessment of Special Educational Needs* (DFE 1994) both emphasise the importance of pupil involvement. Indeed the Code of Practice requires that pupils should be involved in both target setting and regular review of their own progress in all areas of learning. While the intention to involve pupils is clear, there has been very little written to provide advice to teachers on how pupils with special needs may be involved, and even less substantive research to examine its efficacy.

Fletcher has moved beyond discourse and debate to examine the pragmatics of pupil involvement. He is concerned not only with a principle which states that pupils should be involved, this was clearly established within the school before their research began, but is far more intent on discovering how this might be achieved. His action research project provided an opportunity to build upon the ideas expressed by other writers and to begin to analyse the challenges faced by a single school in enabling pupils with severe and complex needs to become effective target setters. In examining the skills and understanding which pupils need to become target setters, he also provides effective guidelines for teachers which could influence their teaching practices and change their approach to pupil involvement.

Examples of other action research projects in special education

'Influences on attitudes towards children with mental handicap'.
Gash, H. and Coffey, D. (1995), *European Journal of Special Needs Education* **10** (1), 1–16.
'Managing behaviour with classroom charters'.
Hedley, I. (1999), *Support for Learning* **14**(3), 129–34.
'Supporting the subject co-ordinator through the process of curriculum monitoring in a special school'.
Rose, R. and Parsons, L. (1998), *Support for Learning* **13**(1), 21–5.

References and further reading

Altrichter, H., Posch, P. and Somekh, B. (1993) *Teachers Investigate Their Work: An Introduction to the Methods of Action Research*. London: Routledge.

Atweh, B., Kemmis, S. and Weeks, P. (eds) (1998) *Action Research in Practice.* London: Routledge.

Cohen, L. and Manion, L. (1994) *Research Methods in Education,* 4th edn. London: Routledge.

Department for Education (DFE) (1994) *The Code of Practice on the Identification and Assessment of Special Educational Needs.* London: DFE.

Department of Health (DoH) (1989*) The Children Act.* London: HMSO.

Elliot, J. (1985) 'Facilitating action research in schools: some dilemmas', in Burgess, R. G. (ed.) *Field Methods in the Study of Education.* Lewes: Falmer Press.

Elliot, J. (1991) *Action Research for Educational Change.* Buckingham: Open University Press.

Gersch, I. (1996) 'Listening to children in educational contexts', in Davie, R., Upton, G. and Varma, V. (eds) *The Voice of the Child.* London: Falmer Press.

Griffiths, M. and Davies, C. (1995) *In Fairness to Children*. London: David Fulton Publishers.

Hutchinson, B. (1998) 'Learning action research and managing educational change – improvement in careers education: a case study of managerialism in action?', *Educational Management and Administration* **26**(4), 379–93.

Kemmis, S. and McTaggart, R. (1982) *The Action Research Planner*. Australia: Deakin University Press.

Kemmis, S. and Wilkinson, M. (1998) 'Participatory action research and the study of practice', in Atweh, B., Kemmis, S. and Weeks, P. (eds) *Action Research in Practice*. London: Routledge.

Lewin, K. (1946) 'Action research and minority problems', *Journal of Social Issues* **2**(1), 34–46.

McNiff, J. (1988) *Action Research Principles and Practice*. London: Macmillan.

McNiff, J., Lomax, P. and Whitehead, J. (1996) *You and Your Action Research Project*. London: Routledge.

Robson, C. (1993) *Real World Research*. Oxford: Blackwell.

Vulliamy, G. and Webb, R. (1992) 'New directions in special educational needs research', in Vulliamy, G. and Webb, R. (eds) *Teacher Research and Special Educational Needs*. London: David Fulton Publishers.

CHAPTER 3

Enabling students with severe learning difficulties to become effective target setters

Will Fletcher

It often seems that in order to encourage teachers to take on new working practices with enthusiasm and commitment, changes and initiatives must produce a tangible and positive impact on teaching and learning. Classroom practitioners should also feel an ownership of the work in which they are engaged and feel able to adapt, improvise and interpret general principles to meet the needs of the pupils under their charge.

This chapter describes a small-scale research project in a school for pupils with severe learning difficulties and the impact it has had on both teachers and learners. It will also describe developments which have taken place since the original project and cite the views of teachers and pupils who currently take an active role in the setting of personal learning targets.

Rationale

The concept of pupil involvement in their education is, of course, well established and its importance has been affirmed in policy and legislation (DES 1981, United Nations 1989). Many schools embrace the aim that their learners should be independent and consistent learners and devise self-assessment and recording activities in order to encourage pupils to reflect on their own progress and achievement. The right of pupils to be involved in decision-making at every stage of the education process is also clearly defined. The *Code of Practice on the Identification and Assessment of Special Educational Needs* (DFE 1994) provided an impetus for such actions and the processes followed by schools has been reviewed in the literature (Francis 1993, Cowie 1994, Davie and Galloway 1996).

The Code of Practice (page 15, para. 2:37) states that schools should consider how they:

- Involve pupils in decision making processes
- Determine the pupil's level of participating, taking into account approaches to assessment and intervention which are suitable for his or her age, ability and past experiences

- Record pupils' views in identifying their difficulties, setting goals, agreeing a development strategy, monitoring and reviewing progress
- Involve pupils in implementing individual education plans.

The principles here expressed build upon those stated in the United Nations Convention on the Rights of the Child (United Nations 1989) and the Children Act 1989, both of which asserted the position of children with regard to having a voice in decisions which affect their future. However, the principles established in legislation and the reality of what takes place in many schools are often separated by a considerable gulf (Rose *et al.* 1996).

There are many perceived advantages of developing pupil involvement, including a greater ownership of their own learning and improved accuracy of judgements by pupils with regard to their own performance (Munby 1995) and the role which it plays in preparing pupils for adult life (Cooper 1993, Marland 1996). Pupils need to be able to identify for themselves areas in which they need help and those where they can make recognisable and measurable achievements if they are to take a more than tokenistic role in their Annual Reviews, and make an informed contribution to determining the content of their Individual Education Plans. There are many obstacles which may make for difficulties in pupils learning the essential skills of self reflection and meta cognition which play an important role in becoming an effective and autonomous decision-maker. These obstacles are particularly challenging for pupils who have a severe learning difficulty and for those charged with responsibility for their education. Nevertheless, if the benefits are seen to be of sufficient value and importance, methods must be sought to overcome some of the perceived difficulties and to examine ways in which these skills can be taught and developed.

Watling View School, which provides a focus for the research described in this chapter, is a day special school for pupils with severe and profound and multiple learning difficulties. Teachers at the school had, over a number of years, been involved in developing pupil self-assessment procedures and recording formats, and had thus built up a practice of pupil involvement. The school staff had a commitment to developing pupil self advocacy and to furthering pupil independence in decision-making. However, there was a general perception among the teaching staff at Watling View School prior to the project that many of the self-assessment and weekly review activities which had been put into place within the school had become routine. The established procedures appeared to be running on a kind of 'auto pilot', with little real development and progression. Pupils regularly identified the same activities they liked and disliked as areas for development and tended to be vague about the areas they needed to work on. In short, the process needed to be redefined in terms that would provide a meaningful focus for planning and learning for both teachers and pupils.

While the staff had a commitment to further development of the area of pupil involvement, the impetus for change came following the provision of an opportunity for schools to become more formally involved in school based research. With the encouragement of officers of the LEA, the author and a colleague applied for a small research grant from Hertfordshire LEA in order to take the concept of pupil involvement further. Funds were made available and a partnership was formed with a colleague from the School of Education at University College Northampton who acted as a research mentor and provided advice on methodology throughout the duration of the project. An action research project was established through discussion between the author and teachers working with secondary-aged pupils within the school who were described as having severe learning difficulties. The initial intention of the project was that of identifying the necessary skills and understanding that would enable pupils to play an active part in setting and monitoring their own learning targets. It was agreed that a standard action research model, based upon the work of Lewin (1946) would be deployed and used as the basis of the work to be undertaken with staff.

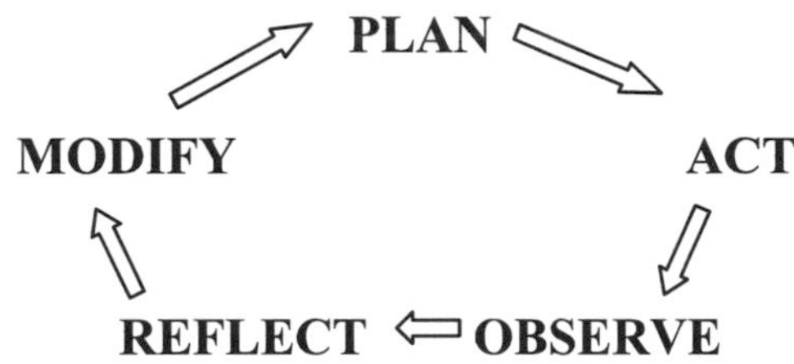

Figure 3.1 Action research cycle used for the project

This recognised methodology (see Figure 3.1) was selected following discussion with colleagues at University College Northampton. It was the most manageable within the school context and would provide the flexibility required for modification of materials within a formalised approach that would ensure consistency.

It was seen as particularly important that staff confidence and enthusiasm was maintained by demonstrating respect for and confidence in the successes that had already been achieved within the school. We aimed to involve staff as much as possible in discussion concerning developments in working procedures. The purposes of the action research project were identified as follows:

- To identify and clarify those processes currently being used to promote pupil involvement in target setting.
- To identify the obstacles that teachers perceive as preventing further pupil involvement.
- To identify the skills, knowledge and understanding required by pupils to become successful in setting and monitoring targets.
- To provide guidance on the means by which staff at the school may further promote pupil involvement in the future.

We agreed that the project would begin with a series of observations of existing practices and procedures. The participant observations largely focused on the conduct of staff and pupils during the pupils' deliberations over the previous week's work and the selection of areas of difficulty to be worked on during the following week. The observers asked questions related to the language used, the respective roles played by the individuals and the ways in which decisions were reached. Video recordings of some of the target setting sessions enabled further clarification and interpretation of the processes taking place.

The observations demonstrated considerable discrepancies in pupils' understanding of the process and their ability to play a full part in target setting. While participants for the most part were enthusiastic, there were also frustrations expressed with the current system. Teachers recognised that some of the pupils involved were highly suggestible and it was often difficult not to lead them in a direction predetermined by the teacher, rather than one that was genuinely established through the pupil's own self-perception of need. Similarly, other pupils had difficulties with communication that inhibited their ability to express ideas and opinions. Some pupils, including those with profound and multiple learning difficulties (PMLD), did not take part in the process in any formal sense as it was universally agreed that certain prerequisite abilities, as yet undefined, would be needed for it to be anything other than a tokenistic exercise.

The 'targets' that were set during the initial observations ranged considerably from the highly behavioural to those linked with their conduct at school, such as 'Next week I won't hit my friends!' or 'I will smile at people each day', both of which seemed to be heavily influenced by staff, and vague statements of intent such as to 'do better at reading'. At times, it was difficult to comprehend where the targets came from. Some appeared to be selected at random, others were familiar, routine and comfortable to the pupil. Similarly, the validity of the targets was at times seen to be problematic. While some pupils appeared to always achieve their targets within the set period of time (usually a week) others appeared to fall short of achievement and would repeat the same target over an extended period of time.

The definition of what should constitute a target was clearly problematic for both staff and pupils. What had been assumed as a simple concept turned out to be one which required much clearer definition. After discussion between staff and with the research mentor, it was decided that a series of key questions should be introduced into the target setting sessions to ensure that the targets being agreed were appropriate to the individual needs of pupils. These questions were intended to exert some consistency over the quality of the targets being set and their validity as a means of promoting pupil development. The questions contained within a simple planning format were used by teachers during each target setting session and were as follows:

- Is it achievable?
- Is it motivating and intrinsically worthwhile to the pupil?
- Is it incremental, i.e. a stage towards greater goals?

- Is it appropriately challenging?
- Is it measurable from a clear baseline, i.e. subject to success criteria?

These five questions were seen as central to the project and it was agreed that they should be returned to at each stage. The difficulties experienced with the question 'Is it appropriately challenging?', which are related to teacher perceptions of pupil needs and abilities, gave the project its greatest challenge. The interpretation of the researchers was that in the past, in order to ensure that pupils succeeded, targets were set which presented insufficient challenge. Establishing a balance of setting targets that were achievable but sufficiently challenging, was seen as a particularly difficult concept for some staff to grasp. For this reason, it was agreed that the researchers should initially monitor each target and analyse its origin in relation to existing pupil needs and abilities.

The key questions sheets were implemented and trialled by teachers for a period of eight weeks. Further observations were conducted to assess any difficulties in using the materials and staff opinions were sought through unstructured interviews. At the end of the eight week trial, there was a period of evaluation in which the views of teachers and pupils were sought to assess the impact of the materials. It was recorded by the teachers and researchers that there was now a greater consideration given to the selection and negotiation of targets and that the questions enabled teachers to focus more clearly on the needs of the individual pupils and to pay closer attention to targets in relation to those that had previously been addressed.

It was decided to continue the trial period and extend the formalised process to other groups within the school and to continue to observe their use. Again, the outcomes of this would be analysed, repeating the process of moving around Lewin's cyclical model.

The introduction of the key questions had addressed some of the issues of target validity but the difficulties of identifying the skills needed to become effective target setters remained. It was decided to examine the kinds of skills and insights exhibited by the pupils who were most fully and effectively involved in the process. The more successful participants appeared to display a number of characteristics that were categorised under three headings which, although not mutually exclusive, seemed to offer a useful framework. These were expressed as follows:

- Negotiation
- Self-knowledge/Recognition of potential
- Prediction skills/Concept of time.

It was noted that pupils who were the least suggestible in target setting sessions were confident enough to state their opinions, disagree with the teacher and, at times, argue for or against the targets under discussion. These pupils also tended to have good listening skills and to be able to initiate conversations on the basis of having identified their own needs. Some pupils were able to identify their achievements while others were unable to assess their own learning strengths and needs and had little understanding of what might be easy or hard to do. The identification of realistic time scales for achieving targets was particularly problematic as was the ability to state what the possible benefits of the achievement of targets might be.

After discussion between the researchers and consultations with others, including the school's Speech and Language Therapist, it was agreed it would be helpful to draw up an assessment format that would summarise the skills of individual pupils based on the three headings. It was felt that this might enable teachers to plan further work and develop pupils' skills in the defined areas.

An assessment schedule was produced that enabled teachers to examine a series of statements on which they could make judgements regarding a pupil's level of performance in relation to the key areas and the possible impact this might have on the target setting approaches currently being used with that pupil. In a number of instances, teachers adjusted their approaches according to their findings. Teachers' feedback on the assessment schedules were collated and, on the basis of their comments, a more formalised system was developed for trial with a greater number of groups. The three main headings remained but some of the statements were modified and a section added asking teachers to provide evidence for their assessments and also to identify steps that would need to be taken to address those areas in which pupils were seen to be lacking.

The statements developed at this stage of the project were as follows:

Negotiation

- Can state an opinion with confidence.
- Can disagree with confidence.
- Takes part in a two-way conversation.
- Can say 'Yes' and 'No' in response to requests.
- Seeks clarification and help when unable to understand.
- Expresses personal feelings and needs.
- Maintains and develops a topic of conversation effectively and appropriately.
- Stands up for self – can represent own views and feelings in an assertive and non-aggressive way.
- Makes suggestions and gives opinions in the correct context.
- Has well-developed skills of refusal which are used effectively and appropriately.
- Achieves a good balance between listening and responding.
- Is able to initiate conversations successfully.
- Adapts behaviour and language to the context and listener.

Self-knowledge/Recognition of potential

- Recognises/identifies personal achievements.
- Knows when something has been achieved.
- Identifies personal strengths and weaknesses.
- Identifies likes and dislikes.

- Identifies possible future leaving (post school) needs.
- Recognition of having had an effect upon decisions.
- Identifies something which cannot be achieved.
- Recognises something which cannot be done yet, but which can be achieved with time.
- Identifies possible learning strategies, including the need for support.
- Recognises something which the target setter could not do, but can do now.
- Acknowledges and identifies difficulties or non-achievement experienced.
- Understands concepts of hard, easy and manageable.

Prediction Skills/Concept of time

- Understands the concept of time in relation to the target set.
- Understands differences in time scales – day/week/term, etc.
- Identifies/recognises/states the benefits of achieving a target.

The assessment schedule was implemented with the project teachers, who were able to develop a bank of evidence related to each of the statements made. These continue to be used in school and are informing teachers' planning for both individuals and groups of pupils by identifying skills related to the statements that need to be taught. They have also been useful in formulating IEP targets relating to the objectives 'To develop skills of choice and decision-making', which all pupils in the secondary phase now have in their Statements of SEN.

Target setting has become an integral part of the curriculum in the secondary phase of the school and individual teachers have developed their own approaches based on the principles and proceedings outlined in the research project. Work has taken place for some pupils in developing a closer relationship between the IEP targets set at their Annual Review and those that pupils select personally on a weekly basis. Some pupils are able to set clearer and more valid targets if the parameters of choice are in some way limited or defined for them. Precise decisions, as the degree to which the process is shaped by the teacher, have to be based on a thorough knowledge of the pupil and on an understanding of negotiation skills.

A particular useful tool for some pupils has been the shared 'breaking down' of targets or task analysis with pupils to ensure achievement is possible over a realistic time scale. For example, recently a 15-year-old pupil had selected 'To make myself a hot chocolate' for a number of weeks with limited success. It transpired that some very basic assumptions had been made which acted as a barrier to success. She did not routinely use the same size spoon, was not confident or consistent as to how many spoonfuls to use and she believed that the kettle was boiled when the indicating light was 'on' not 'off'.

A sequence of steps was discussed with the pupil, based on the difficulties as she saw them, and within the first week a successful hot drink was made without error; a process that has been repeated every day since. This is, of course, neither rocket science nor a radical new approach to the teaching of pupils with severe learning difficulties but it does serve to remind us that often it is the pupils themselves who can help identify the steps they need in their own learning. Not only is it likely to be more effective, but the process of discussion and negotiation can prove to be valuable in its own right.

The research project and its support in developing school procedures has made a considerable impact on the curriculum and implications for planning and teaching. Most teachers have extended their learning and study skills sessions that encompass target setting from half an hour to one hour, as they have found it counter-productive to rush the process in any way. While the whole process of pupil involvement in target setting has proved time consuming, the benefits which have been reaped have been acknowledged by all staff and the time is considered well spent. Teachers also report that pupil evaluation and target setting on a Friday, informs the planning for the following week. If targets are successfully negotiated and agreed for any given week then there needs to be a joint responsibility to ensure that there are sufficient opportunities during the week for them to be regularly addressed. In all classes, pupil targets are compiled and typed up, using symbols where appropriate, and posted on the pupil notice board. The pupils are reminded of their targets on a daily basis and are encouraged to find opportunities in which they may be addressed, given the timetable for the day.

The views of the teachers and pupils most closely involved with target setting were sought through recorded unstructured interviews and by written submission. These are a few examples of their accounts:

Teacher 1

Although you are facilitating the dialogue, I increasingly feel it is very personal and meaningful for my students. It can take a long time but we believe it is valuable for the session to take as long as it needs. It carries over to other sessions and they now take a more active role in finding ways of tackling them.

I now build in their own targets, in addition to those from IEPs, into my planning, though many of them are becoming increasingly similar. Some students have moved on to a lesser degree and often choose activities as targets related to classroom jobs and tasks such as putting the chairs away or collecting the milk. This is fine as it still gives them some control and responsibility and they get the same kind of sense of achievement at the end of the week as the others. The most difficult aspect of target setting for my group is helping them to describe how they will know when they have achieved something and trying to involve them in establishing criteria for successfully completing a target. Some students still need encouragement to ask for help when it is needed and, of course, there are some who think they can do everything well – this is probably when we need our negotiating skills at the best!

Teacher 2

We all have dreams and aspirations, things that we want to achieve in life. For most of us, these dreams are grounded in reality and so we know for example that we probably will not play for England or win an Oscar. However, each day we set ourselves smaller goals, ones that are achievable and give us a great deal of satisfaction when we have mentally ticked them off our list.

These can be tasks such as sending a 'Thank you' card, making a phone call or cleaning the cooker; or more personal goals, such as being nice to the next door neighbour, not drinking for a week or not getting angry in the traffic jam on the way to work.

By achieving these goals, we feel confident and more in control of our lives. We are working towards a goal and we are making it happen. Why should our pupils be denied this?

It is important for our pupils to develop the ability to set some of their own goals; to gain this sense of achievement and a sense of being in control of some parts of their lives. Our job, as teachers, is to give them the tools for this, such as communication, choice and decision-making, and to set up simple ways of enabling them to state their goals. We need to ensure they are grounded in reality and in small enough sets to be achievable.

All the work done throughout the school from the moment a pupil starts should be leading them towards setting their own goals and developing the skills of self-advocacy. We cannot just expect any pupil to suddenly become target setters. Thus we give them choices in as many areas as possible and more importantly we try to let them see the consequences of their choice; we help them to develop a range of skills and develop their self-confidence and self-esteem. In this way, it is hoped that they will be ready in the senior years to become more independent learners, whatever their level of ability.

It is always easier for the more vocal, independent pupils to set a target for themselves, as they have become used to speaking up, giving their opinions and they feel comfortable with this. For our pupils, termed as PMLD, it is harder, as they are used to their lives being adult led, usually out of necessity, but part of our role as special needs teachers is to act as advocates for our pupils. Therefore, whatever their ability, we should be able to set targets with them.

Having taught in schools both with and without pupil targets has enabled me to see the advantages. Yes, it can be difficult to ensure the targets are achievable and appropriate to each pupil and that they are not 'stuck' on a target for too long, but part of teaching is to be creative and work through these difficulties. Ultimately, I have seen pupils gain a real sense of achievement on reaching their targets; they become excited and enthusiastic about learning and it helps them to see that they *do* have some control and some say in things that happen to them. It also sets them on the road to the future where big decisions will have to be made but setting targets such as 'This week I will pour my own drink' or 'This week I will be helpful' may eventually help them to set goals such as 'This week I will visit the cinema' or 'This week I will work hard on speaking to the cashier in Tescos', when they are living independently in the community.

Teacher 3 (Recently transferred from a mainstream secondary school)
I think that teaching and learning of self-advocacy is one of the most difficult and complex areas for both staff and students, whether in mainstream or special education.

However, I would argue that it is one of the most important issues in education as it enables students to feel empowered and to have to take on board the idea of ownership. Education is not just something that is done to them as a passive audience and self-advocacy requires students to take responsibility for themselves.

In secondary education, we had begun the process which required pupils to consider for themselves appropriate targets in each subject at the end of every unit of work and this required a lot of one-to-one work as they often preferred to be 'told' what they should have as a target, other than think for themselves, negotiate and take responsibility for their own learning. How much more challenging will this be in a special school?

My experience of target setting within special needs education suggests that it is very time consuming, requires a great deal of patience and gentle encouragement. Therefore, it needs a lot more time so there are profound implications for the curriculum; we all know there is not enough time to cover everything we would like at present, let alone setting aside even more time for self-advocacy.

However, the benefits of self-advocacy are immense, for example Thomas' mum told me recently how weekly target setting this term has had a very positive impact on him and how proud he was when he achieved a target.

A selection of pupils' comments during an informal videoed discussion about their target setting sessions is as follows:

I'm working on telling the time to ten past the hour. I chose it with a bit of help. When I leave school, I want to be able to tell the time properly. Some bloke might ask me the time – it would be nice to tell him.

We look through our folders, choose what we've found difficult and then think it over with a member of staff. A lot of people need a lot of help, I need a bit too.

You have to practice all week.

I find it a bit hard but we get used to it. It's a bit of a problem to do. It can be hard or easy. It's hard when you're not sure what target you want – your brain turns off. You ask for help when you're stuck.

It's important so when you leave school you know what you want to do and what you don't.

You should choose things that are hard. I feel sad when I've not done my target. It's better when you choose something that you're interested in.

There was a general consensus that they were involved in something that affected the whole of their week, not just the designated review slots on the timetable. The pupils were also aware of their own responsibility in the process and were keen to achieve. It was also apparent that the pupils were conversant with the terminology used such as 'target' and 'achievement'.

Of course, barriers for pupils becoming effective target setters still exist and the researchers readily acknowledge weaknesses in the methodology deployed. Teacher interpretations of material varied at times; partly because the instructions provided lacked clarity and partly because teachers varied in terms of how systematically approaches were undertaken. Nevertheless, the notion of target setting is now as firmly embedded in the curriculum of older pupils as are the statutory and transitional elements such as Maths and English.

There is a general agreement among staff that a greater ownership of the pupils' learning could be facilitated by a range of new initiatives that are currently being piloted as a result of our work on this project. These include:

1. Producing pupil-friendly versions of IEPs incorporating symbols and other augmentative systems.
2. Regular timetabled tutorials during which learning targets are reviewed as part of their Records of Achievement work.
3. Time given to students to discuss and produce draft targets prior to attending their review.

Issues have also been raised concerning the role of learning support assistants and the necessity of establishing an agreed philosophy towards self-advocacy that achieves a balance between guidance and negotiation. LSAs are often at the forefront of this work and have required specific training in order to ensure consistent management of the processes involved.

It is planned to produce a training and guidance pack for existing and new staff, the production of this will be as collaborative as possible in order to maintain a shared understanding and sense of purpose. The pack may contain the following kinds of material.

- Video clips of pupils and staff setting targets together, emphasising successful exchanges and negotiation.
- Observation training materials.
- Examples of target setting profiles and a range of targets selected by pupils over a period of time and their evaluations.
- A variety of possible planning formats and frameworks.
- Activity examples likely to develop pupils' awareness and skills in setting targets.

The implementation of these guidelines may well lend themselves to further action research which could be used to assess the effectiveness of both content and implementation.

Involvement in an action research project had a number of benefits for the school. For many staff it brought the relevance of research to classroom practice much closer to home. Having the support of colleagues in higher education assisted in providing a critical overview and in asking the difficult questions which it would have been easy to avoid. Following the research, reports of the work undertaken appeared in academic journals (Rose, Fletcher and Goodwin 1999, Rose 1999) bringing some recognition of the school and the hard work of staff. Teachers have been provided with important insights into the importance of systematic enquiry to support school development, and some are keen to become more involved in classroom research. This is not to say that there are no difficulties in becoming involved in action research projects of this nature. It is certainly time consuming, and at times it is frustrating to have to constantly review in detail the progress which is being made. However, overall the benefits which staff, pupils and the school as a whole gained from this work far outstripped the disadvantages.

References and further reading

Cooper, P. (1993) *Effective Schools for Disaffected Students*. London: Routledge.

Cowie, H. (1994) 'Ways of involving children in decision making', in Blatchford, P. and Sharp, S. (eds) *Breaktime and the School*. London: Routledge.

Davie, R. and Galloway, D. (1996) *Listening to Children in Education*. London: David Fulton Publishers.

Department for Education (DFE) (1994) *Code of Practice on the Identification and Assessment of Special Educational Needs*. London: DFE.

Department of Education and Science (DES) (1981) *Education Act*. London: DES.

Department of Health (DoH) (1989) *The Children Act*. London: HMSO.

Francis, H. (1993) *Teachers Listening to Learners' Voices*. Leicester: British Psychological Society.

Lewin, K. (1946) 'Action research and minority problems', *Journal of Social Issues* **2**, 34–6.

Marland, M. (1996) 'Personal development, pastoral care and listening', in Davie, R. and Galloway, D. (eds) *Listening to Children in Education*. London: David Fulton Publishers.

Munby, S. (1995) 'Assessment and pastoral care: sense, sensitivity and standards', in Best, R. *et al.* (eds) *Pastoral Care and Personal Social Education*. London: Cassell.

Rose, R. (1999) 'The involvement of pupils with severe learning difficulties as decision makers in respect of their own learning needs', *Westminster Studies in Education* **22**(4), 19–29.

Rose, R., Fletcher, W. and Goodwin, G. (1999) 'Pupils with severe learning difficulties as personal target setters', *British Journal of Special Education* **26**(4), 206–12.

Rose, R., McNamara, S. and O'Neil, J. (1996) 'Promoting the greater involvement of pupils with special needs in the management of their own assessment and learning procedures', *British Journal of Special Education* **23**(4), 166–71.

United Nations (1989) *Convention on the Rights of the Child*. Brussels: United Nations Assembly.

CHAPTER 4

Observation

The use of observation in educational research presents a number of advantages to the researcher. In particular, observation is a very direct method which provides the researcher with close contact with the subject, behaviours or events being studied, thereby enabling a 'real life' picture to be achieved. It lends itself well to the researcher who wishes to gain an understanding of what is happening, for example in a classroom, on the playground, or during a school visit, and in combination with other data collection methods such as interviews or document scrutiny it can be a particularly useful part of the researcher's battery of techniques.

There are, however, a number of difficulties which may be presented to the small scale researcher in relation to using observation. One of the greatest obstacles is the time which is necessary to conduct observations as part of a research project. In order to use observation effectively, the researcher needs to familiarise themselves with the environment in which the observation is to take place, and to enable the subjects of observation to become familiar with him or her. This may entail a teacher researcher spending time in a classroom with a group of pupils who are to be involved prior to conducting the observation. For many small-scale researchers the possibilities of devoting a great deal of time to a direct approach like observation is not possible.

Croll (1986) has discussed some of the difficulties of conducting effective classroom observations. He particularly notes the problems of interpretation which the observer may experience, and the amount of data with which the observer is inevitably confronted in a busy classroom. Hopkins (1992), Tilstone (1998) and Wragg (1999) have emphasised the importance of observation having a focus and a well defined purpose. Having a clear understanding of what is required from the observation can enable the observer to ignore peripheral activity and to obtain maximum relevant information. Of course, use of video recording enables the researcher to observe an event several times, possibly with a different focus for each observation. However, before considering the use of video the researcher needs to recognise the possible attendant difficulties associated with this approach. Decisions need to be made regarding whether a static or moving video camera is to be used. In the case of a static camera it goes without saying that any event or behaviour which occurs out of shot will not be recorded. A moving camera allows the researcher to follow a particular pupil or group of pupils, but can be quite disruptive in a busy classroom. It is often easier for the observer to shift focus from one part of an activity to another when observing directly rather than being dependent upon video recordings.

A key question for the observer must centre upon the type of observation to be conducted. To participate or not to participate?

In participant observation the observer attempts to become a part of the group to be observed. Such an approach demands that the researcher gains the confidence of the subjects to be observed and becomes accepted as an integral part of the activities which these subjects are undertaking. For the educational researcher this may be seen to have some advantages. By 'blending in' to the classroom an observer is likely to be seen as a part of the normal activity of the group and may be in a good position to get close to the action to be observed. However, there are several draw backs to this approach which need to be given careful consideration. Firstly, it is extremely difficult to maintain field notes when closely involved in participant observation. Robson (1993) suggests that in this form of observation the researcher may have difficulties separating the data collection from the analysis phase of the research. Similarly, there are dangers that in becoming part of a group, the observer may influence the activities and behaviours of the observed and could create a false impression of what would normally happen without his or her presence. An important issue for the participant observer is that of behaving ethically. It would be possible to conduct some forms of participant observation without the subjects knowing that they were being observed, or being aware of the motives and purpose of the research. Such action in indefensible in educational research, and it is beholden upon all observers to ensure transparency of purpose and honesty in dealing with subjects. Indeed, many researchers would wish to follow practices in which their field notes were made fully available to the subjects of their observations.

A contrast to the participant observation is the non-participant approach whereby the observer attempts to be the 'fly on the wall' in the classroom, sitting at the edge and taking field notes. This form of observation generally follows a rigid structure and may be accompanied by formal observation schedules which indicate precisely what the observer intends to record. Such observation lends itself to methods such as event coding, where the observer records every time a specific behaviour or event takes place, or time sampling where the observer notes what happens at particular times with specific intervals between each observation. Similarly, the observer may find it convenient to use tally sheets or checklists to record for example occurrences of the use of particular language forms or speech types. Non-participant observation is generally easier to manage than participant observation but may also have some difficulties. In particular, the presence of an observer sat at the side of the classroom taking notes can make both teachers and pupils self conscious and may result in behaviours which are not a true reflection of what would normally happen in the observed situation. It may be argued that since the onset of OFSTED inspections teachers have become more used to having someone observing their lessons in this way. It may be equally valid to say that the nature of these inspections is such that teacher anxieties about such approaches have been increased.

Robson (1993) suggests that it may be possible to achieve a happy medium between participant and non-participant observation. He describes marginal participant observation as an approach in which the observer remains on the periphery of activity, but may from time to time be drawn in to activity by those being observed. This form of observation can often prove successful in schools, being less formal than non-participant observation but still enabling the researcher to maintain an observation schedule or follow a set recording routine.

Ethical considerations in undertaking observations as part of research are extremely important. Issues of informed consent may be particularly taxing to the researcher. If the purpose of your research is to observe the activity of a whole class and the parents of all of the pupils except one gives consent, how will you proceed? Researchers who work in schools often seek the consent of parents or carers to make observations which involve their children. The same researchers often forget that the pupils themselves have rights to be consulted and to be informed about the purpose of the research. Griffiths (1998) writes about collaboration in research as a means of promoting social justice. She suggests that the role of the educational researcher is always to work *with* rather than *on* or *for* people. In acknowledging that true collaboration is hard to achieve, Griffiths asks the researcher to examine their motives for undertaking their work and to consider all of the individuals who are involved. She recognises that there is much that can go wrong, such as failing to involve specific groups or individuals, sometimes by accident, but sometimes because of the assumptions which we make about them. In observing pupils with special educational needs, we should not assume that because they have communication problems or learning difficulties we should not seek their consent or share with them in the research process. Similarly, we should never assume that our interpretation of their understanding or expectations mirror our own. Good collaborative research provides opportunities for discussion and negotiation within a climate of honesty which recognises the individuality and rights of all who are involved.

In the use of observation such openness may in itself lead to difficulties. It may be that the researcher's interpretation of what they see does not exactly coincide with that of the teacher or the pupils observed. The well organised observer will be working to well established criteria which enables him or her to make decisions about what is seen. However, this should not preclude opportunities for open discussion with partners in the research and consideration of the views expressed by the subjects of observation.

Educational researchers who intend to use observation in research related to special educational needs should consider a number of issues:

- What are my motives for conducting observations?
- How can I conduct observation which is of least intrusion upon the lives of those to be observed?
- How can I ensure that the dignity of pupils and staff is maintained at all times? (For example, if a child in a class being observed has an epileptic seizure how can I best help the situation, what role will I play in supporting the teacher?)

- When will be the most appropriate times to conduct my observations? Are there specific times when the events or incidents I wish to observe are most likely to occur?
- If the school is equipped with two-way mirrors, how will I ensure that the observed are comfortable with their use, and how will I let them know that they are being observed?
- How will I dress in order not to appear out of place in the observation situation?
- With whom do I need to share information and data?
- How will I feed back information to interested parties?
- Whose consent do I need to carry out observations?
- What kind of field notes will I keep?

Researchers conducting observations in schools need to be aware that it is a privilege to be a guest in a teacher's classroom. The classroom is the domain of the teacher and the pupils in the class and they have a right to feel comfortable and secure within this environment. Observers need to be prepared to withdraw from a classroom if their presence becomes disruptive or if it is likely to cause embarrassment. For example, if a parent arrives in class to discuss a personal problem associated with his or her child, it may not be appropriate for the researcher to be present.

Observation can be a source of rich data and has been at the heart of some of the most influential educational research (Galton *et al.* 1980). Through observation we have one of the most direct methods of learning about teaching and learning, and possibly one of the most difficult methods to organise and manage.

Ann Fergusson and Trudy Duffield's use of observation

Fergusson and Duffield use classroom observation to gather qualitative data in a particularly difficult area. When observing pupils with severe or profound and multiple learning difficulties, researchers need to establish a good understanding of what constitutes the usual behaviours of the pupils under scrutiny. In this study the researchers were looking for comparative data which could inform them about the effectiveness of mother tongue teaching to a group of pupils whose responses were often non-verbal in nature. Such observation is most easily conducted when the observer has a good understanding of the pupils, and is familiar with the context in which the pupils are working. Non-participant observation was the logical choice in this particular study because of the need for the researchers to be vigilant in looking for small interactions or reactions from pupils with profound and multiple learning difficulties. This particular approach also ensured that the observers did not become a distraction or cause any difficulties for pupils through changes in their routine.

Data gathered through observation often needs to be substantiated through triangulation achieved by using other sources of information. In Fergusson and Duffield's study, informal interviews with parents and with the learning support assistant who conducted work in mother tongue was critical in aiding interpretation of observation data. Robson (1993) points out that where the main purpose of research is to be descriptive, as was the case in the work of Fergusson and Duffield, it often provides a useful primary source of data collection. However, in areas where there are complexities associated with the nature of the pupil's needs, abilities and culture, there is always likely to be some difficulty of interpretation. Fergusson and Duffield are careful not to generalise from their findings in this small-scale study. The work which they continue to undertake within the study school is still at an early stage of development. The information which they have gained tends to confirm their belief that mother tongue teaching is providing benefits for pupils from Panjabi speaking homes. It is easy to make assumptions about the value of such approaches with pupils of such severe and complex needs, and it is therefore essential that further research of this nature is undertaken, which may ultimately lead to greater understanding of the potential benefits of work of the type described by these researchers.

Examples of other observational research projects in special education

'Bridging the communication gap (for pupils with profound and multiple learning difficulties)'.

Detheridge, T. (1997), *British Journal of Special Education* **24**(1), 21–6.

'Can the use of background music improve the behaviour and academic performance of children with emotional and behavioural difficulties?'

Hallam, S. and Price, J. (1998), *British Journal of Special Education* **25**(2), 88–91.

'Comparing instructional contexts of students with and without severe disabilities in general education classrooms'.

Logan, K. R. and Malone, M. (1998), *Exceptional Children* **64**(3), 343–58.

'Efficacy of intensive interaction: developing sociability and communication in people with severe and complex learning difficulties using an approach based on care-giver-infant interaction'.

Nind, M. (1996), *European Journal of Special Needs Education* **11**(1), 48–66.

References and further reading

Cavendish, S. *et al.* (1990) *Observing Activities.* London: Paul Chapman.

Cohen, D. H., Stern, V. and Balaban, N. (1997) *Observing and Recording the Behaviour of Young Children.* New York: Teachers' College Press.

Croll, P. (1986) *Systematic Classroom Observation.* Lewes: Falmer Press.

Galton, M., Simon, B. and Croll, P. (1980) *Inside the Primary Classroom (The Oracle Study).* London: Routledge and Kegan Paul.

Griffiths, M. (1998) *Educational Research for Social Justice*. Buckingham: Open University Press.

Hopkins, D. (1992) *A Teacher's Guide to Classroom Research*. Buckingham: Open University Press.

Robson, C. (1993) *Real World Research*. Oxford: Blackwell.

Simpson, M. and Tuson, J. (1995) *Using Observations in Small-scale Research*. Glasgow: The Scottish Council for Research in Education.

Taplin, P. S. and Reid, J. B. (1973) 'Effects of instructional set and experimenter influence on observer reliability', *Child Development* 44(4), 547–54.

Tilstone, C. (1998) *Observing Teaching and Learning*. London: David Fulton Publishers.

Wragg, E. C. (1999) *An Introduction to Classroom Observation*, 2nd edn. London: Routledge.

CHAPTER 5

Promoting cultural, religious and linguistic diversity in a special school

Ann Fergusson and Trudy Duffield

Introduction

This study reviews the practice developed by a small, inner-city special school in supporting pupils whose home language is not English. A variety of methodologies were employed; some planned, while the need for others 'evolved' as the review progressed. Initially it was thought that the use of structured observation of pupils, together with the use of some published assessment material, would provide quantitative data on pupil communicative responses in order to make comparisons. However, it soon became apparent that this data would form only a small part of this research. The work presented here, has provided the foundations for a longer-term review process.

The school studied is located in the developing town of Peterborough. It is one of two special schools which share the city as their catchment, with pupils being placed either by geography (one school is in the old part of the city, the other in the more recently developed new townships) or based on parental preference. The school has a roll of 45 pupils and is situated in an older suburb of the city. It tends to reflect the multicultural nature of local communities, having more than 40 per cent of pupils from ethnic minority groups. These pupils in the main are from families of South Asian origin (the majority of families being of Pakistani descent and Panjabi speaking).

This review examines current practice in school, but uses the historical perspective as a baseline for evaluation purposes. The writers were involved in a collaborative school development project ten years previously (focusing on access to the then newly introduced National Curriculum), and had spent time in discussing this same issue of effective support for pupils who did not have English as a first language. It seemed an appropriate strategy to map the school's progress relating to this area, over this period.

An audit of current practice was also conducted as part of the review process. Through this we hoped to identify all aspects of the school's procedures or work that was thought to impact on this group of pupils, directly or indirectly.

In the initial stages of planning this work, the route we were expecting to take was to examine pupil responses in contexts with and without home language support. At that time, we also had intentions of investigating the perceptions of this particular aspect of pupil support from all involved (staff, parents and the pupils themselves). However, as the work progressed it became apparent that we would need to be flexible in our approach and in response to the demands of the school.

Background to the study

The origins of this work came about through discussion by the authors, of the impact offered by the home language support for pupils who do not have English as a first language. As part of another school based research project, the support of pupils in their home language had been explored (National Curriculum Development Team (NCDT) 1990). At that time the LEA funded Section XI staffing (multicultural support staff) to schools was purely on a 'numbers basis', rather than proportional representation. Despite the study school's population at the time being of between 40 to 50 per cent from families with Asian origins, this special school had relatively small pupil numbers compared to mainstream schools and was not considered eligible for funding. The head teacher of the school had been fighting this cause for some considerable time and the school had introduced many necessary initiatives from its own resources.

The school based project at the time was working with school staff to introduce the National Curriculum and focused, in part, on issues of access. The findings of this project (NCDT 1990) were that pupils who did not have English as their first language were seriously disadvantaged; many of these pupils needed home language teaching to gain access to most aspects of the curriculum.

Over the next ten years, the school made considerable advances in providing for religious, cultural and linguistic diversity within their pupil population. The LEA began supporting the school in 1992, by providing Section XI funding for bilingual support to the school, for 15 hours per week. A bilingual support assistant was assigned to the school. This was the first time support staff from the local Multicultural Service had been involved in supporting pupils with severe or profound and multiple learning difficulties. New demands were made upon both the school and the support worker, as to how best deploy newly available expertise to support pupils and school staff, in each class across this all-phase school.

The appointment of this bilingual support worker was to be the start of a range of initiatives taken by the school to meet the needs of its ethnic minority pupils and their families.

The present context

The positive developments towards meeting multicultural diversity made by the school, were recognised by the LEA. This together with changes in funding arrangements for multicultural support (Ethnic Minorities Achievement Grant or EMTAG), led to the school's allocation of support hours being increased – initially to 20 hours and then in 1998 to 25 hours per week. Funding arrangements changed again in 1999, with funding in the main, being devolved to schools. Once again, because of the relative, small numbers of pupils supported by this school, funding did not meet the cost of their present provision and there was a financial shortfall. Monies will be fully devolved to schools in the near future and it is anticipated that this shortfall will be greater. This has lead to uncertainty in ensuring there will be adequate funds to secure a bilingual support assistant and to maintain the present level of home language support.

Methodology

From the outset of this study we adopted the position of Reflective Practitioners. We wanted to take stock of what current practice comprised, but we proposed to do this with the intention of changing or developing that practice in light of our research, to improve effectiveness of the provision. This methodology was viewed as the most appropriate to meet the needs of the investigation. It met definitions of teachers working as reflective practitioners as described by Singh (1994) and Elliott (1983) (cited Singh 1994). Elliott talks of teacher researchers as being concerned with improving practice 'by means of their own practical actions and by means of their own reflections upon the effects of those actions' (page 7). Also the notion of 'enhancing understanding' with the purpose of effecting change as being all important to the investigation.

We were aware that our study could not be viewed to have a neutral status. As stated by Singh (1994), investigations of this nature are not neutral in their value commitments to the research. Our intentions were to look for good practice, as well as being inspired by a vision for improvement. Guided by our reading of the relevant literature, we planned to adopt a systematic and critical thinking approach, in our reflections. We hoped this reflection would help us as 'teachers to sharpen … perceptions of the everyday realities of [their] work' (Ruddock 1989). This was the very focus of our study – the 'everyday realities' formed the data that we were attempting to collect and interpret. Murray and Lawrence (2000) explore the role of the Interpretive Researcher, suggesting that although apparently relatively unconcerned with 'subjectivity', qualitative data gathering techniques can be a means of 'placing value' on the daily experiences … in defined … organizational contexts (page 30). They continue by clarifying their definitions of data to include information about 'organizational minutiae, the subtlety of social interaction and perceptual variation'. These were the types of data we expected to be considering.

We identified a range of data gathering methods according to the type of information we were seeking. Again, the work of Murray and Lawrence was influential. They listed 'discussions, direct observations, interviews, case study, ethnographic descriptions, content analysis of documents and anecdotal data' as 'processes all … favoured by the interpretive researcher'.

Easen (1985), in his work on school based developments, raised our awareness of the different kinds of changes we might experience in our review process. He identified three types of change:

- *incremental change* (bit by bit)
- *pendulum change* (abandon beliefs)
- *paradigm change* (reorganise knowledge and transform views).

We were open to the reality that we may experience one, two or perhaps all three of these types of changes in the ways we thought and worked. The catalysts for these were varied; in some instances the sequence of events formed the basis of our review of progress, in others we were influenced by reading from a range of sources.

While endeavouring to work as reflective practitioners the researchers could not ignore the dilemmas arising out of their own backgrounds and those of the children and families within Panjabi speaking homes at the school. We were aware of notions, throughout the literature, of people becoming equated with objects for the purpose of research. Mirza (1995) has discussed how easily children or parents can become the 'objects' of a study by a more dominant group. South Asian children with learning difficulties and their parents could be conceptualised as powerless, oppressed and marginal in society, in relation to more dominant groups. Macintyre (2000) stresses that it is essential that children's rights are not infringed although she acknowledges the validity of school based research and its ability to help practitioners assist specific groups of children within schools.

It is difficult to give voice to the respect we feel for these families without sounding insincere, however, we hope to demonstrate this through further developing practices within school to enhance the learning environment for these children. It may be that as teacher researchers we can demonstrate an overt and political commitment to the ability of research to improve teaching and learning for all pupils.

We acknowledge that we do not share the same cultural, religious and linguistic backgrounds as the children at the centre of the study. Finch (1984) has discussed this complex relationship between the researcher and the researched, while Mirza (1995) emphasised the need for shared meanings to occur between both groups. To proceed further we had to take another view and envisage another reality. As Claudette Williams has stated: 'I am careful not to say "if you don't experience it you can't do anything about it because it is not true"' (Williams 1995:153). Chaudhary (1990) has emphasised that working as a researcher can be difficult when you do not share major common religious beliefs or the same cultural background. We hope our subjectivity is explicitly placed and the limitations of our research are clearly acknowledged.

These cultural considerations were particularly important when planning the classroom observations which were used to gain information about pupil reaction in taught situations. Observations were conducted of pupils taught solely in English, and of other times when they were taught in mother tongue. In order to verify our interpretations of what was observed, we discussed these with staff concerned after each lesson.

The Panjabi group at the study school: the rational

An examination was made of the school documentation that underpinned the ethos and practice of support for this pupil group within the school. One of the researchers had previously examined the value of mother tongue support for pupils with SLD/PMLD (Duffield 1996). The purpose of revisiting the school's rationale was to explore new literature, and to see if educational research continued to promote the practice of mother tongue teaching. An immediate difficulty was the dearth of research looking at these issues with a SLD/PMLD population. The literature, that exists, tends to focus on cultural or discriminative issues rather than pedagogical (Vehma 1999, Tait 1999, Wolf 1999, and Wellard 1999).

When the school's rationale was developed, seven key principles were established. These were shared with teaching staff and governors and all other staff through both the staff handbook and curriculum policy documentation. Shamsa's (the bilingual support assistant) attendance at weekly meetings meant ongoing concerns could be discussed and recorded.

The review of the literature for this study continues to support the rationale for supporting learning in mother tongue at the study school. Furthermore, new principles are evolving which will be discussed in the final part of this chapter.

Principle 1
To develop cognitive functioning in first language by teaching key concepts in mother tongue to support other curriculum areas

Condie and Virani (1993) have illustrated how when the status of community language is high within education, it is invaluable in enabling learners to clarify thoughts and change knowledge into understanding. All teachers of pupils with severe learning difficulties endeavour to devise effective methodologies to consolidate understanding for their pupils. Collier (1995) emphasised that children can only work at their actual level of cognitive maturity in the language they know best. Wright *et al.* (2000) urge that within education practical and financial support must be made to make schools a place where all pupils have equal access to learning.

Principle 2
To observe and assess pupils' communicative functioning in home language

It is important to know how pupils respond in their mother tongue, which we believe is central to their social, emotional and cognitive development.

The National Oracy Project (1991) and Wright (1992) had emphasised how assessment of pupils' work should not be affected adversely by any (comparative) weakness in English. It is important to use dual language materials to assess existing skills and abilities. These may help to reveal that the pupil knows more than assumed. Parsons (1996) reminds us how our home language is an integral part of our identity and should always play a part within the work of the classroom.

Principle 3
To use adult commentary in first language to provide emotional support and develop self-esteem during learning. To recognise and celebrate pupils' achievement using their mother tongue

Collier (1995) stated that confidence was promoted among language minority pupils when their home language was promoted within the school. Parsons (1996) argues that children need to be aware of the teacher's interest in their culture and language. Language is an integral part of the culture of each child and hence the denial of a child's language or culture is also a denial of the child's essence.

Principle 4
To enable pupils to have role models from their own communities working alongside other adults within the school

Otten (1999) describes the importance of pupils within Special Education being given opportunities to develop respect for diversity within schools, families and communities. This provides a foundation for developing pupils' self-esteem and ultimately, good self-advocacy. Wright *et al.* (2000) described how black pupils frequently stress the importance of having black educators in their schools.

At the study school a Muslim Assembly is led by a member of the Peterborough Muslim Community. Brown (2000) comments on the importance of schools encouraging religious observance through everyday attitude to hygiene, dress or diet.

Principle 5
To provide opportunities for pupils to communicate choice, needs or preferences in their home language environment

In May 2000 *Curriculum guidance for the Foundation Stage* (QCA 2000) illustrated the need to provide bilingual support to enable pupils to practise and extend their communication skills. Scott (1997) for the Collaborative Learning Project supports the notion that children are always able to express themselves more effectively in their mother tongue until they are very advanced English users. Abrol (1990) argues that for pupils in special schools it is essential that the child's mother tongue should be retained at school if at all possible, rather than attempting to teach English. This is of paramount importance if the pupil is to be cared for by the family on leaving school.

Principle 6
To provide opportunities within school to reflect the rich history of oracy among the Peterborough Pakistani Muslim Community

We recognise that our pupils live in two languages, Panjabi at home and English at school. It does not mean that our pupils are competent, fluent or literate in their mother tongue. We do believe, however, that Panjabi has more meaning than English for these pupils and should be used within school whenever possible.

Abrol (1990) reminds us that it is very easy and understandable for the majority culture in a school to foster a single system and pay only lip-service to the needs of the minority. However, we should be providing equal status for the culture, customs and languages for all the communities represented in our schools (Diniz 1997 and Chambra *et al.* 1999).

Principle 7
To enable parents a termly opportunity to attend a curriculum workshop in school

Through observing the curriculum 'in action' during the Panjabi group parents are given the opportunity to ask questions and see the setting, teaching activity and social context of their child's learning in school. Hart (1996) and Tait (1999) discuss the need for schools to make the curriculum accessible to parents. Wright *et al.* (2000) argue it is essential to involve parents in the life of the school. Schools should not neglect the needs of disadvantaged groups of pupils and parents within school. The DfEE (1998) urged schools to provide for the cultural needs of their pupils by working closely with parents. Chambra *et al.* (1999) and Tait (1999) both describe the disadvantage minority ethnic parents face within the school system. Brown (2000) emphasises the need for good communication between schools and parents. This will ensure that families will not be treated as homogenous groups, with teachers drawing inaccurate or inappropriate conclusions about their needs. 'Colour blind' treatment is unacceptable and teachers need to encourage diversity. Treating any group of pupils as if they are homogenous without reference to individual characteristics is both racist and insulting (OFSTED 1999). The small size of the study school makes it easier to avoid unthinking conformity.

An audit of practice

Our observations and reflection on the continuing support for this pupil group needed to take account of the many developments that had transpired and were now established as current practice within the school. In order to do this we undertook an audit of present practice.

Staffing

The senior management team (SMT) work closely with the governing body when appointing staffing across the school. The aim is that the cultural, linguistic, and religious backgrounds of the staff reflect those of the children within the school. Although the school has been able to attract members of the Pakistani population to work as learning support assistants (LSAs) and midday supervisors, they have not been able to shortlist teachers to date. At present the Bilingual Assistant works closely with the teaching staff to deliver teaching in home language. It is the opinion of the researchers that attracting suitably qualified teachers into the SLD/PMLD field is difficult in many schools and is compounded when looking for teachers who share similar backgrounds to the pupils discussed.

Pupil grouping

Individual pupils are allocated 2.5 hours mother tongue support, per week. This time is planned and shared between the Bilingual Assistant and teaching staff, to be delivered on a one-to-one basis (for example IEP work) or to support group work in core subjects (thus enhancing pupils' conceptual development). In all work, the aim is to make the learning environment both multilingual and multi-modal. The school believes it is enriching for all children to hear a range of languages in the classroom and essential for children whose mother tongue is not English to have their learning environments supported with multi-modal communication systems and concrete learning experiences.

In addition to this, the pupils meet as a discrete group supported by parents, once a week and in a more formal teaching situation, to support the identified topic of the term. For example, a science lesson taught to a class might be repeated in mother tongue to consolidate earlier learning. Classes with a higher number of children from Panjabi speaking homes receive more bilingual support. Allocation is reviewed on a yearly basis when the Deputy Head and the Bilingual Assistant look at pupil groupings across the school.

Parental involvement

The school has initiated another discrete Panjabi group, led by some parents, who also work in school as lunch-time supervisors. Three Panjabi speaking parents come into school on a weekly basis to work with this group. Initially school staff made suggestions for the focus of work for this group, selecting areas they thought would interest the children (at the parents' request) and which reflected their culture and ethnicity. However, as their confidence grew, the parents began to plan the sessions themselves (in consultation with the Bilingual Assistant), to reflect what was happening in the local community. Any resources purchased by the parents are reimbursed and parents are paid for their time from the school's non-teaching supply budget. Many of the activities are oral in nature and centre around storytelling but this does not diminish the learning and enjoyment the children derive from these sessions.

Subject coordinators offer 'workshops' to parents on a regular basis. These usually take the form of demonstration lessons, planned by the SMT and delivered in home language to the pupils. Governors are often present and time is allocated at the end for parents to discuss what they have seen and to ask questions over refreshments. A minibus is made available to collect and take parents home to enable as many to attend as possible. Attendance at these workshops is high and the parents report that they value these sessions highly.

Pupil assessment

A 'new to school pack' and baseline communication assessment is completed with parents and the Bilingual Assistant when the children start school. Teachers are encouraged to be involved with these meetings. The Bilingual Assistant attends the termly parents' evening to discuss their child's Record of Achievement (ROA) file. An audiotape of the file, translated into Panjabi, is sent home before this meeting to alleviate the difficulty of families having to read their second language. As part of their directed time, teachers and the Bilingual Assistant home visit any family who has not been able to attend parents' night. Religious festivals and parties are regularly arranged and hosted by school staff, governors and parents as appropriate.

Resources

Subject coordinators are encouraged to ensure that materials reflect the diverse pupil backgrounds within school. The Bilingual Assistant manages her own resource budget and has chosen to focus on literacy, RE and PHSE resources. Many school-produced resources are also supported with Urdu text, especially symbol-based materials.

Policy documents

The school staff continue to review documentation to ensure the backgrounds and needs of this group of pupils are reflected. These are clearly articulated in the whole-school Curriculum Policy document and a copy of the rationale for the Panjabi group is included in the staff handbook.

Cultural sensitivity

School staff continue to increase their knowledge and understanding of and about the cultural differences of their pupils, through working with ethnic minority staff and parents. This cultural and ethnic awareness has lead to increasing sensitivity by staff when supporting pupils. An example of good practice which was observed can be illustrated by describing approaches to the personal care and hygiene routines observed for this pupil group. Wherever possible, pupils who are dependent on others for eating and drinking are given the support of a bilingual lunch-time supervisor; where possible personal care and toileting are supported by an adult of the same sex; religious artefacts are carefully removed before swimming and pupils are given the opportunity to wear shalwar kameez for swimming or clothing to cover their legs for PE. An area of the school entrance hall has been designated as a 'gallery' for some works of art donated by relatives in Pakistan; Pakistani staff and parents selected the frames and display design to best reflect their origins.

The school ethos

It is difficult to articulate how the school's ethos reflects its value in effectively supporting this pupil group. Like many schools, LEA policy is adopted on issues of Equal Opportunities, Inclusion and celebrating cultural diversity within school. The school's last OFSTED report (OFSTED 1995) commented very highly on the positive school ethos, with specific reference to this pupil group.

Some issues of assessment and measuring effectiveness of support

A focus of our investigation was to explore how we could measure the impact of home language support on pupil responses on a daily or sessional basis and on their overall achievements. We decided to look at the school's present means of assessing skills within the realms of communication for this group of pupils, both in their home language and the language of the school.

As part of our studies we looked at the efficacy and reliability of these assessment materials and considered the available literature on this issue. We were made aware of the ongoing debate of whether it is in fact possible to devise assessment procedures which are not biased linguistically, culturally or in terms of social class. It is not a legal requirement to assess linguistic minority pupils in their first language in this country, (unlike the USA), and very few assessment tools exist in mother tongue or community languages.

A significant text within this field (Cummins 1984) advocates a holistic view of assessment, in order to differentiate between learning difficulties and difficulties with bilingualism. Cummins offers a model that proposes pupils are supported by ensuring activities that are new or cognitively demanding be 'context embedded' and supported in mother tongue; in the case of less cognitively demanding tasks, the context can be reduced. This model is in some aspects similar to that adopted as good practice within the SLD field, and we were able to identify with his principles.

Another influential source for our study was the recent work of Cline (1999), who made many recommendations about the entitlement to appropriate assessment for bilingual pupils. He detailed the necessity for a full bilingual assessment to be made from the outset of educational placement and which informs all other decisions; the need for the materials used to have been formally reviewed for bias and, that pupils are 'dealt with by workers who, whatever their own background, are knowledgeable about and sensitive to key features of the children's culture and language' (Cline 1999).

These ideals supported our current beliefs about effective support for this group of pupils. However, the aspect that moved the direction of our research route was a resolve that bilingual assessment, in particular of pupils with special educational needs, should formally 'go beyond' the usual concentration on only the pupil, the teaching programme and what Cline refers to as the 'zone of potential development'.

One suggestion was the addition of curriculum-related assessment, but we were aware that, historically, cultural needs were not always brought into curriculum planning.

In order to be fully aware of the 'challenges' presented by individual pupils, Cline suggested any assessment includes an additional focus on the learning environment and its influence. The importance of the two-way nature of this influence was highlighted, and the value on having a clear vision of the 'dynamic interaction between the individual and the context in which they are placed' was stressed.

This line of thinking was not at all new to the 'SLD culture'. We were very familiar with the importance of a responsive, learning environment (Ware 1996, Duffield 1996, Fergusson 1994), in particular for those pupils at the earliest stages of development. However, it had not been formally acknowledged as an area for investigation, until this point.

The study school began using some published assessment materials (Hall 1995, Hall (for Beatrice Tate School 1994)), following a conference disseminating their function. The focus of these specific assessment schedules was to gather information relating to communication skills of pupils in both their home language (Language 1) and English (Language 2). The assessments were established as a routine procedure, providing an initial baseline for every pupil placed in the school whose home language was not English. This was updated annually. Parents (and often the wider family), the bilingual support worker and school staff (including specifically an LSA who was also a Panjabi speaker), were involved in the procedure.

Without exception the assessment evidence, from this school context over the last three years, has proved every pupil from this group as being communicatively more skilled in their mother tongue than English – including pupils with PMLD. Another influential factor to our research findings was that of differing perceptions or expectations. Teachers and parents were both involved in the same assessment process, yet parents in every case viewed their child's language and communication as being at a higher level than that perceived by the teachers. Our view of this was that parents were able to identify the subtleties of responses from their children in mother tongue or with mother tongue support. The school's Record of Achievement evaluations (termly review of IEPs, and aims and objectives for each area of the curriculum) also provide evidence of subtleties of higher functioning in mother tongue than in English. For example, a pupil might be quicker to respond when supported in his or her home language or they may show anticipation in mother tongue but not in English.

Classroom observation revealed that some pupils' responses, particularly those with PMLD, were more open to interpretation and difficult to 'measure'. When with a Panjabi speaker Nadia smiles more frequently and widens her eyes, Ghulum is awake more. These interpretations were influenced by how well the observer knew pupils and how 'tuned in' they were to the idiosyncratic and subtle responses these pupils demonstrated.

In using non-participant observation for gathering information by which to evaluate the impact of the mother tongue support, we were faced with a great number of difficulties in validating our evidence. It was not possible to replicate situations with and without support in home language and gain reliable evidence. Pupils were more responsive some days than others; staffing and other factors could change; pupils were sometimes quicker and more responsive when involved in an activity they had done before. We believed that it was not ethical nor truly comparable to have a 'control' group who received no support in their home language. In addition, we needed to consider whether it was strategies of mother tongue support or the good practice of multi-modal communication support (in the form of objects of reference, sign or symbol for example) that were the most effective channel of support for individuals.

Moving forward

Our first recommendation to where the next phase of this research goes has to be to return to the parents of this pupil group and collect and consider their views. As practitioners we need to consider what we can do to make support for this pupil group as effective and as available as possible. We need to make assessment processes more appropriate to bilingual learners, in order that our evidence be more valid. We need to find assessment mechanisms that look at a wider focus than communication alone. Cline (1999) and Cummins (1984) stressed that context is absolutely essential when assessing bilingual pupils. They highlight the danger in making assumptions of prior pupil experience and that the learning sequences of a task for minority ethnic individuals may differ from that of an indigenous child. Cummins has argued that decontextualising meaningful task content, as a result of task analysis for example, may have particular disadvantages for bilingual pupils.

Contemporary research (Latham and Miles 2001, QCA 2001) may provide one way forward, in being able to gain information about pupil functioning and progress across wider parameters and within varying contexts. The work of Latham and Miles provides a developmental approach to examining communication together with cognition, with an added dimension of emergent literacy. If this were used in both mother tongue and English, it may give more insight as to whether individual pupils think and learn most successfully in English or their home language and give an indication as to preferred learning style and the most appropriate teaching style. The recent QCA (2001) publication, developed to offer guidance to support the revised National Curriculum (DfEE/QCA 1999a and b) for pupils with learning difficulties, while not an assessment tool, offers much in the way of a continuum of learning across the subjects and other elements of the curriculum. Again, offered in home language and English, a more accurate picture of pupil achievement and progress may be made available.

The classroom observations which were undertaken as part of this research provided sufficient evidence to suggest that teaching in mother tongue has been beneficial in eliciting response from pupils and encouraging participation. Future research will consider how such benefits may be measured and sustained.

References and further reading

Abrol, S. (1990) 'Curriculum and Culture', *Special Children*, February, 8–10.

Babbage, R., Byers, R. and Redding, H. (1999) *Approaches to Teaching and Learning. Including pupils with learning difficulties*. London: David Fulton Publishers.

Brown, E. (2000) 'Effective collaboration to support the needs of pupils with profound multiple learning difficulties from minority ethnic groups', *The SLD Experience*, Spring, 2–6.

Chambra, R. *et al.* (1999) *On the Edge. Minority ethnic families caring for a severely disabled child.* Bristol: The Policy Press.

Chaudhary, A. (1990) 'Problems for parents – experiences of Tower Hamlets', in Orton, C. (ed.) *Asian Children and Special Needs. A report from ACE Advisory Centre for Education.* London: ACE.

Cline, T. (1999) 'The assessment of special educational needs for bilingual children', *British Journal of Special Education* **25**(4), 159–63.

Collier, V. (1995) 'Acquiring a second language for school', *Directions in Language and Education. National Clearinghouse for Bilingual Education* **1**(4).

Cummins, J. (1984) *Bilingualism and Special Education: Issues in Assessment and Pedagogy*. Avon: Multilingual Matters.

DfEE (1998) *Meeting Special Educational Needs: A Programme for Action*. London: DfEE.

DfEE/QCA (1999a) *The National Curriculum. Handbook for primary teachers in England*. London: DfEE.

DfEE/QCA (1999b) *The National Curriculum. Handbook for secondary teachers in England*. London: DfEE.

Diniz, F. A. (1997) 'Working with families in a multi-ethnic European context: Implications for services', in Carpenter, B. (ed.) *Families in Context. Emerging Trends in Family Support and Early Intervention*. London: David Fulton Publishers.

Duffield, E. T. (1996) 'Exploring the part that the use of mother tongue can play in supporting learning in a school for pupils with severe learning difficulties: a case study of one school. Unpublished M.Ed. Thesis, University of Cambridge.

Easen, P. (1985) *Making School-centred INSET work*. Milton Keynes: Open University Press.

El-Hadi, A. (1996) 'The inner life of children from ethnic minorities: the impact of cultural differences', in Varma, V. (ed.) *The Inner Life of Children with Special Needs*. London: Whurr Publishers.

Elliott, J. (1983) 'Paradigms of educational research and theories of schooling'. Paper presented at Westhill Sociology of Education conference, January. Cited in Kelly, A. 'Action research: what is it and what can it do?', in Burgess, R. G. (ed.) *Issues in Educational Research*. Lewes: Falmer Press.

Fergusson, A. (1994) 'Planning for communication', in Rose, R. *et al.* (eds) *Implementing the Whole Curriculum for Pupils with Learning Difficulties*. London: David Fulton Publishers.

Hall, S. (1995) *An introduction to Collaborative Learning: extending thinking and creating contexts for developing academic language in multilingual classrooms*. London: Collaborative Learning Project.

Hart, S. (1996) *Beyond Special Needs: Enhancing Children's Learning through Innovative Thinking*. London: Paul Chapman.

Latham, C. and Miles, A. (2001) *Communication, Curriculum and Classroom Practice*. London: David Fulton Publishers.

Macintyre, C. (2000) *The Art of Action Research in the Classroom.* London: David Fulton Publishers.

Mirza, M. (1995) 'Some ethical dilemmas in fieldwork: feminist and antiracist methodologies', in Griffiths, M. and Troyna, B. (eds) *Antiracism, Culture and Social Justice in education.* Stoke-on-Trent: Trentham Books.

Murray, L. and Lawrence, B. (2000) *Practitioner-Based Enquiry. Principles for Postgraduate Research.* London: Falmer Press.

National Curriculum Development Team (SLD) (1990) '*Report on School Block at St George's School, Peterborough*'. Unpublished project report, Cambridge Institute of Education.

National Oracy Project (1991) *Teacher Talking and Learning in Key Stage One.* York: National Curriculum Council.

OFSTED (1995) *Inspection Report of St George's School, Peterborough.* London: OFSTED.

OFSTED (1999) *Educational Inequality: Mapping Race, Class and Gender.* London: OFSTED.

Otten, L. (ed.) (1999) *A Curriculum for Personal and Social Education.* London: David Fulton Publishers.

Parsons, Y. (1996) 'Story-Telling and Home Language, in Southwark Council', in *Learning in Culturally Diverse Classrooms.* Southwark: Southwark Traveller Education Project.

QCA (2000) *Curriculum guidance for the Foundation Stage.* London: DfEE.

QCA (2001) *Planning, teaching and assessing the curriculum for pupils with learning difficulties.* London: DfEE.

Ruddock, J. (1989) 'Practitioner research and programmes of initial teacher education', *Westminster Studies in Education* **12**, 6–72.

Singh, B. R. (ed.) (1994) *Improving Gender and Ethnic Relations. Strategies for schools and further education.* London: Cassell.

Tait, T. (1999) 'Doubly Disadvantaged? The Challenge', *Link Up* , Spring, 4–5.

Vehma, S. (1999) 'Discriminative Assumptions', *Disability and Society* **14**, January, 37–52.

Ware, J. (1996) *Creating a Responsive Environment. For people with profound and multiple learning difficulties.* London: David Fulton Publishers.

Warner, R. (1999) 'The views of Bangladeshi parents on the special school attended by their young children with severe learning difficulties', *British Journal of Special Education* **26**(4) 218–23.

Wellard, S. (1999) 'Caring about culture', *Community Care*, November, 26–7.

Williams, C. (1995) 'How black children might survive education', in Griffiths, M. and Troyna, B. (eds) *Antiracism, Culture and Social Justice in Education.* Stoke-on-Trent: Trentham Books.

Wolf, F. (1999) 'Celebrating diversity', *Talking Sense*, **45**(2), 14–17.

Wright, C. (1992) *Race Relations in the Primary School.* London: David Fulton Publishers..

Wright, C., Weekes, D. and McGlaughlin, A. (2000) '*Race*', *Class and Gender in Exclusion from School. Studies in Inclusive Education.* London: Falmer Press.

CHAPTER 6

Using documents

Documentary research is a valuable method for understanding and explaining social relations. All research projects will involve at some stage the use of documentary evidence, but what is a document? Scott (1990) provides a useful starting point for answering this question:

> a document in its most general sense is a written text ... Writing is the making of symbols representing words, and involves the use of a pen, pencil, printing machine or tool for inscribing the message on paper, parchment or some other material medium ... Similarly, the invention of magnetic and electronic means of storing and displaying text should encourage us to regard 'files' and 'documents' contained in computers and word processors as true documents. From this point of view ... documents may be regarded as physically embodied texts, where the containment of the text is the primary purpose of the physical medium. (Scott 1990:12–13)

This definition celebrates the diversity of documentary sources. Documents can be classified in a variety of ways:

- as *primary* sources, that is produced at the time of the event that they describe;
- as *secondary* sources, that is produced after the event;
- as *public* documents, generally official records produced by national and local governments;
- as *private* documents, produced by individuals not by the state;
- as *solicited* documents, produced for a research project;
- as *unsolicited* sources, produced for personal use.

These classifications clearly overlap, but the researcher needs to be clear about the provenance of his or her documentary evidence (Yin 1984, Burgess 1990, Scott 1990). In addition, documents can also be categorised according to their public accessibility: closed, restricted, open-archival and open-published (Scott 1990). If documents are held in the public domain (a national or local archive) this accessibility is usually determined by the state.

Educational researchers generally work with documents associated with educational settings, such as policy documents, school records, curriculum materials, textbooks, the incidental everyday documents associated with teaching and so on; or with documents produced as part of the research process, for example the solicited diary or journal of a head teacher asked to keep a record of daily events and the proportion of time given over to each event, or the field notes of a classroom assistant recording their day-to-day response to incidents in the classroom. Whatever the document, the same critical research practice applies. A simple maxim may be helpful here: 'no document is innocent.' All documents carry values and ideologies: they do not simply reflect social reality, they also construct it. Documentary analysis proceeds through careful evaluation; this involves asking questions about a document's authenticity, credibility, representativeness and meaning (Platt 1981a and b, Scott 1990). Forster (1994) usefully summarises the questions the researcher should ask about authenticity:

> Are the data genuine? Are they from a primary or secondary source? Are they actually what they appear to be? ... Can authorship be validated? Are the documents dated and placed? Are they accurate records of the events or processes described? Are the authors of documents believable? (Forster 1994:155)

Credibility relates to the accuracy of the information recorded in the text and involves the researcher in locating the document in the wider social and political context in which it was produced. Representativeness relates to the 'typicality' of the document in terms of its type and the instance that it portrays. The meaning of a document can operate in different ways: there is the meaning the author intended, the meaning given to the text by its audience, and the 'content meaning' which refers to the relationship of elements within the text to each other and to other texts.

Content meaning can involve the use of discourse analysis. Briefly, discourse is a key concept in Michel Foucault's philosophical project. For Foucault, discourses are 'practices that systematically form the objects of which they speak'. They do not identify objects, they constitute them:

> [a] discourse finds a way of limiting its domain, of defining what it is talking about, of giving it the status of object – and therefore making it manifest, nameable and describable.

Discourse is structured by a 'group of rules', assumptions and procedures that are immanent in its practice and 'define it in its specificity'. This body of rules has to be followed if the writer is to convey meaning within a particular discourse at a particular time. These rules of discourse determine how knowledge about a topic can be represented. It is through discourse that the social processes that produce meaning function. Further, for Foucault, discourse marks the conjunction of power and knowledge. The possibilities for meaning and definition are determined by the social and institutional position from which it originates. Thus discourses for Foucault are about 'Who, among the totality of speaking individuals' has the right to speak or write and with what authority; and why, at a given moment of time 'one particular statement appeared rather than another?'(Foucault 1972:27–8, 41–50). Green and Grosvenor (1997) applied Foucault's theoretical apparatus to explore how a range of educational texts produced over a 20-year period conceptualised and presented the black experience of schooling in the UK. They were able to demonstrate that the texts studied constituted a distinctive discursive practice and to document how 'race' was 'put into discourse' in the field of education. In short, documentary evidence can be used to explore how social practices become sedimented and, in turn, how those practices structure later activity.

Finally, returning to Scott's definition of a document as 'a written text', photography has been called 'light writing' (Clarke 1997:11). A photograph has both a temporal and physical presence. What was in front of the camera existed and is captured as a moment. It is a moment open to scrutiny. As Alan Sekula observed, the viewer of a photograph 'is confronted not by historical writing, but by the appearance of history itself' (Sekula 1983: 198). Photographs should be included in the definition of documents. There is a growing interest in the use of photography in educational research (for examples, see Prosser 1998). However, as with written texts, the 'documentary' nature of photographs has generated critical discussion and the researcher thinking about using photographs as documents could valuably engage with this literature (Solomon-Godeau 1991, Prosser 1998, Grosvenor 1999).

Kaikkonen's use of documentary research

Kaikkonen reflects upon the efficacy of a training programme through an analysis of journals kept by a group of mature students. In so doing she is able to provide examples of teacher reflections and opinions as they are expressed by the individuals being studied. This primary information then enables her to search for similarities and trends within the documents and to gather comparative data for analysis. By examining personal learning plans (PLPs) and examining the student journals, Kaikkonen was able to reflect upon the efficiency of the training, and to make observations about student perceptions of their own progress, changing levels of understanding, and appreciation of the nature of their new roles.

As with any research methodology, the analysis of documents has strengths and weaknesses. In Kaikkonen's research the collection of data which is permanent and therefore reusable is undoubtedly a strength. She is able to extract information from the journals, returning to them at a later date in order to ask more questions or examine issues from a different perspective. The very personal nature of the student journals enabled Kaikkonen to gain an immediate picture of student reflections, but does, of course, raise issues of partiality which need careful consideration during analysis. Robson (1993) has described the distinction between 'witting' and 'unwitting' evidence which may be revealed by the authors of documents. Students participating in this research were aware that their journals would be seen and eventually used by Kaikkonen. Had they been unaware of the researcher's intentions there would have been major ethical issues to be considered.

The nature of 'teacherhood', which is in common parlance in Finland, is an interesting one, with connotations of professionalism and reflective practice. The role of the student in becoming a reflective practitioner who measures his or her own progress and also provides data which may influence further development of a course, or changes of teaching approach, is one which has implications for teachers throughout their careers. Kaikkonen reminds us of the important role which student teachers can play in measuring their own performance and providing valuable feedback on the effectiveness of training.

Examples of other research in special education using documents

'Special educational needs in primary and secondary school brochures in England'.
Copeland, I. C. (2000), *European Journal of Special Needs Education* **15**(3), 241–54.

'Research on inclusive education programs; practices and outcomes for students with severe disabilities'.
Hunt, P. and Goetz, L. (1997), *The Journal of Special Education* **11**(1), 27–32.

'Technology, literacy and disabilities: a review of the research'.
Okolo, C. M., Cavalier, A. R., Ferretti, R. P. and MacArthur, C. A. (2000), in Gersten, R., Schiller, E.P. and Vaughn, S. (eds) *Contemporary Special Education Research*. Mahwah, New Jersey: Lawrence Erlbaum Associates.

References and guide to further reading

Brown, A. and Dowling, P. (1998) *Doing Research/Reading Research*. London: Falmer Press.

Burgess, R. (1990) *In the Field: An Introduction to Field Research*. 4th imp. London: George Allen and Unwin.

Clarke, G. (1997) *The Photograph*. Oxford: Oxford University Press.

Forster, N. (1994) 'The analysis of company documentation', in Cassell, C. and Symon, G. (eds) *Qualitative Methods in Organisational Research*. London: Sage.

Foucault, M. (1972) *The Archaeology of Knowledge*. London: Tavistock Publications.

Gilbert, N. (ed.) *Researching Social Life*. London: Sage.

Green, M. and Grosvenor, I. (1997) 'Making subjects: history-writing, education and race categories', *Paedagogica Historica* XXX111(3), 883–908.

Grosvenor, I. (1999) 'On visualising past classrooms', in Grosvenor, I., Lawn, M. and Rousmaniere, K. (eds) *Silences and Images. The Social History of the Classroom*. New York: Peter Lang.

May, T. (1997) *Social Research. Issues, Methods and Process*, 2nd edn. Buckingham: Open University Press.

Platt, J. (1981a) 'Evidence and proof in documentary research: some specific problems of documentary research, *Sociological Review* **29**(1), 31–52.

Platt, J. (1981b) 'Evidence and proof in documentary research: some shared problems of documentary research, *Sociological Review* **29**(1), 53–66.

Prosser, J. (1998) *Image-based Research. A Sourcebook for Qualitative Researchers*. London: Falmer Press.

Robson, C. (1993) *Real World Research: A Resource for Social Scientists and Practitioner-Researchers*. Oxford: Blackwell.

Sekula, A. (1983) 'Photography between labour and capital', in Buchloch, B. and Wilkie, R. (eds) *Mining Photographs and Other Pictures*. Halifax, Canada: Nova Scotia, School of Art and Design.

Scott, J. (1990) *A Matter of Record: Documentary Sources in Social Research*. Cambridge: Polity.

Solomon-Godeau, A. (1991) *Photography at the Dock. Essays on Photographic History, Institutions, and Practices*. Minneapolis: University of Minnesota Press.

Yin, R. K. (1984) *Case Study Research: Design and Methods*. Newbury Park, CA: Sage.

CHAPTER 7

Studying the development of 'teacherhood' in trainee teachers for the education of adults with severe learning difficulties

Leena Kaikkonen

The principle of educational equality was written into Finnish vocational education legislation at the end of the 1970s. The law concerning vocational education as established in 1991 states that all students on completion of secondary education should be afforded the opportunity to receive vocational education in line with his or her needs or abilities. By the end of the twentieth century this principle was clearly established in practice within the Finnish education system.

The achievement of educational equality within Finnish education has been largely successful and for the most part students do progress through a clearly structured pathway, which aims to meet their needs, even though there remains much which could be improved. It may be suggested that those who are described as having severe and complex learning difficulties are among the least accounted for by the legislation which endorses principles of educational equality. This is not a large group, but does comprise a population many of whom were denied all but the most basic of education in the past. Those who were provided with the foundations of an appropriate education often found that further education was denied to them. Despite assertions regarding the right to equality in education it was only after 1997 that responsibility for students with severe learning difficulties transferred from social welfare administration to education, thus enabling them to become part of a truly comprehensive school system. This resulted in far greater consideration being given to the facilitation of further education for this section of the population.

There is now a recognition that full rights to education will only be fully realised when teachers are trained to meet the specific needs of these students. In the spring of 1992, the Finnish National Board of Education appointed a team to plan basic recommendations for implementing teacher education for those who were to teach adults with severe and complex learning difficulties (known as ASSEN teachers). This resulted in a pilot study based in the Vocational Teacher Education College and financed by the National Board of Education from 1993 to 1997 (Opetushallitus 1993a).

The research here described aimed at finding out how the participants of this pilot experiment built this kind of new 'teacherhood'[1] and more importantly, how they analysed and described their own professional growth. Before examining teachers' experiences of the course, it is necessary to provide a brief description of ASSEN teacher education context and structure.

ASSEN teacher education

The growth in demands for equal educational rights for all also clearly strengthens the demands for developing each teacher's skills for meeting the individual needs of learners. With a new concentration upon the needs of students with severe and complex needs, there was some uncertainty with regards to what the development of these skills might mean for teacher education. If we have an intention to address all learner needs, according to Greenleaf, Hull and Reilly (1994), only one thing is certain and that is that we must address demands for change in teacher education. In this case a wider examination of the nature of teaching and the basic assumptions which have been made about it are wholly justified (Hansen 1997, Ojanen 1997, Simola 1997).

In his study of Finnish teacher education, Simola (1997) suggested that attention has traditionally been orientated towards classroom activities and didactic-psychological classroom behaviour. Simola's conclusions indicated that within their training teachers do not acquire the 'readiness' to perceive schools as socio-historical and cultural institutions and are unable to break out from a mechanistic and technical view of teaching. He describes a problem within Finnish teacher education which has persisted over decades – that of the removal of a study of education which develops an understanding of the principles behind learning, and a socially orientated knowledge related to the teacher's working context which moves beyond a narrow focus upon content and mechanics. Based upon his observations Simola claims that learning difficulties were perceived throughout the 1970s and 1980s as simply presenting pedagogical problems. In the 1990s the focus shifted towards seeing the difficulty as being one of school organisation – a managerial view. Neither of these perspectives has given teachers adequate knowledge or understanding in recognising or addressing the individuality of learners, or aided them in solving problems that arise from their diverse and complex life situations.

One may assume that by taking account of the individuality of learners and recognising the realities of life situations, teachers will be addressing a more complex task than that suggested by current approaches to teacher education. In the experimental ASSEN teacher education programme it was anticipated that current practice would be revealed which had begun to take account of such issues. Although the starting point for the experimental programme was to educate teachers for working with adults with severe and complex learning difficulties, it was not

[1] The concept of 'teacherhood' is common within the Finnish education system. It refers to an idea about the development of those professional competencies, attitudes and understanding(s) which enable a teacher to function at the highest possible professional level.

considered to be simply special needs training. The focus of courses was upon providing every student with an understanding of adulthood and adult learning including an appreciation of special education issues, as opposed to a concentration upon teaching approaches specifically aimed at those with special needs. The education provided was described as being in pursuit of reflective teachers who would be able to promote the development of pedagogical actions which took full account of both their learner's needs and their social backgrounds and context. These curricular aims stemmed from the fundamental requirements of vocational teacher training (Opetushallitus 1993b) but were emphasised from the perspectives of adults with special educational needs.

The ASSEN teacher education experiment was implemented as an on-the-job learning programme. The programme was aimed at professional colleagues who through changes in the legislation and organisation of health and social services found themselves being required to adapt from their previous roles as carers and into a new and unfamiliar role of vocational teacher. It contained ideas from action research and developmental work research, but it did not purely represent either of these approaches. Education included contact sessions at the teacher's vocational education college backed up by tasks defined through distance on-the-job learning periods. Learning tasks consisted of working on personal learning plans (PLPs) and carrying out a workplace specific development task. With the help of these, ASSEN teachers were enabled to concentrate upon developing a more analytical approach to their work. The aim was to strengthen each teacher trainee's pedagogical skills alongside cultivating general readiness for teachers to respond to the challenges posed by a swiftly changing range of societal demands.

Foundations for this developmental work were applied through three thematic learning modules, these being:

- Adults with severe special educational needs in Finnish Society
- The adult as a learner
- Learning and teaching.

In addition to these modules an additional course called 'Self confidence and interaction' was included in the programme. This focused upon enabling teachers to consider their role in relation to making decisions and exercising control which affects the lives of other individuals. The course encouraged teachers to inspect their own thinking and working methods and their potential impact upon students. Teaching methods included the use of drama, and expected that teachers should construct a portfolio of their experiences, which enabled them to assess their own personal and professional growth and informed their PLP.

Trainees worked independently on their tasks and received guidance and advice personally and directly from their teacher trainer as well as in small locally defined tutor groups. The tasks were also approached through directly taught sessions. The learning tasks made it possible for each trainee teacher to analyse his or her own current teaching approaches and to address the issues raised through the course in direct relation to his or her own working situation. This type of training implementation has been common within the Finnish teacher education system throughout the 1990s. A balance between reflective practice and work specific tasks is emphasised, and through this approach it is hoped that teachers may become more focused upon the relationship between theories of learning and classroom practice.

Using learning journals as a methodology

The ASSEN teacher education pilot programme at Jyvaskyla Vocational Teacher Education College took place between 1993 and 1997. The research here described was conducted upon a cohort of trainee teachers, seventeen female and one male, from across Finland who were involved in the programme from 1995 to 1997. The age distribution of the participants was between 25 and 48 years. The qualifications and experience of the trainees varied. Most had experienced a long professional career in the care and education of adults. All participants were working with adults with severe and complex learning difficulties in their day to day employment, this included work in residential units and in vocational special schools. The research set out to consider how the trainee teachers assessed their own progress in changing their approaches and gaining a changed 'teacherhood' and professionality in relation to their working practices.

Preliminary tasks, PLPs and learning journals

Participants in the programme were each sent an instruction package and curricula of the ASSEN teacher education programme before starting their tuition. Alongside these they were also sent preliminary orientation tasks which required them to conduct personal self assessments and assisted them in designing personal learning plans. In order to start their learning process and to assist with the development of PLPs, the preliminary tasks contained widely ranging questions with which the ASSEN trainee teachers could contemplate, among other things, their learner roles and learning needs. The tasks also contained a couple of short essay questions. The first of these asked trainee teachers to contemplate 'what is modern teacherhood?', the aim of which was to direct their thinking towards reaching their learning needs and readiness for teaching. The second essay title 'Me as learner, and other adults as learners', aimed at teachers assessing themselves in a learning context and exploring suitable study methods to address personal needs while beginning to consider the educational needs of their adult learners with special educational needs.

In order to begin addressing their tasks, the trainees were required to organise a discussion session at their own work place, where together with colleagues they discussed the work of an ASSEN teacher and how this role might be more clearly defined. The task also included a preliminary contemplation of the basic principles of understanding student learning needs. However, this chapter will focus less upon the work specific tasks and more upon the ways in which trainees came to reflect upon and assess their own teacherhood.

The trainee teachers assessed their own progress in many ways throughout the programme period. They maintained a journal which researched their own feelings and thoughts, and which they used to inform their PLPs. As the programme proceeded they carried out a number of PLP assessments which were used to enable them to reflect upon personal change and progress. In addition to their journals, the trainee teachers also took advantage of the portfolios which they had constructed for the course and which promoted self-awareness to assist in writing their own final assessments. The journals and portfolios were for personal use, and each trainee teacher could decide what information they would disseminate to others and to myself as researcher. Thus, their personalised accounts, entailing their own professional learning analysis, when shared, became a rich source of data for the researcher which were analysed in order to inform further discussion of the impact of the course and the perceptions of trainee teachers of their roles and responsibilities.

Within this chapter I intend to depict some of the experiences of the trainees' own concepts of teacherhood and the ways in which it changed during their teacher education period by using their own views and words as much as possible. In so doing I will reflect upon the value of journals as a research tool. From the outset I challenge the reader to consider Goodson and Cole's assertion that:

> if we are to develop valued models for teacher development, we first need to listen closely to the teacher's voice. We need to continue, almost obsessively, that act of listening. Hence we feel the best way to develop sensitive models of professional development is first of all to listen to the professionals at whom the development is aimed. (Goodson and Cole 1993:71)

In so doing I also invite the reader to assess the experiment's success in building teacherhood through listening to the voices of trainee teachers and the students in their charge. In order to do this I will begin, in the next section of this chapter, by summarising how the trainee teachers described teacherhood at the outset of the programme. This will be followed by a reflection upon how this view changed as they progressed through the teaching programme.

Outcomes of the programme

Outlining modern teacherhood

In their preliminary task the ASSEN trainees were asked to contemplate 'modern teacherhood'. They did this through several methods; some focusing upon teacherhood in general, some reflecting upon teacherhood in relation to their personal professional experiences while others sought a view through a review of the current literature. The curriculum materials which were mailed to the trainees aimed to direct their thoughts through this reflection period. It was therefore interesting to see that at this initial stage the trainees did not hold a unified picture of the nature of modern teacherhood. Some congruence, however, could be found in some of the characteristics which they associated with this concept. Teacherhood was commonly seen to include elements of teacher interpretation of knowledge and information, an understanding of general and special teaching demands and also as a process of network generation which encouraged learning from each other.

Views related to knowledge and information were quite strongly held. Seven trainees described this as an important area of teacherhood by saying, among other things, that a teacher must have a firm understanding of the subjects to be taught coupled with an appreciation of learning and teaching and the ability to combine theory with sound classroom practice. Their texts inferred that the demands on the work of a teacher in a rapidly changing society and an increasing plethora of information, requires that teachers gain an ability to recognise what is relevant and act upon this, while circumventing that which is not wholly pertinent to the quality of their teaching. The descriptions provided emphasised teachers as 'contextual experts' and masters of the management of classroom activity. When the descriptions were focused more distinctly in terms of their role as vocational teachers working with students with special educational needs, the demands of understanding specific pedagogical factors in relation to this population received a greater emphasis. Recognition of the importance of individuality in teaching, especially related to specific special needs, and a focus upon improvement of the quality of life for students were also identified as essential attributes. Other desirable factors in teacherhood which were identified by the study group included the importance of critical analysis and reflection upon all aspects of teaching, adaptability to a range of teaching and learning situations, and personal development, were seen as significant by a number of the trainees. Perhaps more surprising was the emphasis given to networking within the work of the teacher. This was seen in terms of sharing ideas among professional colleagues and also in enabling teachers to act positively on behalf of the students in their care.

Sketching goals for personal teacherhood

It became apparent that in defining modern teacherhood, the ASSEN trainees were beginning to express their personal interpretation of this concept. They inspected their own professional routines and assessed the skills required of an ASSEN teacher in personal terms. This enabled them to comment upon their own present levels and to consider the priorities which they might address during the course. One student's journal records:

> My workplace was transformed from an institutional ward to an assisted residential home. The traditional role of the nurse had to be buried. From

nursing we had to move towards guiding and counselling ... the teaching viewpoint for severely disabled adults I'm lacking...

Comments such as this indicate the need for a radical shift of professional perspectives, from a role which is seen largely as one of carer, to that of teacher in the more traditional sense of the term. There are several factors which can be discerned from the identification of these developmental needs. Perhaps the most crucial of these is the process carried out in Finland since the 1980s whereby institutions which were originally built for the 'mentally retarded' were dismantled and decentralised. This has inevitably affected the work of all staff and has brought with it a shift of focus from care to education. Another significant factor can be seen in the changed view of learning and an increased expectation upon the learning abilities of persons with severe special educational needs. As a consequence of these changes, staff have reached the conclusion that their own know-how has proven inadequate, as evidenced in the above journal extract. However, it was noticeable that at the outset of the course, the trainees had not yet developed the ability to interpret exactly what their 'know-how' needs would be.

During the process of setting personal goals for their own growth towards teacherhood, the ASSEN trainees often stated their desire to deepen or broaden their professional skills and knowledge (10 mentions). However, even when these were described more specifically, their desires were limited to general aims and questions of how to support adults with special educational needs towards participation or activation and how to improve their self-determination and quality of life (7 mentions). In setting more content specific aims, trainees hoped that the programme would deliver greater understanding of the disabled adult (5 mentions), how to teach and function efficiently as a teacher (8 mentions), as well as developing improved interaction skills with both colleagues and students in the workplace (3 mentions). Some expressed a wish that they should acquire more skills and readiness to become an efficient motivator of students (4 mentions).

At this stage of the process no more specific description of the concept of teacherhood in relation to the ASSEN teacher was forthcoming. ASSEN trainee teachers considered the task before them to be a critical one, but still had difficulties in concluding how their role might change, and the skills and understanding which they would require in order that this might happen. When describing the future of their role their comments tended to focus upon narrow pedagogical issues such as the mechanics of teaching or the classroom tactics which they may deploy. Very little attention was given to socially or societally orientated questions such as setting goals for learning in relation to need, or considering the future demands which would be made upon students with severe or complex learning difficulties. In describing teacherhood in general terms, the trainee teachers were able to discuss some of these issues, but when reflecting upon their own needs they tended to revert to the practicalities of classroom management issues.

Moving towards personal teacherhood

The overall purpose of the ASSEN teacher training programme was to improve the quality of life of adults with severe and complex learning difficulties by providing a more professional approach from teachers. For this reason it was seen as essential that the ASSEN teachers consider changes in the demands of society as well as increasing understanding of learning processes. Around the mid-point of the programme one trainee's journal described this process as follows:

> It became apparent to myself as I dug into history, that societal development, social politics, human conceptualisations of each dominant time period, concepts of learning and concepts of knowledge, direct those attitudes of how to relate to and deal with those less fortunate for each of those time periods. I also began to see those conformities which could be linked in this timeframe to the marginal groups ... I wanted to see and graph more carefully in my own municipality and N's special care district area, how education of those with special needs is carried out.
>
> Why do I specifically want to work in this area? ... The current structure of services is guided by an open care model. Persons with special educational needs are becoming more and more visible as members of this municipality ... what is the position of those with severe special educational needs in our ever changing, networking society? Throughout history the 'mentally disabled' have been cleared away from our eyes, our sight. The place for the severely disabled has been in institutions. According to traditional nursing ideologies they have been cared for well. Life has proceeded in safety and seclusion. As the economic situation became more stagnant, we were forced to find new solutions. But are we returning to the same situation as in the previous century; a new rationalised system? Are persons with special educational needs now threatened with abandonment instead of 'labelling'?
>
> How do I as a private citizen through my own work affect the position of the mentally disabled in this ever changing and networking society?
>
> How have I taken hold of these challenges?
>
> I want to be able to influence in my own municipality so that the persons with special educational needs could, as much as possible, find their own individuality through assisted services.

At the same time another trainee wrote:

> In all, the entire study time had been full of active thought refinement, change seeking and a time for finding understanding ... both past and future have received new meaning during this educational period...
>
> Generally, Finnish future views or societal development have opened in different ways during the course. I have frankly been disinterested in societal issues, but

> now I follow up events in different ways. Work with people with severe special needs is not an 'isolated case', but in association with time ... and I am able to influence things, so that they could themselves better cope amidst other people.
>
> The last definition of humanity that I've heard is 'humans grow amidst humans'. To me that was an important thought and an advice that clarifies my actions as well as effectively offering influential insight into some of my solutions.

Both of these assessments were written halfway through the programme. The broader concept of societal influences has taken on a more significant position for these trainee teachers. These short extracts from their journals combine a reflection upon human development and professional functions. The writers have recognised how both are strongly related to time contexts and our understanding of the development of human beings and society. These questions may be perceived as being fundamental to the growth of teachers and the development of teacherhood (Patrikainen 1999).

Because the period of training was relatively short, decisions needed to be made about its structure. It was believed that through contemplating the basis of teachers' work they were given opportunities to explore a variety of classroom practices, and to contextualise these within a wider framework of teacherhood. One trainee teacher writing in a journal commented:

> anyhow, teacherhood had felt foreign to me and to see oneself as a teacher is difficult. I have thought that a teacher was a very wise person who knows much and is knowledgeable of many exclusive methods of teaching, which seem rather mystical to normal people, but of which functions or teachings have nothing to do with everyday life...
>
> Because my picture of teacherhood was what it was, therefore when I started in the programme I expected it to be more concerned with teaching methods, rather than being a course on philosophy. That is why, for example, some of the preliminary tasks felt rather surprising, and the literature that I carried home last summer I had never thought to read. Luckily enough for me, I did, for example Liekki Lehtisalo's book *Towards a New Educational Thought* was one really thought awakening book despite first impressions. As I was grinding on the preliminary tasks I realised one thing about this education, that it forces me to think and it is not an easy task. But only up until I chewed on the task relating to adulthood (including my own adulthood, concept of human beings and life in general) I thought I understood that theory indeed had something to do with practice and how strongly my work is affected by e.g. concepts of human beings, life, adulthood and learning.
>
> I have learned much during this time about myself as a learner. Self-directedness, contrary to my previous assumptions, was more demanding and agonising than I had expected. I have often sighed and wished that the book pile I had in front of

> me could just be read and tested and forgotten after that. Although at the same time I had to accept that this was a better way to learn, even if it was more laborious!!! It was also irritating how thoughts of work and education spun and hummed in my head from morning till night, and sometimes even in my dreams, not because I was stressed by my studies, but because the topic was so exhilarating. I have a feeling that now, I can really get something done and that we as a working community could build positive changes and therefore I am very excited and on the other hand uncertain at times, especially about the working community's reaction to development. It is exciting as we could never be sure about that…

It was in the author's interest to gather information from the trainees' self-assessment of their growth towards teacherhood. Their descriptions were not 'objectively' evaluated, instead they were taken at face value. The trainees were asked to elaborate and justify their views through mentoring sessions both in verbal and written form. They were asked to verify their statements about what they had learned, and the ways in which their thinking had changed. Such sessions enabled the students to conduct self analysis and to report on how they had begun to behave differently in their working practices. Thus the trainee whose journal was quoted immediately above also wrote:

> at the same time, however, I have noticed annoying contradictions between how I claim to think and how I behave in practice, e.g. in my opinion I can vouch for humanistic views of a person, in other words a person is a value in itself. Why don't I always behave that way, however? The same thing applies for my working community.
>
> Is it so that I just presume to think this way and yet in reality my understanding of human beings is something totally different? Or have I not earlier on assessed my actions critically enough and thought about its foundations?
>
> Is this the transformation that takes place in 20 credit weeks from nurse to TEACHER; clarifying the basis for one's actions and after that, beginning to critically compare one's own behaviour with a theory that is adapted?

Journal records indicate quite clearly the ways in which ASSEN trainees were becoming aware of the need to move beyond a simple contemplation of teaching skills and to incorporate wider philosophical issues within their professionalism.

> Today I went to the health centre with one resident. (This trainee worked in a supported residence.) We went there by taxi. The resident sat on the front seat beside the driver and I myself sat in the back seat. The resident had her purse in her pocket and after some guidance from me she resumed to pay the fare. At the health centre she checked herself in at the booth. We went inside to the reception

> room. The doctor asked and the resident answered. The doctor spoke to her in the normal fashion. Then came a question which the resident was not able to answer herself, therefore I answered for her. After this the doctor mainly spoke to me only. After that, he spoke more slowly and in a slightly raised voice to the resident; 'would you please climb on the examination table?'
>
> What do we learn from this? Previously I would have just, without much thinking, sat with the resident's purse in the front seat and let her sit in the back seat. Similarly, I would just walk into the health centre and check her in at the booth that she had arrived. As we saw the doctor I would just normally explain her condition at times better than I could explain mine. I really regret having answered for her. Perhaps, after some thought, she would have been able to answer for herself. I would also have been polite enough to point out to the doctor, that he could stress his point directly to the resident. Perhaps I might be wiser next time. Through this education I had become more sensitive in observing people's behaviour and reactions when they meet a person with special needs.

Reflections and emerging ethical considerations

The learner's special educational needs must be only one consideration when we consider the training of vocational teachers. In the case of the learner with severe and complex learning difficulties, our mind is often bound in such a way that prevents us from seeing beyond these difficulties, as is suggested by the trainee quoted above. Another trainee expressed the view that being asked to take this more holistic approach to education had led to a rethink of the entire function of her working unit.

> During the autumn we arrived at a thought, that places that were built only for the disabled would itself feed the behaviour of those with such needs, and we ourselves become entangled into weird issues. We must dare to rip ourselves out of the entire system.

Building this type of courage was one of the basic foundations of the ASSEN teacher education programme. The programme wanted to state to these teachers-to-be that there are no ready solutions to the education of adults with severe and complex learning difficulties. As teachers they are faced with the lifelong task of considering the most sensible goals for learning and teaching. The basic question, however, is about human life and learning – even if it takes place more slowly for those with severe special needs.

The way in which we understand learning also opens up goals for ourselves and requires that we consider the ways in which these may be achieved. In the above journal extract, the trainee also sees the consideration of goals as one of the more central issues. Because the education of adults described as having severe and complex needs has been poorly organised in Finland, adjusted working practices for these people do not seem to exist. Concrete development work in ASSEN teacher education thus meant developing the innovative learning and guidance of basic ideas and working methods applicable to this work. The significance for ASSEN trainees is that they felt able to apply their general discussions and development tasks into practical work for the benefit of adults with severe and complex needs.

> I was really satisfied with finally being able to study for the work that I was already doing for a long time … In the beginning of the programme I wandered almost entirely at the mercy of book knowledge, and always experienced that the text did not answer to what I sought for in severe special needs education. Only up until I began to translate the idea of 'teacherhood' in general to our 'speciality field' did it start to flow for me.

Importantly, this development task takes place in collaboration with each ASSEN trainee teacher's own working community, whereupon the aim is to develop its entire pedagogical functions.

> I incorporated everything possible with my working community. We considered human concepts first from its theoretical background and then from the practical point of view. The discussion was quite a ramble at first and set thoughts into motion … The group thought of their own concepts of learning and teaching practices, while writing their thoughts down. Together we went through them and at the same time I wrote down the emotions that I felt. I also made a questionnaire for the community, wherein everyone thinks about actions in the working community from their own current point of view.

The changes towards improvements in the quality of life for those with severe special needs starts primarily from changes occurring in their environment. The starting point for ASSEN teacher education was to begin to change the attitudes of those working with adults with severe and complex learning difficulties, to realise opportunities for learning and find clear aims and methods for reaching these. For this the teacher must have the sensitivity to detect the personal needs of someone who is dependent upon them. Several ASSEN trainee teachers contemplated how this might be achieved:

> Now, through this education I have begun to 'listen' to the resident himself. What developmental and educational objectives could be individually set on his part? In addition, upon setting goals, I have started questioning the goals being set. Who does it? Whose needs and standpoints? I have thought of the use of power before, but my views have acquired depth through my education for me to be able to more thoroughly touch its different functions. Even in my own teacherhood, I have thought of elements of the use of power, what is taught, and

> why? I have myself aspired towards reflectiveness in my own actions, as well as tried to question currently valid action models. Now in my own working unit, I hope that there will be more ethical and moral considerations than before on how we act as advisers in an environment that is our client's home. This contemplation makes work more challenging, but at the same time the accountability over the effects of one's actions on the life of residents bears more emphasis.

It is evident from this journal extract that the challenges for ASSEN trainee teachers in developing their own teacherhood were targeted largely upon gaining more personal understanding. To learn to acquire more autonomy is a lifetime challenge – both to those with special educational needs themselves and to those who are close to them.

Conclusions

In this chapter I have described ASSEN trainee teachers' feelings during the process of their education. By listening to their opinions and reflections and through studying their journals, we intended to gain information about the suitability of the methods deployed within the programme. However, the activity of listening with sensitivity to the trainees' voices, both orally and through their journals, had another and possibly more important pedagogical objective. It was hoped that by valuing the opinions of these trainees, and showing them the importance of this reflective approach, they might be encouraged to apply the same principles to their students.

The key question to ask at the end of the programme was, did the method as implemented work? In other words, did the assessment of personal learning and experience expressed through a journal generate the necessary strength and sensitivity for listening to the voice of the adult learner with severe and complex learning difficulties?

One teacher described how both the writing of learning tasks and the maintenance of a journal have supported her self development even through the most difficult passages of the training.

> For me it was extremely important to work on the preliminary task 'myself as learner'. To go through my own background history from childhood milieu to date. The process was very personal and much pain surfaced ... That process also helped me to understand the meaning of the first thematic task. Why is it important to be knowledgeable of one's own history and backgrounds, because they affect us today...
>
> Through this learning process I have grown to be more conscious of my own shadow. I have had to ponder the struggle between good and bad in humans. Ethical questions are altogether more strongly brought forth. What is my

> concept of human beings? How do I continually communicate more strongly those values which I've learnt through my own actions?
>
> Writing a journal has helped me analyse more visibly that pain where my vulnerability is high. At the same time I was able to go through self assessment that has also organised my understanding of theoretical knowledge.

Besides being a tool through which trainees could track their own progress, the journal also proved useful to tutors in maintaining a record of their growth.

> I have marked a journal entry during our group discussion sessions for each participant separately ... at the same time I have described my own insights ... of the project and its progress ... attention on my group or thoughts pertaining to the applicability of this experiment.

The learning journal was valued as a method by trainees who found it valuable in enabling them to focus upon the need to develop sensitive working approaches.

> The most that I have received from my education for my current work ... is perceived as a fact that nowadays I think more about how I am acting in whichever situation. Could I have taken better care of this situation? Would I still remember tomorrow the mistakes I made today? I have thought about using a learning journal to record these types of thoughts...

ASSEN trainee teachers' primary experiences regarding their participation in this programme were positive. Many of them explained their phases of confusion and anxiety, but also commented on their renewed educational insights through their final assessments.

> Although writing has occasionally been very painstaking, it was worth doing ... In my own working environment, I was able to develop observational skills in relation to my learners ... I have discovered that I don't have to know everything. My learners and I could both be learners together. The meaning of knowledge has changed. The theoretical framework I have acquired during my ASSEN teacher education has created a strong foundation, which has freed me for improved interaction.

A noteworthy point would perhaps be the lack of negative descriptions of learning through this approach which came from trainees. Thus, one could easily presume that everyone's learning journey ended successfully. Unfortunately such an interpretation may not necessarily be true. The working method of keeping a journal did lead to many positive experiences being expressed, but it may be that negative ones were just not expressed. My interpretation of the journals maintained by trainees would suggest that the learning experiences for the trainees and the impact of the programme were positive. Listening to the stories of these trainees and trying to read between the lines remains as a continuing challenge to teacher educators.

References and further reading

Ammatillisista koulutusta koskevan lain täydennys. (1991).

Goodson, I. and Cole, A. (1993) 'Exploring the teacher's professional knowledge', in McLaughlin, D. and Tierney, W. G. (eds) *Naming Silenced Lives: Personal Narratives and the Process of Educational Change*. London: Routledge.

Greenleaf, C., Hull, G. and Reilly, B. (1994) 'Learning from our diverse students: helping teachers rethink problematic teaching and learning situations', *Teaching and Teacher Education* **10**(5), 521–41.

Hansen, S. E. (1997) Lärärutbildnig och lärararbete I postmodern tid. *Kasvatus* **28**(1), 13–23.

Laki ammatillisista oppilaitoksista 487 (1987).

Laki ammatillisista koulutuksesta 630 (1998).

Ojanen, S. (1997) Nykymuotoisen opettajankoulutuksen kehityssuunnasta. *Kasvatus* **28**(1), 7–12.

Opetushallitus (1993a) Vaikeimmin kehitysvammaisten aikuisten opettajaksi valmistavan opettajankoulutuksen opetussuunnitelman perusteet. Työryhmän muistio: *Opetushallitus*.

Opetushallitus (1993b) Ammatillisen opettajankoulutuksen opetussuunnitelman yleiset perusteet. *Opetushallitus*.

Patrikainen, R. (1999) Opettajuuden laatu. Ihmiskäsitys, tiedonkäsitys ja oppimiskäsitys opettajan pedagogisessa tominnassa, Jyväskylä: PK-Kustannus.

Simola, H. (1997) Pedagoinen dekontekstualismi ja opettajankoulutuksen opetussuunnitelmat. *Kasvatus* **28**(1), 24–37.

CHAPTER 8

Case study

Case study is concerned with an in-depth investigation into an individual, group or collection of individuals which have similar attributes. It can be undertaken using a variety of data collection methodologies, but is generally concerned with developing a detailed understanding of a particular institution, individual or phenomenon. Yin (1993) has described case study as being an empirical inquiry that investigates a contemporary phenomenon within its real life context, especially when the boundaries between phenomenon and context are not clearly evident. Case study research lends itself well to the small scale researcher as it encourages a focus upon a small sample or even a single individual and can often be carried out within a single institution. Bassey (1999) has argued that there are at least three different forms of educational case study each of which may have a specific purpose in assisting the researcher to gain increased knowledge and understanding of the phenomenon studied. The first of these Bassey calls 'theory-seeking and theory-testing case study'. In this form of case study the researcher begins with a hypothesis related to the case, such as 'lack of playground equipment is the cause of poor behaviour at lunchtimes', and constructs a method to test this out. This may involve the use of a variety of data gathering methods, such as observation of the playground both before and after the introduction of playground equipment, interviews with pupils, or regular examination of an incidents book, and is most likely to call upon a combination of these. Bassey's second type of case study he refers to as 'story-telling and picture-drawing'. In this form, the case study has the intention of providing an accurate picture of events and may be concerned with clarification of what 'really happens' within an institution. This information can then be used to confirm or inform the people within the institution and may lead to a changing or reinforcement of practice. Such an approach may be particularly helpful when constructing comparative studies in which, for example, the behaviour of a group of pupils in one location is compared with that observed in another. This is, of course, only a legitimate exercise when the researcher conducts an analysis which takes account of the many variables which are likely to exist in the differing situations under review.

The final form of case study described by Bassey is what he refers to as 'evaluative'. This is more concerned with making decisions about the value or effectiveness of a system, event or intervention. It may, for example, be used to evaluate if a newly adopted home–school diary scheme is having the desired impact of increased contact between parents and teachers, or to assess whether the implementation of Assertive Discipline is perceived by teachers as having made classroom management easier.

Each of Bassey's three formats can play a valuable role in educational research. By categorising case study in this way, the researcher is encouraged to focus upon the intended purpose of the study and may thereby examine which data collection methodologies may prove to be most helpful. Other writers have established similar categories. Stenhouse (1988) described four styles, ethnographic, evaluative, educational and action research case studies. The first of these Stenhouse equated with the methods commonly deployed by the anthropologist, and is most often associated with participant observation by an individual who *lives* among the subjects being studied. Hence individual teacher researchers may conduct a study of staffroom behaviours while themselves being a regular participant in staffroom activity. Critical ethnography is an approach which has been utilised by a number of researchers (Hammersley and Atkinson 1983, Carspecken 1996). Cohen and Manion (1994) suggest that an attempt to understand social institutions, such as schools, from within, may be important for some educational researchers. Such researchers are likely to be concerned to 'rationalise' the behaviours and events of an institution or a group within that institution, and case study may well provide opportunities to do this in a systematic manner.

Ethnographic case study does have a number of potential dangers, and there are several ethical considerations which must be taken in to account. The researcher who studies his or her own community may well be treated with some suspicion by subjects under observation and will need to be mindful of the need to share information and intentions at all stages of the project. Similarly, there may be difficulties in reporting findings, particularly when individuals may be able to identify themselves or their colleagues. The need for careful planning is an imperative for all research, but in studies of this nature it may be even greater.

Stenhouse's distinction of 'educational case study' as a distinct form is worthy of some comment. He comments that in this particular use of case study: 'many researchers using case study methods are concerned neither with social theory nor with evaluative judgement, but rather with the understanding of educational action' (Stenhouse 1988:72). This bears some comparison to Bassey's story-telling approach as it is concerned to see what happens in a given situation in order possibly to inform further action or to confirm a view.

Robson (1993) suggests that when designing case study research the researcher needs to have:

- A conceptual framework
- A set of research questions
- A Sampling strategy
- Clear methods and instruments for data collection.

He points out that a distinguishing feature of case study research is that it concentrates solely upon a specific case in its context. This may be achieved, he suggests, by adhering either to a relatively loose structure, which may assume that all information gathered along the way is important, or through a more selective and structured approach, which clearly identifies what will be examined and how. There are strengths and weaknesses within each approach. The researcher who decides to observe everything and discard nothing will have enormous quantities of data to collate and analyse and may have some difficulties in distinguishing the useful from the irrelevant. On the other hand, beginning with a clearly defined framework may result in discarding information which may have been of value. Making decisions about which route to follow is one of the major challenges for the case study researcher, which is why Robson suggests that time should be given to each of his four key elements highlighted above. In particular, the development of a conceptual framework, through which the researcher considers who the key players may be, which relationships may be of greatest significance, what are the key features of the case to be studied, and when events are most likely to take place, may ultimately make the research more manageable.

An important consideration for the case study researcher is that of generalisation. From the outset it is necessary that the case study researcher is clear about the purpose of the research. Who is it for? A single school case study which examines instances of bullying on the playground, or the use of the school's rewards and sanctions system may have great intrinsic value to that school. It may enable a school to change its policies and actions or may confirm the effectiveness or otherwise of existing systems. What it is unlikely to do is provide information which is generalisable beyond the confines of the school being studied. Bassey (1995) has discussed the difficulties of generalisation in some detail. However, Bassey (1999) has also proposed that from such studies it may be possible to gain some form of 'fuzzy generalisation', whereby statements related to the findings of small scale studies may have 'built-in uncertainties'. For example, the researcher may say that in a given school the introduction of a rewards and sanctions system has been very well received by the pupils. While the research cannot conclude that because of this finding such a scheme would be equally well received in other schools, the researcher may suggest that this may be the case, and that it is worthy of further research in other establishments.

Many teacher researchers undervalue their own research because it is small in scale and possibly conducted only within their own schools. If, however, this research provides important information which confirms beliefs, identifies issues or may result in improved performance within the school, this in itself is justification for the work undertaken.

Marie Howley's use of case study research

The case study research described by Howley (in Chapter 10) provides a good example of the examination of a specific intervention undertaken in a single school. Howley's hypothesis, that social stories may lead to an increase in appropriate social behaviours in a group of pupils with autistic spectrum disorders, was investigated by examining a specific group of pupils in one school. Her work, though small in scale, is particularly important when considering the dearth of empirical evidence to support the efficacy of social stories, which have come more and more into use in recent years. The studies reported by Gray (1998) into the use of social stories were conducted wholly within the USA and Howley is concerned to see how this approach has transferred into a UK primary setting. She is careful to suggest that her findings may not be readily generalised beyond the confines of this case study, but in identifying further areas in need of research she provides other researchers with the basis for more work in this important area. In Bassey's terms the case study conducted by Howley may be described as evaluative, being concerned to assess the effectiveness of an intervention programme put into place for a specific group of pupils. The choice of methodologies including interviews and observation lend themselves well to this particular study and the purpose behind each of these is clearly articulated and was well established from the outset of the research. Within Howley's study it is possible to trace the four elements of effective case study proposed by Robson (1993), and to see quite clearly how these combine to provide an effective research framework.

Liz Waine's use of case study research

Liz Waine's research (Chapter 9) has many characteristics which are similar to those deployed by Howley. Just as Howley studied a specific identifiable population of pupils with autistic spectrum disorders, so has Waine given her attentions to pupils with dyslexia. Waine follows a well established tradition of basing her research approach upon that of a previous study (Dutton 1991). In so doing she is able to obtain information within her case study which may provide an opportunity to derive some form of 'fuzzy generalisation' (Bassey 1999). Waine is able to compare her results with those from other studies and can therefore justify a claim that her findings *suggest that* any pupil with a writing speed of less than ten words per minute should be identified as having 'slow' handwriting. She recognises that her own sample is small, but by relating her own conclusions to those of other researchers she is in a position to make suggestions and recommendations on the basis of empirical enquiry.

Waine provides us with a good example of how case study research carried out with a limited sample can add to the canon of information which exists within an area of study, thereby reinforcing or supplementing the information provided by other researchers. Her study is also valuable in providing information which may guide the work of teachers and examiners and enable students with dyslexia to receive more equitable approaches to assessment procedures.

Further examples of case study research in special education

'The educational attainments of pupils with emotional and behavioural difficulties'. Farrell, P., Critchley, C. and Mills, C. (1999), *British Journal of Special Education* **26**(1), 50–3.

'Introducing Feuerstein's Instrumental Enrichment in a school for children with social, emotional and behavioural difficulties'.
Head, G. and O'Neill, W. (1999), *Support for Learning* **14**(3), 122–8.

'Choosing to campaign: a case study of parent choice, statementing and integration'.
Paige-Smith, A. (1996), *European Journal of Special Needs Education* **11**(3), 321–9.

'Using classroom support in a primary school: a single school case study'.
Rose, R. (2000), *British Journal of Special Education* **27**(4), 191–6.

References and further reading

Bassey, M. (1995) *Creating Education Through Research*. Newark: Kirklington Moor Press.

Bassey, M. (1999) *Case Study Research in Educational Settings*. Buckingham: Open University Press.

Bromley, D. B. (1986) *The Case Study Method in Psychology and Related Disciplines*. Chichester: John Wiley.

Carspecken, P. F. (1996) *Critical Ethnography in Educational Research*. London: Routledge.

Cohen. L, and Manion, L. (1994) *Research Methods in Education*, 4th edn. London: Routledge.

Dutton, K. P. (1991) 'Writing Under Examination Conditions: Establishing a Bassline', *SED/Regional Pyschological Services: Professional Development Initiatives 1989–90*. Scottish Education Department.

Gray, C. (1998) 'Social stories and comic strip conversations with students with Asperger syndrome and high functioning autism', in Schopler, E., Mesibov, G. and Kunce, L. (eds) *Asperger Syndrome or High Functioning Autism?* New York: Plenum Press.

Hammersley, M. and Atkinson, P. (1983) *Ethnography: Principles in Practice*. London: Tavistock.

O'Donnell, C. (1996) 'The role of the resource teacher: case studies in collaborative good practice', *REACH, Journal of Special Needs Education in Ireland* **10**(1), 14–23.

Robson, C. (1993) *Real World Research*. Oxford: Blackwell.

Stake, R. E. (1995) *The Art of Case Study Research*. London: Sage.

Stenhouse, L. (1988) 'Case study methods', in Keeves, J.P. (ed.) *Educational Research Methodology and Measurement: An International Handbook*. Oxford: Pergamon.

Watson, J. (1999) 'Working in groups: social and cognitive effects in a special class', *British Journal of Special Education* **26**(2), 87–95.

Yin, R.K. (1993) *Applications of Case Study Research*. London: Sage.

Yin, R. K. (1994) *Case Study Research: Design and Methods*, 2nd edn. London: Sage.

CHAPTER 9

Writing speed: what constitutes 'slow'? An investigation to determine the average writing speed of Year 10 pupils

Liz Waine

There are many pupils taking external examinations at school or college who, although they may have coped with the learning demands of a course, may, because of their special educational needs, be unable to demonstrate their attainment under standard assessment arrangements. The Joint Council for General Qualifications, the regulatory body for all examination boards, recognises this fact and publishes guidelines for teachers and tutors who wish to apply for special arrangements during examinations for these pupils. In such cases the Joint Council document (1999) *Regulations and Guidance relating to Candidates with Special Requirements*, amended and published annually, provides detailed guidance relating to which pupils it is appropriate to consider making special arrangements for, and how to apply for permission to make those arrangements.

The Joint Council requires examination centres to have a 'systematic approach to identifying all candidates who may be eligible to special arrangements'. Centres should keep 'relevant records' showing 'the candidate's history of literacy difficulties and the way the centre has made arrangements to enable the candidates to overcome these difficulties'. There should also be 'formal assessment' that 'should be carried out immediately before or very soon after the courses begin'.

For some pupils, in particular those whose difficulties are of a dyslexic or a dyspraxic nature, the 'special arrangements' are required to provide extra time, permission for the pupil to use a word processor, or for an amanuensis, in view of the pupil's slow handwriting. This requires teachers or educational psychologists to make a judgement about the writing speed of individual pupils in relation to their peers.

Requests for special arrangements should be based on an analysis of objective evidence of literacy difficulties. The use of recent editions of standardised tests is recommended, with results given as standard scores or percentiles, with a standard score of below 85 taken to represent 'below average'.

For reading and spelling this presents no difficulty. There is a range of standardised tests on the market providing evidence of 'below average' attainment. However, there is as yet no standardised test for assessing pupils' writing speed. This presents teachers with the difficulty of establishing which pupils should be put forward for special arrangements. How slow does their writing have to be to be seen as 'below average'?

The application for 'special arrangements' is made in the form of a report. Prior to 1999 this report had to be compiled by an Educational Psychologist. However, in October 1998 Terry Davies, Secretary to the Standing Committee of the Joint Forum for the GCSE and GCE, wrote to all Examination Centres informing them that the 1999 version of the *Special Arrangements and Special Considerations* document contained 'important changes to previous arrangements'. These included the agreement that holders of the OCR (formerly RSA) Diploma for Teachers of Learners with Specific Learning Difficulties were authorised to write the reports. Providing detailed guidance to these OCR Diplomatists on how to assess pupils in order to gather the information needed to write the reports for special arrangements, Backhouse (1998), chartered psychologist and OCR Assistant Chief Verifier for the Diploma, noted that there was 'very little normative data' in relation to handwriting speeds. She suggested that 'a rule of thumb norm for 15–16 year olds should be taken as 14 words per minute'. She did note that 'this may prove to be wrong' and that 'research is needed here!'.

Alston (1994) reviewed the research into writing speeds carried out throughout the twentieth century up to 1990. She identified two major groups of pupils whose specific difficulties were causing concern in recent years, namely those with reading, writing and spelling difficulties identified as dyslexic, and those with motor learning difficulties thought to be dyspraxic. She recognised that although some pupils will be affected by only one of these conditions, the two groups were not mutually exclusive. She concluded that when considering writing speed there was 'no reliable assessment with normative information, for either group'.

The research she reviewed consisted of studies requiring pupils to copy from a text, and others that were based on an analysis of pupils' 'free' writing on a specified topic under 'test' or examination conditions. In the latter series of studies the length of time the pupils were required to write varied between 20 and 30 minutes. The age groups in the reported studies included primary (Y3 to 6, i.e. pupils between the ages of 8 and 11 years), some studies involving whole secondary school populations and others involving single year groups. In all studies precise instructions were given to both the teachers who administered the test and to the pupils.

In the same article Alston then reported the results of her own study on a sample of 68 fifth year pupils in a Guernsey Secondary Modern School. She reported results indicating a mean words per minute rate, over a 20-minute period of free writing, of approximately 14 words per minute.

Dutton (1991) reported results from a similar study carried out in a Scottish secondary school, the main difference being that in his study pupils wrote for half an hour. He summarised his results as follows:

1. A typical senior pupil writes approximately one sentence per minute of about 18 words.

2. That rate can be maintained for at least half an hour.
3. A writing rate of less than 12 words a minute would be considered abnormally slow and would warrant further investigation and possible intervention with respect to examination presentation. (Dutton 1991:203)

Dutton based his conclusion that a rate of less than 12 words per minute should be considered 'slow' on the statistical calculation of two standard deviations below the mean for the S4 year group (equivalent to Year 10 pupils in English schools). His results were based on an analysis of only ten boys and ten girls from each of five senior year groups.

Dutton concludes his report by suggesting that there is a need for a 'more precise definition of what is expected of pupils in respect of writing ability'. Alston reflected this in her study, suggesting that a further 'more precisely controlled validity study' when pupils were required to write for one hour under examination conditions 'would be of interest'. She concluded her report with the statement that:

> As the number of students requesting special examination arrangements increases, the need for objectivity in the granting of extra time, rest periods, use of a word processor, or similar, is paramount. (Alston 1994:11)

This view was supported by Sawyer, Gray and Champness (1996) who, in reporting on the use of copying tests by some psychologists to measure writing speed for examination special arrangement reports, concluded that 'there is no accepted criterion below which special arrangements are made', and that 'additional work also needs to be carried out in determining just what motor co-ordination speed in handwriting is required for GCSE examinations'. The research described in this chapter is based on quantitative methods of data analysis. Since the aim of the research was to provide objective data relating to writing speed there was no qualitative analysis of the content of the pupils' writing. Similarly the quality of the handwriting was not taken into consideration, other than to take the decision not to include any papers in the analysis where the writing was not legible. Any pupils unable to produce legible handwriting would be eligible for special arrangements either because their handwriting deteriorated under time pressure, or because their scripts may be illegible despite their being allowed to write more slowly.

Handwriting speed survey

The study described in this chapter was carried out to provide one school with writing speed data about their Year 10 pupils in order to inform decisions about support during course work and possible application for special examination arrangements. It was a collaborative study between the researcher and the staff of the school, a mainstream urban comprehensive school. A senior teacher in the school worked closely with the researcher to facilitate the study and liaise with other teachers in the school. There were 166 pupils in Y10 at the time of the study. However, due to absences only 152 took part in the study.

The aim of the study was to provide objective data that could be analysed using statistical conventions to provide not only a mean writing speed for the year group, but also to identify the standard deviation of the sample. This is an important factor when considering which pupils could be deemed to have a relatively 'slow' writing speed. Mean speeds, as reported in many studies, give no indication of what range of writing speed may be considered average. By computing the standard deviation of the sample it is possible to use this to identify the slowest speed within this average range. Any pupils writing at a speed below this pace could then be viewed as appropriate candidates for consideration in relation to special arrangements.

Thus the objective data collected through this study could then be used to provide statistically valid comparisons between pupils in this school. By applying further statistical analysis the reliability of the results in relation to Dutton's (1991) findings were also calculated in order to judge the validity of the findings on a wider scale.

When used in conjunction with more subjective information relating to performance in class and on other school based assessment, the study data provided the basis for discussion relating to decisions on which pupils it would be appropriate to apply for special examination arrangements. This in turn lead to consideration of how the pupils thus identified should be supported in class and prepared to use the special arrangements that would be available to them during their end of course examinations. Furthermore, such data may also be used to facilitate discussion relating to suitable courses for the pupils and staff to consider. These issues will be discussed further when the analysis of the results is considered.

After studying the details of other research referred to earlier in the chapter, it was decided to follow a similar approach to that of Dutton's (1991) research. This was because it appeared to provide a clear model for administration that could easily be replicated in order to provide a valid basis for comparing results.

Issues for consideration when designing the study included:

- How long should the pupils be required to write?
- What should they write about?
- Under what conditions should they write?
- Who would administer the 'test'?
- Ethical issues of confidentiality.

How long should the pupils be required to write?

As discussed earlier, previous research into this topic (Alston 1994) was based mainly on pupils writing for either 20 or 30 minutes. Roaf (1998) reported a study in her school where pupils were required to write for only ten minutes, plus 2.5 minutes for correction. The longer the pupils are expected to write, the more words they would write in total and the greater the task of counting these words for analysis. Weighed against this is the fact that some pupils would find it difficult to write for an extended period of time because they would not have enough to say! It was decided to follow Dutton's (1991) model and ask the pupils to write for 30 minutes. Since the main purpose of the study was to measure how fast pupils could communicate their knowledge on paper under timed examination conditions, it was considered that the longer period of time would give a better result in terms of how fatigue affected their total output. A further consideration in deciding on the 30-minute task was the organisation of the school timetable. In the school used for the research the lessons were in 40-minute blocks. Allowing for ten minutes to introduce the task, and 30 minutes for the writing, the exercise could be fitted into one period, making the task of finding suitable slots in the timetable easier.

What should they write about?

The main consideration was that no pupil should be prevented from writing by not knowing what to write. In examinations they are of course expected to answer questions set to judge their knowledge and understanding of the subject being examined. Inevitably many pupils will write less not because they have a slow writing speed but because they have only limited knowledge of the subject. In calling for more research into writing speed, Backhouse (1998:5) suggested three possible titles: (1) My favourite person/personality; (2) A person I know well; (3) Something in which I am very interested.

After discussion with the senior member of staff at the school collaborating in the study, Dutton's (1991) title, 'My Life History' was chosen. Although we had some reservations that a small minority of pupils may not want to write about personal details, it was agreed that this title was the one about which the majority of pupils would have enough to say to write for 30 minutes. By introducing the topic to the pupils and suggesting they could discuss where they were born, their hobbies and interests and other relatively non-personal details, we hoped to eliminate the possible reluctance to discuss sensitive issues.

Who would administer the 'test'?

Under the overall guidance of the senior teacher the task was administered by class teachers during a single period of English. The teachers were given precise instructions regarding organisation and instructions to be given to pupils. Since it was not possible for the researcher to speak to all the teachers involved, a single A4 information sheet (Figure 9.1 at end of this chapter) was provided, briefly explaining the purpose of the task and the administration details. Teachers were asked to spend a few minutes introducing the title, 'My Life History', providing a few prompts or 'starter ideas' to help the pupils begin to consider what they might write. As discussed above, they were asked to encourage the pupils to consider non-sensitive aspects of their lives, such as interests and hobbies, rather than intimate family relationships.

In a busy school timetable it was likely that some teachers would see the writing activity as irrelevant to the curriculum as a whole. It was therefore important that the individual teachers understood the philosophy behind the task and the relevance to their school. It was also important that they recognised the need for standard methods of administration of the task, including the need for accurate timing. Any individual queries were dealt with by the senior teacher on a personal basis. In the event all members of staff saw the value of the study and took part willingly.

Under what conditions should the pupils write?

Following Dutton's (1991) model, the pupils were required to write in conditions as close to those found in examinations as possible. This included a formal presentation of the task, the requirement to use paper provided and, of course, the timing considerations (Figure 9.2). Pupils were instructed to treat the task as an examination, and not to communicate with each other at all during the 30 minutes writing period. They were instructed to write their details on the first sheet of paper before starting the timed writing. Before papers were collected in the pupils were asked to add their identification details to any additional sheets of paper they had used.

Pupils were asked to mark their paper with two forward slashes (//) every three minutes. This would give an indication of those pupils who were unable to write for a full 30 minutes, rather than writing slowly but consistently throughout the whole period. For the purposes of the discussion of the results in terms of which pupils would benefit from having extra time in an examination in order to demonstrate their knowledge and understanding of the subject, this would be particularly relevant.

Ethical considerations

It was important that the teachers administering the task were reassured that any publication of the results would be anonymous with regard to pupils, themselves as administrators and the school. This was made clear on the information sheet provided by the researcher for each teacher, and was reinforced verbally by the senior teacher when she requested their cooperation in involving the school in the study.

To support discussion following the analysis of results it was deemed necessary to be able to identify the class groupings of any individual pupil in the sample. The teachers were asked to collect the papers from pupils and collate them as a class set at the end of the task. They were asked to identify the class by using their own initials on a front cover attached to the set of papers. The senior teacher would then be able to identify each set of papers and corresponding class group. The researcher would not have this knowledge and would therefore not be able to identify individual teachers.

Similarly the pupils completing the task were reassured that their writing would be anonymous. This was particularly important considering the possibly sensitive nature of the essay title. Dutton (1991:194) stated that he had 'no interest in individual pupils' and therefore could have allowed complete anonymity. However, he suggested that allowing this might 'not result in the best motivation from pupils'. He therefore compromised by requiring the pupils to write their names on their paper, but asked the teachers to cut the name off each paper prior to submitting them for assessment.

Since the results of this study would be used to inform discussion relating to future support and possible application for special examination arrangements for some of the pupils, it was necessary for the senior teacher to be able to identify individual pupil's results. However, since for the purposes of the study only writing speed was under consideration, it was not necessary for the school to have access to the content of individual papers. The pupils were therefore asked to write their initials and their date of birth on each sheet of paper they used. The pupils were assured that no teachers would read any of the papers, and that the researcher would not have access to full names. In this way the pupils were reassured that the content of their writing would remain anonymous. It was a lucky coincidence that no two pupils in any one class had the same initials. Had this not been the case, the dates of birth provided further identification.

Analysis of data

The papers were collated into class groups by the teachers as described above. These were passed to the researcher who then labelled each paper allocating a class and pupil number to each paper. There were seven classes in the year group, with class sizes at the time of the task varying between 30 and 11. The papers were therefore labelled from 1.1 to 7.11 there being only 11 pupils who wrote papers in class 7. In this way, although anonymous to the researcher, each paper could be identified in discussions between the researcher and the senior teacher.

The researcher counted the number of words written by each pupil and entered the data onto computer using Microsoft Excel software. Using this software, the mean writing speed and standard deviation for the sample was then calculated. The table of results is shown in Figure 9.3. From the table the researcher was then able to identify the speed for any individual pupil, and tell the senior teacher the initials and date of birth on that paper. Using class lists the senior teacher was then able to identify the pupil. The researcher then gave details of that pupil's writing speed to the senior teacher, but no information relating to the content of the writing, thus protecting the interests of the pupils.

The results

The mean writing speed was calculated to be 14.9 words per minute. There was a standard deviation of 4.9. For practical purposes these speeds were rounded to the nearest whole number of words, giving a mean speed of 15 words per minute and a standard deviation of 5. Therefore any speed between 10 and 20 words per minute could be accepted as 'average'.

From the total number of 152 pupils in the study, 20 pupils wrote slower than 10 words per minute and 20 wrote faster than 20 words per minute, i.e. outside the figure representing one standard deviation either side of the mean. As a percentage of the whole sample, these figures represent approximately 13 per cent of the year group at each extreme. Looking at the curve of normal distribution, 68 per cent of all observations lie within one standard deviation either side of the mean, with 16 per cent above and 16 per cent below this range. Comparing this with the figures for the study, a normal distribution would have given 24 pupils in each of the groups above and below average. The results of the study are therefore close to a normal distribution.

Five pupils wrote at a speed that is below two standard deviations below the mean (below five words per minute), and five wrote at a speed that is above two standard deviations above the mean (above 25 words per minute). Again, comparing this with the normal distribution curve, where one would expect 2.5 per cent (i.e. four pupils) to be in each group, the results are close to the normal distribution.

The results of this study compare favourably with previous research described in this chapter. This suggests that the 14 words per minute speed suggested as a 'rule of thumb norm' for consideration for special arrangements suggested by Backhouse (1998) in the guidelines referred to above, is correct for a mean writing speed. However, by calculating the standard deviation, it would appear that a speed between 10 and 20 words per minute should be considered average, and that a speed of less than 10 words per minute would be a better figure to use in considering applications for pupils to be allowed extra time in examinations.

Since the completion of this study, a similar study has been reported by Allcock (1999). She reported a mean speed of 14.7 words per minute for Y10 pupils. No figures were given for standard deviation. This appears to be an important omission, since it is the point at which a pupil's speed falls below *average*, not below the *mean* that should indicate consideration of the need for special arrangements.

Discussion of results

As well as adding to the bank of knowledge and data available for calculating a reliable measure of writing speed, the purpose of this study was to provide the school with data on individual pupils to inform discussions about the application for special examination arrangements.

Having calculated the mean and standard deviation, and identified those pupils whose writing speed was below average, the researcher provided the data on these pupils to the senior teacher. She was able to compare the statistical data with the subjective information available on each pupil. All these factors would be taken into account when deciding, together with curriculum colleagues, which pupils would be likely to benefit from the provision of extra time, or other special arrangements.

Of the 20 pupils identified as having a writing speed below average, 11 failed to write for a full 30 minutes. From curriculum records and discussion with staff, it was clear that these pupils were all having difficulty acquiring the knowledge base for the majority of their examination subjects, and they would not therefore benefit from any extra time.

Of the remaining eight pupils, one had a statement of special educational needs for dyspraxia and was already being taught to make full use of an amanuensis. This is an important issue for both special needs and subject teachers when considering special arrangements. Special needs staff have a duty to identify pupils needing special arrangements, and which particular arrangements best meet the needs of individual pupils. Some pupils will need to be taught how to utilise extra time effectively. Others will need to be taught keyboard skills in order to make the best use of word-processing facilities. Some will need to learn how to work with an amanuensis. All of these options require early identification of need in order to enable the pupils to have sufficient time to practise using them in order to make effective use of the special arrangements during examinations.

Subject specialist staff need to consider what special arrangements best meet the needs of slow writers in their curriculum area and how they will prepare pupils to make use of these arrangements within their subject time. The implications for close liaison between special needs staff and subject specialists are clear. There is likely to be a need in many schools for staff training, not only to raise levels of awareness of the issues involved, but also to support staff and give them the necessary knowledge, skills and understanding of how to meet the needs of those pupils who, due to a slow writing speed are unable to effectively demonstrate their knowledge of the curriculum under examination conditions.

As discussed at the start of the chapter, when applying for special arrangements, schools must provide 'historical evidence of the candidate's needs and an indication of how the centre meets these needs' (Joint Council for General Qualifications 1999:8). The implication here is that teachers must be able to recognise those pupils with 'slow' writing speeds as early as possible in the pupil's secondary schooling, and know how to provide appropriate support for those pupils across the curriculum. Early identification and intervention will therefore provide the historical evidence that may be needed as the pupils approach external examinations.

Evaluation of the study

Having identified a need for a statistically accurate assessment of what constitutes 'slow' handwriting, the most difficult aspect of this study was finding a school willing to take part. Many of the schools approached by the researcher were unwilling or unable to find the necessary time for pupils to write for the study. The researcher is therefore particularly grateful to the senior teacher from the school used for her support, and to the individual teachers who supervised the writing task.

The need for accurate timing made it essential that all the teachers involved fully understood the rationale behind the task. The provision of information to teachers (Figure 9.1) and of clear instructions for those teachers to read verbatim to pupils (Figure 9.2) enabled the researcher to communicate indirectly with all the teachers involved. However, it was essential that one member of staff, the senior teacher, was willing and able to speak directly to the other teachers and answer individual questions if necessary.

The most difficult aspect of the study was counting how many words the pupils wrote. Dutton (1991:194) commented that although he had originally planned to have each script double marked, 'time factors subsequently made this impossible'. Dutton eventually resorted to only marking a sample of the scripts available. The researcher was determined to base the results on as large a sample as possible and therefore did mark all 152 scripts. A colleague supported this marking, but the task was still very time consuming. Since the information was numerical and did not involve making any subjective judgements, the use of two markers did not produce any difficulties.

Following publication of Allcock's (1999) study the Professional Association of Teachers of Students with Specific Learning Difficulties (Patoss) recognised the 'pressing need for a much broader sample which can be analysed to establish proper benchmarks of writing speed for different year groups' (Greenwold 1999:21). Patoss agreed to support further research by providing funds and supporting the analysis of the data collected (Patoss 1999). In providing the instructions for this further research it was suggested that since counting words is so time consuming 'it would be sensible to instruct the students to do this'. As discussed above, the number of individuals involved in counting the words should not cause any judgemental difficulties. However, if allowing students (pupils) to mark the scripts it would be necessary to second mark a sample to check the accuracy of their counting. It is not a particularly interesting activity and boredom could well lead to inaccuracies if any individual marker was not aware of and supported the importance of accuracy in the task.

Conclusion

Many pupils are unable to demonstrate their knowledge and understanding of the curriculum in examinations due to their relatively slow handwriting. To enable these pupils to achieve results commensurate with their abilities they need to be given the special arrangements that they are now entitled to. In order to do this schools need to first identify these pupils. It is necessary to know what rate of handwriting may be taken as 'slow'. The results of this study indicate that 15 words per minute is the mean writing speed for Year 10 pupils, and that anything between 10 and 20 words per minute may be taken as average. Therefore the researcher is suggesting that any pupil writing slower than 10 words per minute should be identified as having 'slow' handwriting. It is then up to the pupil's teachers to make a judgement about whether that pupil would benefit from special arrangements for examinations. This judgement should be based on information gathered from a wide range of sources, both objective and subjective. Having reached agreement on those pupils for whom special arrangements will be made, it is then essential that the pupils are prepared to make effective use of whatever arrangements have been agreed. This has implications for all staff, in terms of the early identification of pupils and the planning and delivery of appropriate support arrangements.

This quantitative study will add to the small body of data available on handwriting speeds. It is hoped that other teachers will carry out further study, possibly by becoming involved in the Patoss (1999) research project in order to provide nationally agreed norms for all ages of pupils. In this way it will be much easier for teachers to identify pupils early in their school career and begin to make appropriate arrangements to support those pupils and enable them to reach their full potential.

References and further reading

Allcock, P. (1999) 'Define "Slow" – the quest for a standardised test of handwriting speed', *Patoss Bulletin* November, 18–20.

Alston, J. (1994) 'Written output and writing speeds', *Dyslexia Review* **6**, 6–12.

Backhouse, G. (1998) 'GCSE and GCE candidates with special assessment needs – specific learning difficulties: special arrangements and special consideration', *Patoss Bulletin* May, 2–7.

Davies, T. R. (1998) *Communication to Heads and Principals of Centres.* Joint Forum for GCSE and GCE.

Dutton, K. P. (1991) 'Writing Under Examination Conditions: Establishing a Baseline', *SED/Regional Psychological Services: Professional Development Initiatives 1989–90*, Scottish Education Department.

Greenwold, L. (1999) 'Handwriting Speed Research Project', *Patoss Bulletin* November.

Joint Council for General Qualifications (1999) *Examinations and Assessment for GCSE and GCE: Regulations and Guidance relating to Candidates with Special Requirements 2000.* London: Joint Council for General Qualifications.

Patoss (1999) 'Group and individual assessment of handwriting', *Patoss Bulletin* November.

Roaf, C. (1998) 'Slow hand: a secondary school survey of handwriting speed and legibility', *Support for Learning* **13**(1), 39–42.

Sawyer, C., Gray, F. and Champness, M. (1996) 'Measuring speed of handwriting for the GCSE candidates', *Educational Psychology in Practice* **12**(1), April.

WRITING SPEED RESEARCH

Each year decisions have to be made regarding the granting of 'special exam conditions' for a number of candidates who have an extreme difficulty in producing written text. This can be in the form of specific spelling difficulty, very poor handwriting ability or a combination of both.

Many norm-referenced tests exist to place spelling ability in context. However, there is little information available to guide decisions on the quality, quantity and speed of handwriting.

This survey, based on earlier research by Dutton (1991) is to measure the 'normal' speed of writing under examination conditions in order to place judgements on this ability in a context. It sets out to find answers to the question:

How fast do pupils write when faced with an examination-type task?

The method and instructions are similar to those used by Dutton. The subject for the essay is 'My Life History', a title chosen by Dutton after discussion with the English teachers in a secondary school. This title should overcome limitations of any pupil's knowledge and ensure as even a starting point as possible.

INSTRUCTIONS

Please provide A4 paper, either lined or blank depending on school and/or pupil preference. You will need a stapler available for pupils to clip sheets together.

Please present the instructions to the pupils verbatim as scripted on the attached sheet. Then briefly introduce the topic, along with some 'starter' ideas. This short discussion may include the types of things that might arise under such a topic heading, i.e. place of birth, significant life events, interests, hobbies, etc.

It is vital that you time the writing accurately. Pupils must have exactly **30 minutes** writing time. They need to be told to make a 'time mark' every **three minutes**.

The results will be returned to your school as soon as papers have been marked and results analysed. Any publication of results will be anonymous with regard to pupils and the school.

Dutton, K.P. (1991) 'Writing Under Examination Conditions: Establishing a Baseline', *SED/Regional Psychological Services: Professional Development Initiatives* 1989–90, Scottish Education Department.

Figure 9.1 Information for Teachers

INSTRUCTIONS TO BE READ VERBATIM TO PUPILS

1. Today, I am interested in seeing how you write. I want to look at how quickly you write, how neatly you write, the ideas you put into a piece of writing and how much you write.
2. In a moment I'll describe what you are to write about and we will give you a few minutes to think about how you will tackle the subject, but first let me describe what you will need and what I will want you to do.
3. You may write with any suitable writing implement of your choice and that you feel most comfortable with.
4. I want you to use this paper (indicate). At the top please write your initials, the date, your year group. On the next line please write your date of birth.

   Now, fill in the details at the top of the page. If you are not sure how, then put up your hand. (Deal with any queries arising.)

   If you need any extra paper as we go simply put up your hand and I will bring it to you.
5. As you are writing during this lesson I will be calling out 'Time Mark' at three-minute intervals. When you hear this, simply mark the point in your writing with this mark // and then carry on (indicate on blackboard by writing 'line of // writing'). It will only take you a second and should not disturb your writing or ideas. No matter how much you have written since the last mark, maybe even no words at all, always put the mark when you are told.

   (At the end of the 30 minute period)
   Stop writing now, even if you are in the middle of a sentence.

   If you have used more than one sheet of paper, please put your initials and date of birth on any additional sheets of paper you used and clip your papers together.

Figure 9.2 Information for Pupils

pupil	words	w/m	<1StDev	>1StDev	<2StDev	>2StDev	
2;1	351	11.7					
2;2	330	11					
2;3	367	12.2					
2;4	545	18.2					
2;5	601	20		1			
2;6	454	15.1					
2;7	443	14.8					
2;8	442	14.7					
2;9	744	24.8		1		1	
2;10	323	10.8					
2;11	391	13					
2;12	560	18.7					
2;13	476	15.9					
2;14	780	26		1		1	
2;20	324	10.8					
2;21	631	21		1			
2;22	492	16.4					
2;23	370	12.3					
2;24	591	19.7					
2;25	557	18.6					
2;26	386	12.9					
2;27	495	16.5					
2;28	476	15.9					
2;29	607	20.2		1			
2;30	595	19.8		1			
4;1	608	20.3		1			
4;2	380	12.7					
4;3	486	16.2					
4;4	350	11.7					
4;5	309	10.3					
4;6	339	11.3					
4;7	518	17.3					
4;8	564	18.8					
4;9	544	18.1					
4;10	**240**	**8**		**1**			
4;11	444	14.8					
4;12	**187**	**6.2**		**1**			
4;13	582	19.4					
4;14	344	11.5					
4;15	303	10.1					
4;16	379	12.6					
4;17	488	16.3					
4;18	553	18.4					
4;19	**207**	**6.9**		**1**			
4;20	**176**	**5.9**		**1**			
4;21	**238**	**7.9**		**1**			
(a)	446.4	(b) 14.9	(d) 20		20	5	5
		(c) 4.9					

Example of data: samples of results from two classes out of the seven

Results from whole sample

Key
(a) Mean numbers of words written in 30 minutes.
(b) Mean number of words/minute.
(c) Standard deviation.
(d) Total number of pupils writing < or > 1 or 2 StDev below or above mean.

Figures in bold indicate pupils writing at a below average speed.

Figure 9.3 Example of data: samples of results from two classes out of the seven

CHAPTER 10

An investigation into the impact of Social Stories on the behaviour and social understanding of four pupils with autistic spectrum disorder

Marie Howley

Introduction – the social impairment in autistic spectrum disorder

The social impairment in autistic spectrum disorder is a critical element of the triad of impairment (Wing and Gould 1979) and lies at the core of the disorder. The need for teachers to address social competence is critical to the development of the individual with autistic spectrum disorder from two perspectives. Firstly, access to so much of the curriculum depends on a child's ability to interact with both adults and peers. Secondly, in order for an individual to be successfully included in both school and in the wider community, he or she needs to develop a degree of social competence (Harris and Handelman 1997). Yet the development of social skills and interaction frequently present the greatest challenge to teachers and pupils alike.

The researcher became particularly interested in the social impairment while teaching children with autistic spectrum disorder. It became clear that while it can be relatively easy to teach 'splinter' social skills, considerable challenges are presented in the development of social interaction within a broader context. The development of social skills in isolation from other aspects of social development is inadequate, as the social deficit in autistic spectrum disorders is significantly greater than simply the acquisition of skills (Howlin 1986, Gray 1998). A number of crucial aspects of social development are frequently not addressed by teaching specific skills in isolation including:

- social judgement
- social prediction
- social understanding (Gray 1998).

Howlin (1986) suggests that 'the essence of social behaviour consists of the ability to relate to others in a mutually reinforcing and reciprocal fashion and to adapt social skills to the varying demands of interpersonal contexts'. Thus social competence depends on an ability to draw upon a range of strategies in an integrated way, as opposed to developing isolated skills. Pupils need to use social judgement and prediction in order to apply and generalise learnt social skills appropriately. Clearly success in this area will vary among individuals and frequently remains a challenge into adulthood, nevertheless it is critical that teachers address these areas if pupils are to begin to utilise their social skills in a meaningful way. Indeed, the development of social skills may be of minimal intrinsic value unless accompanied by the development of social understanding.

Social understanding may be defined as an understanding of the underlying messages that underpin social interaction, described by Gray (1998) as a 'hidden code'. Social understanding depends on an understanding of explicit and implicit social rules that govern everyday social encounters; it requires an ability to make decisions about the social skills we have in terms of 'when' and 'where' to use them. These areas of social development became a focus for the researcher's teaching and provided the impetus for this research.

The introduction and development of Social Stories

Gray (1998) suggests that Social Stories focus on the development of social understanding in order to enable individuals to use their social skills more appropriately. She states that:

> the goal of a Social Story is to share relevant information. This information includes (but is not limited to) *where* and *when* a situation takes place, *who* is involved, *what* is occurring, and *why*. (Gray 1998:171)

Social Stories attempt to develop a greater understanding of the social world in addition to teaching appropriate social behaviour. However, apart from anecdotal reports, there is to date a lack of empirically based research that examines the impact of Social Stories on social development. Of the research that does exist (Kuttler *et al.* 1998, Rowe 1999, Swaggart *et al.* 1995) some issues arise that need careful consideration. For example, Swaggart *et al.* used a combination of approaches, thus complicating any conclusions drawn. In addition, some of the Social Stories used did not follow the sentence ratio recommended by Gray (1998). The impetus for this research was provided therefore from both a pragmatic and theoretical perspective.

The hypothesis

The hypothesis for this research was derived directly from Gray's (1998) view that Social Stories may be used by teachers (and others) to develop social behaviour and understanding in individuals with autistic spectrum disorders. The hypothesis formulated suggests that:

> The development and implementation of individualised Social Stories may lead to an increase in appropriate social behaviours and to improved social understanding in pupils with autistic spectrum disorders.

Research approach

This research uses case study as its main strategic research strategy in that it can be described as a 'relatively formal analysis of an aspect of classroom life' (Hopkins 1985:81). It is essentially interpretative, an objective being to 'describe and interpret the phenomena of the world in attempts to get shared meanings with others' (Bassey 1995). The purpose of this research was to describe and interpret the events of the project and to share the findings with teachers and others who may have an interest in this area. This is a particularly important part of the research as the findings may have a direct influence on classroom practice. Finally, the research is qualitative in its approach. Howlin (1986) criticises research into the social behaviour of people with autistic spectrum disorder for being primarily concerned with quantitative data collection, measuring frequency of specific behaviours. This research focused on teacher perceptions of the impact of the Social Story approach and compared these perceptions with observational field notes, thus allowing for a qualitative approach and analysis.

Generalisation of findings

While the findings of this investigation may not be generalised due to the small sample of cases included in the study and the diverse range of needs within the autistic population, this does not mean that the findings are not of interest to others. Bassey (1999) proposes the notion of 'fuzzy generalisations', suggesting that it may be possible for research findings to be of general interest to others while accepting the inevitable uncertainty within such a generalisation. He goes on to suggest that this offers others the opportunity to 'try it and see if the same happens for you'. While it may not be possible to offer generalisations from this research, the outcomes of the study do serve to illuminate our understanding of the use of Social Stories and there are implications for the way in which teachers might best use the approach.

Research context

The research was carried out in a primary school in Northampton. The school has designated special provision (DSP) for children with a range of special educational needs, some of whom have a diagnosis consistent with autistic spectrum disorder. The research involved liaison with the teacher in charge of the DSP, learning support assistants working with individual children, an autism specialist, a speech and language therapist, and one parent.

Choice of sample

Four pupils, three males and one female, were selected each of whom were having difficulties during periods of integration within the mainstream classrooms. All had a diagnosis of autism and had specific difficulties with aspects of social functioning. All four pupils spent some time in a specialist classroom base using the TEACCH (Treatment and Education of Autistic and related Communication handicapped Children) approach. The children also spent a considerable amount of time in mainstream classes with learning support assistants; three children were placed in a year group below their peers, one child was placed with his peer group.

Methodology

As the approach was essentially interpretative it was appropriate to collect data of a qualitative nature. This included:

- Semi-structured interviews with the DSP teacher, learning support assistants working with each pupil and a specialist speech and language therapist. One parent was also interviewed by telephone.
- Observational field notes – kept by DSP staff.

Interviews

Interviews were carried out before the introduction of the Social Stories and again at the end of the project. The teacher and the learning support assistants were interviewed as a group in order to promote discussion and to explore a range of opinions. The specialist speech and language therapist was interviewed separately in order to follow up some of the issues raised during the group interview. One parent was interviewed by telephone in order to explore her opinions with regard to the impact of the Social Story used at home. The purpose of the interviews was to gather information in relation to several elements:

- Information about each child's current social skills and understanding.
- Information about the behaviours to be investigated, including opinion with regards to frequency of behaviour prior to introducing a Social Story.
- Information about how the Social Stories were implemented.
- Information about the perceived effectiveness of the approach.

The specialist speech and language therapist was interviewed as a consistent element across all four cases.

All interviews were recorded to aid transcription, in addition to the researcher taking notes relating to the critical points raised. The interview schedule combined both tightly-structured questions requiring specific answers and open-ended questions to facilitate discussion, with the use of prompts and probes to further explore issues raised.

Observations

The observations took place in a natural setting with people who already have a relationship of trust with each child. The children were observed generally as an everyday feature so this requirement fitted well into usual classroom practice.

Observational field notes were kept for each child prior to introducing the Social Stories and at intervals of one, two and four weeks following their introduction. Frequencies of target behaviour were recorded, but more importantly, individuals recorded comments relating to each child's behaviour and possible understanding of the situation.

The data gathered using these methods were coded into key areas:

- data about the implementation of the Social Stories;
- data about the perceived impact of the approach in relation to social behaviour and understanding.

Behaviours investigated

The difficulties identified by the teacher were specific behaviours occurring at times of integration either in mainstream classes or at whole-school break times. The teacher and the speech and language therapist provided a description of the purposes of each Social Story during the semi-structured interview (Figure 10.1). The four children were observed in relation to a specific behaviour and individualised Social Stories were written for each child (see Appendix A at the end of this chapter). Gray's (1998) guidelines for producing Social Stories were adhered to, including the sentence ratio. Each story was written in a book format, as all the children were able to read.

	Target social behaviour	Purpose of the Social Story	Visual presentation
Michael Age 7.0	Michael used a voice that was too loud in the (mainstream) classroom, thus disrupting his peers, especially when reading.	To enable Michael to read aloud at an acceptable level of volume. 'To know there are different volumes of voices … to develop an appropriate reading voice' (Speech and Language Therapist).	Written Social Story. Visual number line 0–10 0 = silence 5 = reading voice 10 = shouting Used in the story and as a bookmark while reading.
Sally Age 9.4	Sally was unable to follow directions given to a group and was unaware that she needed to listen when the teacher addressed the whole class.	To enable Sally to listen to whole class directions and respond appropriately. 'To tell her when it's important to listen to group instructions' (Speech and Language Therapist).	Written Social Story. Symbol line drawing representing listening in a group – used as a cue in the story and as a prompt card in the classroom.
Max Age 7.5	Max had difficulties at break times. He was unable to stay in the designated play area and constantly wandered into areas he should not have been in. In addition, he had no idea of how to occupy his time at break times.	To enable Max to stay in the designated area, i.e. the field at play times and to begin to join in simple activities. 'To let him know the rules of where to play and what to do' (Speech and Language Therapist).	Written Social Story.
George Age 8.1	George liked to play turn-taking games but was fixated on winning – he was anxious throughout the game, worrying about whether he would win/lose.	To reduce George's anxiety relating to winning or not, when playing games. 'To let him know you won't always win, you might another day' (Speech and Language Therapist).	Written Social Story.

Figure 10.1 Difficulties with social behaviour targeted for Social Stories

Ethical considerations

Informed consent was sought in the early stages from all of the adults who took part in the study. The researcher required access to the identified school and permission was given from the governors, head teacher, teacher in charge of the DSP, DSP staff involved in data collection, speech and language therapy service and the parents of each child. In order to gain confidence and acceptance of those involved, in particular the parents, the researcher outlined the research proposal to all concerned, supported by an opportunity for face to face discussion and reassurance.

The researcher liaised extensively with a specialist speech and language therapist who played a key role in identifying suitable children for the study and in supporting the teachers in the development and implementation of the Social Stories. All were fully informed in order for them to feel able to support the project. The informed consent of parents was considered to be critical, particularly as the sample group of children was from a vulnerable population due to the nature of their disorder.

Findings

Implementation of the Social Stories

Key questions were asked to identify how the Social Stories were implemented for each child:

- Was any additional visual information used to supplement the Social Story?
- Who read the Social Story?
- In what context and when was it read?
- Was the Social Story maintained throughout the observation period?
- Did the pupil like the Social Story?

The findings are summarised in relation to each pupil in Figure 10.2.

Perceived impact and effectiveness of the approach

The findings in this area are summarised for each pupil in relation to the:

- immediate impact and perceived effectiveness of the Social Stories on specific social behaviours;
- perceived level of social understanding of each pupil.

	Additional visual cues	**Who read? How often? Context**	**Maintained throughout?**	**Did the pupil like the story?**
Max	No	• LSA (all lunch time staff had copies) • Daily 10 minutes prior to break time Max also read the story to himself whenever he wanted to	Yes	Mostly Less keen on days when he was feeling 'stressed'
Sally	Visual icon for 'group, listen'	• LSA • Prior to group lessons (different subject areas)	No Sally said she no longer needed the story after two weeks	Yes, especially when it was first introduced
Michael	Visual number line presented as a bookmark: 0 = silence 5 = reading voice 10 = shouting	• LSA • Prior to Michael reading to an adult	Yes	Yes – very much
George	No	• LSA • Prior to group games	Yes	No

Figure 10.2 Summary of findings in relation to implementation of Social Stories

Max

Max was reported to wander around at break times and seemed unaware of the areas he should not use. The teacher said that Max had been anxious at break times, as he did not understand the social rules governing the situation. Prior to introducing his Social Story, Max was observed on six occasions. The teacher observed Max outside at lunch/break times and recorded how frequently he entered an incorrect area. During this period, Max was reported as 'hovering around the borders of each of the designated play areas'. He frequently entered the out-of-bounds area and was sent back to the field. Max was described as upset on a number of occasions and was sometimes in tears. Although various resources were available in the field for pupils to play with Max did not attempt to play with any of the items available on any occasion. There were also markedly infrequent interactions with other pupils. An extract from the field notes illustrates this behaviour:

> Onto playground from grass. Edge of grass, sitting on floor in tears. Holding hands with dinner lady. Onto playground. Brief chat with 2 pupils – 30 seconds. Edge of playground. Looking at the ground – joined by another child so moved off but still on playground. Moving along railings. Walking along border.

Following the use of the Social Story the teacher and the speech and language therapist reported that Max was more able to stay on the field and began to 'explore other areas of the field'. Max was described as playing with apparatus and was able to ask lunchtime supervisors for items to play with. The teacher was particularly pleased that Max seemed to be happier and showed much less anxiety about wandering to the playground. The speech and language therapist raised two further issues that were felt to have had an impact on the success of the approach. Firstly, the rules governing break times had to be clearly defined for **everybody** concerned and secondly, she felt that in order to achieve consistency of responses to Max, every adult needed to read the Social Story, in order to familiarise themselves with the information in it.

The observational data supported the information offered during the interviews. Max was observed on seven separate occasions following the introduction of his Social Story. Analysis of the field notes shows a gradual and progressive change in Max's behaviour. He was observed in the 'out of bounds' area less often and he spent the majority of his time in the field, with only isolated visits to the playground area. This change is apparent from the first observation following the introduction of Max's story: 'On field with 3 other children. Played game, running round group. 8 children in group now – still playing.' Max's behaviour appeared to alter immediately following reading his story. He was observed on three consecutive days during this period and each of the observation periods showed a reduction in playground wandering. Max was observed two weeks later when again wandering was minimal. Max was also observed in areas of the field that he had not visited before: 'Well into the middle of the field (never been there before on other observations).' The final notes state that 'I do feel that Max feels more comfortable on grass now'. Max was also observed engaging in activities with other children two weeks following the initial reading of his story. The field notes show a progressive development during this period that includes playing with materials provided and interacting with other children e.g.:

> Max came to get a skipping rope out of the equipment bag and went onto the field.
>
> Running with skipping rope onto field. Brought into game by another child.

Both the interview and observation data show progressive changes in Max's behaviour following the introduction of his Social Story. The teacher was also questioned about Max's level of social understanding at playtimes. The teacher reported during the interview that she believed that Max had developed an understanding of the rules, 'he knew to stay on the grass' and that he seemed as a consequence 'to be more comfortable with the rules'. The speech and language therapist also suggested that Max had developed an understanding of the rules and that he seemed happier 'because he understood **why** he had to stay on the field'.

Sally

Sally was reported as having difficulties with listening and responding to directions in whole-group situations, regardless of the content of the lesson. During the initial interview the teacher suggested that Sally 'masks her difficulties with a confident air'. She was described as using strategies to hide her difficulties and was able to 'look busy'. The teacher also explained that Sally 'aims to fit in and please'. The speech and language therapist believed that Sally did not know that when directions were given to the whole class she was supposed to listen. Consequently she was then unable to follow the instructions, as she had not heard most of the information presented.

Observations of Sally prior to the introduction of her Social Story supported this information. Sally was observed by an LSA in the classroom on five occasions during different whole-class lessons. Observations show that Sally used a variety of strategies as cues and prompts in order to follow class directions including:

- peer prompts;
- copying other children's work;
- additional verbal prompting from the teacher;
- instructions repeated by LSA.

Extracts from the field notes demonstrate Sally's behaviour at this time:

> *Science lesson*
> Verbal prompts from teacher as not understood what was required of her. Teacher had to sit and talk through again what she needed to write.

> *English lesson* – class instructions only.
> [Sally] looked anxiously at other children. Began to copy information sheet only – not as requested. Sally began to cry.

During joint interviews with the teacher and the LSA, following the use of the Social Story, both expressed opinions that Sally had made marked progress in relation to listening to and following class directions. The LSA described Sally's story, combined with the visual cue card, as 'very helpful'. She felt that Sally experienced a decrease in tension and stopped relying on additional prompting during the lesson. Again this was supported by the observations of Sally who was observed by the same LSA on five occasions, one week after the introduction of her Social Story. The first observation notes following the reading of the Social Story show progress in Sally's ability to listen and follow instructions directed at the whole class:

> *Science*
> Class sitting and listening to teacher. Sally listening attentively. Teacher held up group card and gave instructions. Sally did as requested. Did not look at other children for reassurance. Listened – answered questions correctly.

Similar responses are recorded in a maths lesson and further English and science lessons. Sally was no longer relying on prompts such as repetition of instructions, but was observed listening to the teacher and following instructions.

Sally was observed on a further five occasions two weeks later. The observation notes described Sally as listening and following instructions consistently with a reduction in anxiety. She is described as 'on task' and able to follow group directions without further prompting. During one observation the class had a different teacher. Such a change would usually cause Sally great anxiety. An extract from observation notes show Sally's response during this lesson:

> *Science lesson*
> Question and answer session on experiment previously undertaken. Sally answered questions correctly. Sally listened and worked as directed.

The speech and language therapist also described the story as being 'effective'. This interview took place after the school summer holiday and Sally was now in a new class. The speech and language therapist reported that Sally was 'listening well in her new class' and no longer needs to read the story. Sally had taken the story home at her own request.

Sally's story was directly concerned with giving her information to develop her understanding of how to behave in group situations – i.e. to listen and to respond to group directions. The teacher reported that Sally was 'looking and concentrating more' and seemed to have grasped the rules relating to listening in a group. The speech and language therapist described Sally's understanding as shifting from 'this is nothing to do with me' (i.e. class instructions) to 'it is to do with me and I should listen'. Sally's understanding of the social situation appears to have changed and this development is reflected in her behaviour. The teacher and the LSA agreed that they would use the Social Story approach again with Sally.

Michael

Michael's teacher reported that Michael shouted most of the time and that this behaviour distracted other pupils. Observations of Michael reading aloud on four separate occasions support this. The teacher recorded how frequently Michael needed reminding to read in a quieter voice and kept notes recording his behaviour. Prior to the introduction of the Social Story Michael was prompted almost constantly during his reading, e.g.:

> Michael shouted most of the words throughout the story.
>
> Read whole passage loudly – continual prompts to read more quietly. Disturbed other children around him.

Following the use of his Social Story the teacher said that it had been very successful with Michael reducing his shouting 'from nine words out of ten to nought to three words out of ten'. She reported that she would extend the approach and write a new Social Story for Michael to use an appropriate voice level in other contexts at school. The teacher also commented that the additional visual cue contributed to the success of the Social Story as Michael referred to it spontaneously while reading. The interview with the speech and language therapist supported the opinions of the teacher. She described the story as 'immediately effective' and having seen Michael after the summer holiday commented that it 'continues to be effective'. The speech therapist also commented that Michael used one of the sentences in the story as a reminder, saying, 'a number 5 voice is a good voice'. She felt that Michael's story was the most effective with the most marked improvement in behaviour.

Extracts from the observations support these views, e.g.:

> Whole page number 5 voice. Read bookmark twice.
>
> 100% number 5 voice with no reminders or prompts. No shouts or any raised voice.

The observation notes reveal a marked change in Michael's reading voice, with a noticeable reduction from shouting throughout his reading to no shouting at all. Subsequently, the teacher and speech and language therapist said that they would certainly use the approach again. The teacher also believed that Michael's understanding had improved in this specific context. During the follow-up interview, she commented that she would like to extend the use of Social Stories to teach Michael 'why you use different volumes in different situations', thus broadening his understanding to other social situations. The speech and language therapist confirmed this, commenting that she felt Michael's understanding had undergone a 'massive shift' in this context.

George

During the initial interview the teacher and George's LSA reported that George was sometimes described as 'naughty' and had problems with 'winning and losing'. The teacher also commented that George had the same problems at home when playing games and that his parents had reported difficulties in this area to the point that they dreaded playing games – although George insisted on playing them. Observations of George confirm the views that winning and losing games caused anxiety for George.

Prior to the introduction of his Social Story, George was observed playing different games on five separate occasions by his LSA and his comments throughout the games were recorded. The following extract is typical of the comments made during every game:

> We don't know who's going to win. I'm never going to win. You don't need to cry, it's just a game.

All entries recorded during the initial observation period repeat the same phrases, reflecting the echolalic nature of George's language when he is under stress.

During the follow-up interview the LSA expressed the opinion that George remained 'stressed about winning games' although she felt there was a 'slight reduction' in his overall anxiety level. The LSA felt that George might need to have the story read for a longer period as 'it became more meaningful as he got to know it'. She also suggested that certain games seemed to cause greater anxiety for George than others do. The speech and language therapist reported that the effect of George's story was 'not so good'. She suggested that George had begun to repeat one of the sentences in the story, 'I might win another time', to replace his previous anxiety sentences. She further commented that she did not feel that George's story was 'right' in that it did not tackle the real issue for George.

Observations one week and three weeks after introducing the Social Story support these views and show a continued use of comments by George throughout each game. The LSA described George's distress throughout the entire observation periods e.g.:

> You're not going to win – (distressed – physically tried to hurt another boy because he was winning). I don't like this at all.

> You have won – who's winning? It's just a game. (At this point the LSA noted that George cried.)

George makes many similar remarks throughout every game, although he did on one occasion say 'well done' to the winner of the game when prompted. George did not say 'well done' to other players on any other occasion, although this was a key sentence in his Social Story.

George took the Social Story home at the end of term and his parents agreed to use it during the summer holiday. George's mother was subsequently interviewed and reported that initially she felt the story 'was helpful and that George seemed less anxious'. However, his anxieties quickly resurfaced and they ceased to use the Social Story. George returned to school after the summer-break with the same worries about winning and losing. All those interviewed were of the opinion that George had not made any progress in terms of his understanding in this situation. The speech and language therapist commented 'there was no shift in his view – his viewpoint did not alter'. The story provided another vehicle through which he could express his anxiety, but was not effective at reducing that anxiety. It was felt that the Social Story approach may still be of some benefit to George, but that clearer assessment of his understanding would be required, together with more detailed specification of a relevant goal. The speech and language therapist felt that further observation and analysis of George in this context would be necessary in order to write a more successful Social Story.

Discussion

A number of issues have emerged from the findings that lead to the formulation of guidelines for teachers considering introducing this approach. These relate to:

- the identification and assessment of social behaviours and understanding;
- details of implementation of the Social Stories;
- the relationship between social behaviour and social understanding;
- assessing social understanding.

While these factors will be considered separately, there is clear overlap between each of the areas.

Identification and assessment of social behaviours and understanding

The Social Stories written for Michael and Sally were perceived to be the most successful of the four stories, both in terms of improving social behaviour and in developing social understanding. In one case (Michael) the purpose of the Social Story was well identified and all were in agreement with regard to the particular difficulty being addressed. This had been an ongoing problem for Michael for some time and it was seen to be a priority area. In Sally's case, the initial purpose of the Social Story was unclear and it was agreed that the teacher would observe Sally at group times before deciding on a priority area to target. Subsequently, this led to the formulation of a very specific goal. In both Michael and Sally's cases, the social goals were clearly identified and the purpose of the Social Story was made explicit. Rowe (1999) similarly identified clear objectives in a single case study also perceived to be effective.

This is supported by the findings of the other cases in this investigation. Although Max's Social Story was perceived to be successful to a degree, it was felt that Max had just begun to understand the social requirements of break times and that he would need further, more detailed information in order for him to develop both his behaviour and understanding. From the outset, it emerged that the rules governing 'break times' were complex and depended on a number of variables, e.g. the weather, number of staff on duty. As a result, Max's original story relating to defining which areas to stay in at break times needed modification. Subsequent stories based upon more specific objectives may be increasingly helpful to Max. This issue is perhaps even more pertinent in George's case. During the interviews it was revealed that those involved felt that the story had not addressed the real issues for George. As a result, the objectives and purpose of the story did not meet George's needs. The speech and language therapist explained that she felt that 'we do not yet know what the problem is'. In George's case, it was suggested by the speech and language therapist that a further period of observation would be necessary to try to establish the nature of his difficulties when playing games before writing a new Social Story.

The evidence from this study supports the hypothesis that Social Stories can provide a useful strategy to enable some pupils to develop appropriate social behaviour and understanding, but only when the difficulties of the individual have been accurately identified. The **process** of developing the Social Story requires careful ongoing assessment (Gray 1999) and stories need modification as they reveal the child's perspective. This process may be equally important as the end product. Thus Social Stories that do not appear to be successful may still be useful in highlighting individual areas of difficulty. While George's story was not successful, the process was perceived as useful and would lead to further assessment and modification of future Social Stories for George.

Details of implementation

Visual information

Much of the detail with regard to how the Social Stories were implemented appears to be similar across all four cases with one clear distinction between the stories – the use of additional visual information. The stories that included additional visual information were perceived to be the most successful. This is corroborated by the body of evidence that exists to support the use of visual strategies when teaching individuals with autistic spectrum disorders (e.g. Gray 1998, Hodgdon 1995, Quill 1995, Kunce and Mesibov 1998).

Sharing information

The success of Max's story depended upon all adults involved with Max at break times being aware of the story content. As social interaction and competence rely upon reciprocity, it would seem essential that others involved with a pupil become familiar with the Social Story. This enables all participants to gain an insight into the child's understanding and to adjust their own social behaviour so as to enhance the child's attempts to interact or follow the social rules.

The relationship between social behaviour and social understanding

Gray (1998) suggests that Social Stories should address social behaviour and improve social understanding by focusing on the underlying cognitive deficits of the social impairment in autistic spectrum disorder. Despite the emphasis on social understanding, other studies have focused on measuring behaviour only (Kuttler *et al.* 1998, Swaggart *et al.* 1995). The findings of this study support Gray's (1998) emphasis on social understanding in a number of ways. The two most successful stories resulted in a change in both behaviour and understanding for Michael and Sally. Rowe (1999) also indicates development in relation to behaviour and social understanding, illustrated by the case study child's comment, 'now I'll know what to do', suggesting that he now has a greater understanding of the social requirements of lunch time.

While Max's story was successful to some extent, his understanding did not undergo the 'massive shift' of the other pupils and the LSA reported that Max's behaviour still appeared to depend in part upon his levels of stress. George's story was not successful possibly as it may have failed to identify his level of social understanding from the start; hence the information he was provided with did not address his difficulties. George's understanding was not perceived to change in any way and consequently his behaviour did not alter. This would seem to support the theoretical view that social behaviour and social understanding are inextricably linked and any improvement in social behaviour depends to a large extent on simultaneous development in understanding.

Assessing social understanding

In order to develop effective Social Stories it is critical to identify an appropriate goal from the outset. This can only be achieved if an accurate assessment of the individual's level of social understanding is established. The final key factor to consider therefore is the need to accurately assess an individual's level of social understanding in order to provide a Social Story that is more likely to lead to success. This factor underpins the whole process with regard to firstly identifying social difficulties and subsequently using Social Stories to improve and develop social behaviour and understanding. It is important therefore to consider **how** social understanding can be assessed for, if assessment is more accurate, then the Social Story may be more successful. Gray's (1998) 'comic-strip conversations' may well be one useful strategy for assessing social understanding. Gray suggests that comic-strip conversations provide 'insights into a student's perspective of a situation' and that the strategy is useful as a prerequisite to the development of a Social Story.

Guidelines for further use of Social Stories

The findings of this investigation would suggest the following guidelines for teachers who are considering the approach:

1. Identify and assess the nature of individual difficulties in relation to behaviour and understanding before writing the Social Story. This process is as important as the Social Story eventually produced. Gray's (1998) comic-strip conversations may be helpful in assessing social understanding.
2. Formulate specific objectives against which the impact of the Social Story can subsequently be measured. Intended outcomes should be defined in measurable terms in order to ensure that progress can be monitored.
3. Include appropriate visual information to support the Social Story.
4. Ensure that the contents of the Social Story are shared with all involved.

These guidelines are reflected in the findings of this study and are supportive of the recommendations described by Gray (1998). Further guidelines may well emerge from subsequent, more in-depth research.

Areas for future research

Jordan (1999) advocates that there is a place for practitioner based evaluative research, suggesting that normal daily monitoring practices should become more systematic in order to produce reliable and valid findings that can be shared with others. Research in the area of Social Stories offers practitioners the opportunity to become actively involved in evaluating the impact of this relatively new approach. A number of research questions arise therefore that may well be of interest to teacher researchers:

1. Is the impact/effectiveness of a Social Story maintained over a long-term time period?
2. Do new skills and understanding generalise to other contexts?
3. Which groups of individuals is the Social Story approach most likely to be effective for?
4. Is the approach effective for individuals who do not have autistic spectrum disorder?

5. How critical is the type of sentence and sentence ratio defined by Gray (1998) in determining the effectiveness of the approach?
6. What other factors recommended by Gray (e.g. visual information, presentation) are critical to the effectiveness of the approach?

Conclusion

Inclusive practices must address the social needs of the individual with autistic spectrum disorder if inclusion is to be successful (Burack *et al.* 1997). Such children are socially excluded by the nature of the social impairment; thus it is imperative that strategies are developed that aim to improve social functioning. The difficulties described in this investigation impact upon both the individual and other pupils in the class. There are clearly implications for inclusion if a child is experiencing these types of social difficulties. As Harris and Handelman (1997) suggest:

> Competent social skills are essential for effective inclusion of children with autism in mainstreamed classes. Even children with Autistic Disorder or Asperger's Disorder who are of normal intellectual ability have grave problems understanding the social transactions of childhood. These limitations make them stand out among their peers and can lead to rejection by other children (Harris and Handelman 1997:665).

It is critical therefore for teachers to develop strategies for developing social behaviour and understanding in pupils with autistic spectrum disorder if they are to be successfully included in a mainstream setting. This research supports the view that Social Stories offer an effective strategy to develop social competence in some individuals with autistic spectrum disorder. Although the case study described is small scale and the findings are therefore limited, nevertheless it offers some insight into the effectiveness of the approach and suggests that it is worthy of further investigation. Social Stories appear to offer an exciting and potentially valuable tool that may have a significant impact on the social development of some individuals with autistic spectrum disorder. However, while the use of Social Stories may well help to develop the social understanding of individuals with autistic spectrum disorder, it remains essential that we also need to develop our own understanding and awareness in order to enhance social inclusion. After all, social reciprocity and competence depends not only on the individual with the autistic spectrum disorder, but also on the 'neuro-typical' individuals within society!

References

Bassey, M. (1995) *Creating Education through Research.* Edinburgh/Newark: British Educational Research Association/ Kirklington Moor Press.

Bassey, M. (1999) *Case Study Research in Educational Settings.* Buckingham: Open University Press.

Burack, J., Root, R. and Zigler, E. (1997) 'Inclusive education for students with autism: reviewing ideological, empirical and community considerations', in Cohen, D. J. and Volkmar, F. R. (eds) *Handbook of Autism and Pervasive Developmental Disorders.* Chichester: John Wiley.

Gray, C. (1998) 'Social stories and comic strip conversations with students with Asperger syndrome and high functioning autism', in Schopler, E., Mesibov, G. and Kunce, L. (eds) *Asperger Syndrome or High Functioning Autism?* New York: Plenum Press.

Gray, C. (1999) 'Social Stories and Comic Strip Conversations: Teaching Social Understanding to Students with Autistic Spectrum Disorders'. Unpublished presentation for The Gray Center for Social Learning and Understanding.

Gray, C. and Garand, J. (1993) 'Social stories: improving responses of individuals with autism with accurate social information', *Focus on Autistic Behaviour* **8**, 1–10.

Harris, S. and Handelman, J. (1997) 'Helping children with autism enter the mainstream', in Cohen, D. J and Volkmar, F. R. (eds) *Handbook of Autism and Pervasive Developmental Disorders.* Chichester: John Wiley.

Hodgdon, L. (1995) *Visual strategies for improving communication.* Michigan: Quirk Roberts.

Hopkins, D. (1985) *A Teacher's Guide to Classroom Research.* Milton Keynes: Open University Press.

Howlin, P. (1986) 'An overview of social behaviour in autism', in Schopler, E. and Mesibov, G. (eds) *Social Behaviour in Autism.* New York: Plenum Press.

Jordan, R. (1999) 'Evaluating practice: problems and possibilities', *Autism* **3**(4), 411–34.

Kunce, L. and Mesibov, G. (1998) 'Educational approaches to high-functioning autism and Asperger syndrome', in Schopler, E., Mesibov, G. and Kunce, L. (eds) *Asperger Syndrome or High Functioning Autism?* New York: Plenum Press.

Kuttler, S., Smith Myles, B. and Carlson, J. (1998) 'The use of social stories to reduce precursors to tantrum behaviour in a student with autism', *Focus on Autism and Other Developmental Disorders* **12**, 176–82.

Quill, K. (ed.) (1995) *Teaching children with autism: Strategies to enhance communication and socialisation.* New York: Delmar.

Rowe, C. (1999) 'Do social stories benefit children with autism in mainstream primary school?', *British Journal of Special Education* **26**(1), 12–14.

Swaggart, B. L. *et al.* (1995) 'Using social stories to teach social and behavioural skills to children with autism', *Focus on Autistic Behaviour* **10**, 1–15.

Wing, L. and Gould, J. (1979) 'Severe impairments of social interaction and associated abnormalities in children: epidemiology and classification', *Journal of Autism and Childhood Schizophrenia* **9**, 11–29.

APPENDIX A: THE SOCIAL STORIES

Where to play at lunch time: a story for Max

(p1)
My name is Max.

I am in class _____ at ___________________________________ School.

Usually all the children go out to play at lunch time.

When the grass is dry some children play ball games together on the playground, some children play on the field.

(p2)
When it is a dry day Mrs ____________________ or a teacher will tell me when it is my turn to play on the playground.

(p3)
When it is my turn to play on the play on the field I can ask a dinner lady if I can play with a piece of equipment out of her bag.

Sometimes she has: hoops
skipping ropes
stilts
or other things.

(p4)
It is important to stay on the field when it is my turn to be on the field.

I will have a turn on the playground another time.

(p5)
On days when the grass is wet, everyone plays on the playground.

APPENDIX A (continued)

Listening to the teacher: a story for Sally

(p1)
My name is Sally and I go to ______________________________ School.

Mrs ____________________ is my teacher.

Sometimes other teachers come to teach my class.

(p2)
Sometimes my teacher talks to **me**.

Sometimes the teacher talks to **me** and everyone else.

Sometimes the teacher talks to **me** and four, five or six other children at the same time. This is called a '**group of children**'.

(p3)
Usually when the teacher is talking to my '**group**' she will show me a card like this

(p4)
It is important to look at the teacher and listen to what she says when she is talking to my '**group**'.
This is because she is usually telling us what to do, or teaching us new things.

(p5)
I will try to remember to look at the teacher and listen when she is listen when she is talking to the group.
The teacher is pleased when I look at her and listen.

(p6)
Sometimes the teacher might ask me questions about what she has said. I can try to answer the questions. The teacher is very pleased when children listen and answer questions.

APPENDIX A (continued)

Reading to a teacher: a story for Michael

(p1)
My name is Michael.

I am in class _____ at ____________________________________ School.

Sometimes I read in school to an adult.

Sometimes I read to ____________________

Sometimes I read to ____________________

Sometimes I read to ____________________

(p2)
A number 5 voice is a good voice for reading to an adult.
I will try to remember to use a quiet, number 5 voice when I read to an adult.

(p3)
Mrs________________, Mrs________________ and Mrs________________are happy when I use a number 5 voice for reading.

(This story was accompanied by a bookmark with a linear scale showing 0–10. 0 meaning silence.)

APPENDIX A (continued)

Playing games: a story for George

(p1)
My name is George and I go to ______________________________ School.

Sometimes I play games at school.

Sometimes I play games at home.

Many people like to play games.

(p2)
Some people who like to play games are:

____

____

____

____

(left blank for George to complete)

and other children in my class.

Sometimes they win.

Sometimes they lose.

(p3)
Most people like to win.

Many people feel a bit sad when they lose.

(p4)
When I lose I can try to say 'well done' to the person who won.

(p5)
I might win another time.

CHAPTER 11

Interviews

Interviews have the potential to yield valuable insights into people's life experiences, attitudes, opinions and aspirations. They are valuable for collecting data which would be inaccessible using other research techniques such as questionnaires and observations. Interviews allow the researcher to explore complex issues in detail, to probe beneath the surface of events, to find out 'how people think' and 'how they construct meaning' (Brown and Dowling 1998:60). Use of interviews in research usually occurs when the researcher decides that the research question requires in-depth information and that data collected from a small number of informants will satisfy the demands of the research project in terms of reliability and validity.

Interviews can take different forms: structured, semi-structured, unstructured and the group interview. A research project might use a mixture of interview forms. In the structured interview the researcher controls the interview through the use of predetermined questions. Data collection is organised through a standardised interview schedule. The interviewer directs the respondent to answer and restricts his or her own involvement to asking questions with little or no elaboration (Fontana and Fray 1994). Structured interviews are usually associated with survey research. The semi-structured interview again utilises a question schedule, but allows a greater role for the interviewer in terms of asking for clarification and elaboration. The unstructured interview is more open-ended and aims to allow the respondent to talk using her or his own frame of reference rather than one imposed by the interviewer. In this sense, the interview becomes one of more 'equal' partnership between the interviewer and the interviewee (Holstein and Gubrium 1995). Group interviews, normally involving about four to six individuals are used when the researcher wishes to explore group norms. Lewis has argued that group interviews have several advantages over individual interviews:

> they help to reveal consensus views, may generate richer responses by allowing participants to challenge one another's views, may be used to verify research ideas of data gained through other methods and may enhance the reliability of … responses. (Lewis 1992:413)

The researcher's role in the group interview is to act as a 'moderator' who 'promotes interaction and assures that the discussion remains on the topic of interest' (Stewart and Shamdasani 1990:10).

Having decided on the interview form the researcher must resolve a number of issues. These include gathering background research data, locating suitable respondents, arranging interviews and agreeing informed consent. The latter relates to clarifying any areas of concern which the respondents might have about the research, issues of confidentiality and the degree of control that the respondent will have over the interview and its use in the research. The researcher will also have to take into account a number of practical considerations: cost, time, location of the interview, interview field notes or taping and transcription. The use of a tape recorder has both advantages and disadvantages. It can inhibit interaction but also allows the researcher to focus on the nature of the interaction rather than their notes. A recording also captures the 'words' of the informant.

On the technical side there are a number of simple procedures which can ensure a good quality audio recording:

- choose a well furnished room, this will absorb echoes;
- avoid unwanted noises; position the microphone about 23 to 30 centimetres away from the interviewee, avoiding a hard surface as this will produce a hollow distorted sound;
- familiarise yourself with the equipment and always check it before the interview;
- have a reliable power source, take spare batteries;
- place the recorder where you can see it so that you can look over occasionally to see that the cassette is turning;
- choose tapes which are long enough to contain the planned interview.

Unstructured interviews in research rarely happen spontaneously. At the beginning of the unstructured interview it is important that the researcher pays attention to the establishment of a mutual trust 'that allows for the free flow of information' (Spradley 1979:78). According to Spradley the development of mutual trust involves a four stage process. The first stage is one of initial apprehension. This apprehension can be overcome by engaging in a conversation where the questions asked are generally of a descriptive nature which allows the respondent to feel at ease with the interviewer. The second stage is exploration, where both parties to the interview begin to gain insights into the way in which the interview will develop. Stage three is cooperation, where each party knows what to expect of one another. Finally, there is the fourth stage, participation, where the respondent takes a more assertive role in the interview as he or she recognises and accepts 'the role of teaching' the researcher (Spradley 1979:83).

During an interview the researcher can use a range of questioning forms. Dillon (1990) provides a very useful exploration of the variety of purposes and forms in which questions can be asked. The text also offers advice on improving questioning skills.

Effective interviewing is a skill that can be learned, but the good interviewer must have 'some essential qualities':

> an interest and respect for the people as individuals, and flexibility in response to them; an ability to show understanding and sympathy for their point of view; and, above all, a willingness to sit quietly and listen. (Thompson 1988:196)

Once the interview is completed the researcher will either write up field notes or engage in the production of an accurate transcription (six to eight hours of transcription for one hour of tape) before beginning text analysis.

In analysing interview data Hitchcock and Hughes (1995) identified nine related areas which the researcher should consider. First, familiarity with the text is a prerequisite for analysis. Second, reading and re-reading texts is time demanding and therefore may act as a constraint in the research process. Third, in making sense of the data the researcher will engage with the method of grounded theory (Glaser and Strauss 1967) whereby they move consciously backwards and forwards between the data and emerging explanations, analyses and theory. Fourth, the researcher will then be able to isolate the broad themes and issues which give meaning to the interview. Fifth, these 'related units of meaning' can then be set against the research focus and sixth, the researcher can explore in greater depth the major themes which emerge from the data and how they relate to the research focus in particular. Seventh, the researcher can then isolate taken-for-granted assumptions presented in the interview and unravel and explain them. Eighth, an interview, particularly an unstructured one, can involve the respondent in the process of self-revelation and the researcher will need to reflect on the issues exposed. Lastly, the researcher will need to validate the data produced by the interview.

In avoiding bias and working towards validity and reliability in the use of evidence gained from interviews Griffiths (1998) argues that in addition to factors identified in standard research texts such as the significance of non-verbal communication, sample frames, and the effect of any previous or continuing relationship between interviewer and interviewed, the researcher's 'openness to other perspectives' and 'reflexivity about the positionality of the researcher' should be taken into account. Gender, ethnicity, social class, sexuality and disability significantly shape social relations, are constitutive of all the other bias factors, and therefore will affect communication in an interview (Griffiths 1998:131).

Phyllis Jones and Pat Gilbert's use of interviews

Jones and Gilbert (Chapter 12) used interviews with parents of pupils identified as having autistic spectrum disorders. They set out on their research with a clear intention of gaining information which would support the process of school development. In so doing they are clearly attempting to address the perceived need for a closer link between research and policy development as identified by several critics of the educational research process (see Chapter 1 by Grosvenor and Rose).

Mason (1996) suggests that interviewing is possibly the most widely used method in qualitative research, but that it is a difficult approach and one which requires careful management. Jones and Gilbert acknowledge that within their own work the use of group interviews was not always easy, but would suggest that it has some advantages when working with parents. In a group situation some parents will feel less intimidated than they might in an individual situation where the focus is entirely upon themselves. However, the researchers do need to have an awareness of group dynamics and the possibility that participants may be led by a strong individual within the group.

In a situation such as that described by Jones and Gilbert, in which the researchers are conducting evaluative work which is attempting to judge the effectiveness of a management procedure, the group interview, with its emphasis upon a 'conversation' between interested parties is a justifiable tool. Powney and Watts (1987) have made a distinction between 'respondent interviews' and 'informant interviews' determined by where the locus of control is situated. Jones and Gilbert conducted their study with a purpose of enabling the interviewees to express opinions which could encourage changes to existing practices and, as such, the emphasis upon an 'informant interview' giving some control of the discussion was important. In their conclusion the researchers state that the research has had a 'significant impact on practice', that the information gained through their study has 'directly influenced the school development planning process' and that the information gained has been of immediate use to practitioners. An important feature of this research is the ability to demonstrate how the researched have been empowered in changing the practices which were scrutinised by the researchers.

Examples of other projects in special education which made use of interviews

'How children with emotional and behavioural difficulties view professionals'.

Armstrong, D. and Galloway, D. (1996), in Davie, R. and Galloway, D. *Listening to Children in Education.* London: David Fulton Publishers.

'Teachers' motives for referring students to special education'.

Pijl, Y. J., Pijl, S. J. and Van den Bos, K. P. (1999), in Ballard, K. (ed.) *Inclusive Education: International Voices on Disability and Justice.* London: Falmer Press.

'The views of Bangladeshi parents on the special school attended by their young children with severe learning difficulties'.

Warner, R. (1999), *British Journal of Special Education* **26**(4), 218–23.

References and guide to further reading

Brown, A. and Dowling, P. (1998) *Doing Research/Reading Research*. London: Falmer Press.

Denscombe, M. (1983) 'Interviews, accounts and ethnographic research on teachers', in Hammersley, M. (ed.) *The Ethnography of Schooling: Methodological Issues*. Driffield: Nafferton Books.

Dillon, J. T. (1990) *The Practice of Interviewing*. London: Routledge.

Dunne, S. (1995) *Interviewing Techniques for Writers and Researchers*. London: A and C Black.

Fontana, A. and Frey, J. H. (1994) 'Interviewing: the art of science', in Dickens, D. R. and Lincoln, Y. S. (eds) *Handbook of Qualitative Research*. London: Sage.

Glaser, B. and Strauss, A. L. (1967) *The Discovery of Grounded Theory*. Chicago: Aldine.

Griffiths, M. (1998) *Educational Research for Social Justice*. Buckingham: Open University Press.

Hitchcock, G. and Hughes, D. (1995) *Research and the Teacher: A Qualitative Introduction to School-Based Research*, 2nd edn. London: Routledge.

Holstein, J. A. and Gubrium, J. F. (1995) *The Active Interview*. London: Sage.

Hull, C. (1985) 'Between the lines: the analysis of interview data as an exact art', *British Educational Research Journal* **11**(1), 27–32.

Kvale, S. (1996) *Interviews: An Introduction to Qualitative Research Interviewing*. London: Sage.

Lewis, A. (1992) 'Group child interviews as a research tool', *British Educational Research Journal* **18**, 413–32.

Mason, J. (1996) *Qualitative Researching*. London: Sage.

Powney, J. and Watts, M. (1987) *Interviewing in Educational Research*. London: Routledge and Kegan Paul.

Ross, E. M. (1996) 'Learning to listen to children', in Davie, R., Upton, G. and Varma, V. *The Voice of the Child*. London: Falmer Press.

Russell, P. (1996) 'Listening to children with disabilities and special educational needs', in Davie, R., Upton, G. and Varma, V. *The Voice of the Child*. London: Falmer Press.

Spradley, J. (1979) *The Ethnographic Interview*. New York: Holt, Rhinehart and Jackson.

Stewart, D. and Shamdasani, P. (1990) *Focus Groups: Theory and Practice*. London: Sage.

Thompson, P. (1988) *The Voice of the Past*, 2nd edn. Oxford: Oxford University Press.

CHAPTER 12

'It's not about just getting by, it's about moving on'

A study exploring a qualitative approach to involving parents of primary-aged children with autistic spectrum disorders in the cycle of school development planning

Phyllis Jones and Pat Gilbert

This chapter concerns a research partnership project between a primary school for pupils with learning disabilities and the University of Northumbria. The fundamental aims of the study were:

> To explore parental perceptions of two dedicated bases for children with an autistic spectrum disorder (ASD) recently set up in the school, and to draw from these, potential targets for development that would feed into the school development planning process.

In doing this the study begins to explore some of the pertinent issues surrounding the involvement of parents in the process of school development planning and offers some initial insights into possible ways that this may be developed. The engagement of parents in the school development planning process is an area that demands much more development and research, and the present study offers an example of how one school attempted to move beyond a quantitative audit of views to a more qualitative engagement of parental perceptions and aspirations. The research is based on two stages of interviews with small groups of parents of pupils with autistic spectrum disorder, one stage discussing views and aspirations generally and another stage offering potential school improvement targets for review, discussion and agreement.

The complex nature of autistic spectrum disorder

The quest for greater understanding of children with autism has always attracted a great deal of academic and pedagogical attention, which, in recent years, has progressed with increasing momentum. The term autistic spectrum disorder (ASD) shows how the understanding of autism has developed to encapsulate a more complex continuum. Autism has, for many years, been characterised by a triad of impairments. The characteristics are difficulties with relationships, marked by problems in appreciating the feelings of others; difficulties with communication, both expressive and receptive; and difficulties with play and imagination, often including obsession with a particular object (Nickles 1995). It is clear that there are fundamental difficulties with the quality of the development of communication, particularly how communication is being used. Links have also been made between autism and more generic psychological theories including theory in mind (Connor 1999), central cohesion theory (Pierce, Glad and Schreibman 1997) and cognitive style (Happe 1995). A definition of ASD is presented in the work of Jordan (1999:6):

> Autism is a severe disorder of communication, socialisation and flexibility in thinking and behaviour which involves a different way of processing information and seeing the world.

This encapsulates the diversity and complexity of the disorder. The very nature of ASD calls for an understanding of the ways in which a child may be using communication, and the people who are in a position to offer comprehensive insight about this area of development are people who are possibly the most frequent and intensive communicating partners, the parents.

School development planning and the role of parents

A child who is displaying a multiplicity of difficulties, not all of them on the ASD continuum, may be a very difficult child for whom to provide in the school setting. Of the children diagnosed with ASD, approximately four per cent attend a school or unit specifically for children with autism: 'Most are taught in schools for children with moderate and severe learning difficulties (National Autistic Society 1995:14). It follows then that these schools should be addressing the needs of this complex group of pupils in their cycle of school development planning. If this were the case it would seem appropriate to involve the parents of these children in this process. The role of parents in the education of their children with special educational needs is well documented (Wolfendale 1997, Beveridge 1997). It has recently received a great deal of government interest in the White Paper *Excellence in Schools* (DfEE 1997b), the Green Paper *Excellence for All* (DfEE 1997a) and the *Action Plan for Special Educational Needs* (DfEE 1998). However, parental involvement in decision-making regarding the educational provision for their child has not been without difficulties. There is a small but growing body of research that has evaluated the involvement of parents in the decision-making process at the Annual Review of the Statement of Special Educational Need. This highlights some of the difficulties, including the level of stress parents experienced at the formality of the process of the actual meetings (Hughes and Carpenter 1991). In addition, the way parents perceived their role was also significant, with many questioning the value attributed to parental perspectives in the review (Armstrong 1995).

If parents have found this highly personalised and individual meeting problematic, there is a challenge to ensure any involvement in whole-school development planning is enhanced to enable parents actively to participate and feel their views are being valued. In school development planning it is not unusual for schools to send out questionnaires to parents to support whole-school audits (Dunkenford 1997). These tend to be quantitative in nature, usually set out as a set of questions with a multiple-choice answer for parents to circle. This may create a rudimentary overview of trends in parental perceptions, but does not present opportunities for parents to offer more detailed insights. Of course, parent governors may be involved in school development planning, providing a group of parents who may be able to offer significant insight into the parental perspective of school development planning. However, there is a paucity of research in the field of parental involvement in school development planning both from a quantitative and qualitative perspective. In the current climate of continual school improvement this is an interesting anomaly. This study explores the process and product of involving parents in a more qualitative way.

Context of present study

The school in the study opened in September 1997 as a result of a reorganisation of schools for pupils with learning difficulties. A number of pupils had autistic spectrum disorder. In summer 1998, with financial support from the LEA, an extra teacher and Specialist Support Assistant (SSA) were appointed. In September 1998 two dedicated autism bases were opened: a KS1 and a KS2 base, each staffed by one teacher and two SSAs. In the present cycle of school development planning, a questionnaire was sent to parents and the response to this was fed into the current school development booklet. It is intended that the present research will feed into the school development planning cycle, beginning in April 2000.

Methodology

There have been two distinct stages to the research. In the first stage a letter was sent to all parents in the school informing them about the research and inviting them to attend one of three group interview sessions. Twelve parents chose to attend one of the three group sessions and, apart from one parent governor, they were parents of children identified as having ASD. The University person conducted these interviews, without school staff being involved. This was to encourage parents to feel comfortable with the opportunity to speak freely; ethics and confidentiality were assured. Prior to analysis by University and school the taped interviews were transcribed with all names taken out. The interviews consisted of questions, which were designed to enable a frank evaluation of the present provision for children with ASD in the school from the perspective of the parents, and to inform future developments in the school. Ethical issues were discussed at the beginning of each interview so that parents were clearly informed about the purpose and potential outcome of the research and the particular role they had to play in it. The analysis was a joint University and school collaboration; the head teacher was the main collaborator but she took the potential targets back to the senior management group for discussion. Potential school improvement targets were developed. The second stage of interviewing offered these targets for discussion and review. Again a letter was sent to all parents. The parents who had previously been involved were also sent a discussion paper including an appraisal of the analysis and the potential targets. Seven parents chose to be involved: three from the original group; two parents of children who had just entered the school, and two other parents who had not been involved at the first stage. It proved difficult to arrange convenient interview times and there were four interviews held to accommodate everyone. Two of these were with individual parents. It was decided that school would be involved at this stage and the head teacher conducted the interviews along with University staff. These interviews were transcribed (University staff) and analysed collaboratively. Again the head teacher discussed the pertinent issues arising from the analysis at the senior management meeting.

The initial targets

The interviews proved to be a rich source of data collection, with parents speaking frankly about their feelings and perceptions of the base provision, highlighting four broad areas.

Attitude and feelings towards the base provision

Interviews with all three groups highlighted the positive views of the base provision held by the parents: '*I would say I think it is excellent*' (Parent, Interview 3). There was a feeling of change for the better from the previous year. The flexibility of provision with integration into the main body of the school appeared to be another element of the organisation liked by the parents. While parents wished the provision to continue and they particularly liked the development of different approaches, they expressed concern about the range of ability in each group. A tentative first target that reflected the general trends in all three interviews was:

> To continue to develop base provision in the light of developing knowledge and understanding of approaches and strategies in relation to teaching and learning for pupils with autism; and also in respect of the wide range of abilities of the pupils with ASD. (Target One)

Knowledge of parents

The thirst for more knowledge about the nature of autism and the specific approaches used was a recurring theme that came out of all three interview groups.

The nature and delivery of training for parents is both complex and sensitive, and it is important to ensure that the 'expert' knowledge that parents have is nurtured and supported. This may not happen in a training scenario where only the professional trainer is seen as an expert. Parents in this study were beginning to offer some solutions to this naturally problematic and sensitive area. It was apparent they would like any training to be focused on the needs of their children and for it to be organised in a way that is convenient for them and their families. A second possible target for future school development planning that was developed through these discussions with parents was:

> To develop training sessions for parents that are accessible and focused on the needs of their children. (Target Two)

Communication and liaison with school

This topic created a great deal of discussion in the course of the group interviews. The use of target setting and individual education plans to ensure individual needs are met was well received by the parents, particularly when parents were involved in the process.

The school uses the home–school diary method of daily communication. For many parents this was their most regular and frequent contact with the school. One parent's comment typified the general positive view towards these diaries: '*I love it, as soon as he comes in … we race to get the book to see what he has been doing*' (Parent, Interview 2). It became apparent, however, that there were some differences between classes; some classes were very consistent in the use of the home–school diary while in others it was less so. It was decided that this might be an area where the school could continue to develop more ways to involve parents and to ensure consistency of practice. From this there were two further targets for consideration for school development planning:

> To continue to develop ways to involve parents in school, from informal contact to involvement in target setting, progress and review. (Target Three)

> To continue to develop effective and consistent ways of informing parents about all aspects of school life. (Target Four)

Support for parents

A recurring theme in all three groups' interviews was the support structures in place for parents. The discussion ranged beyond the base provision to LEA and Health Authority provision and illustrated the lifelong pressure and stress that children with severe disability can bring to bear on a family. After-school provision received a great deal of attention from the parents. Parents wanted a place where children and parents could come together to relax and enjoy being with each other.

The school already has some parental support systems in operation but this area would offer the school opportunities for significant development. From this a possible fifth target for consideration was therefore:

> To consider extending the support networks available for parents and families. (Target Five)

Parents' reaction to the targets

During the second stage of interviews parents discussed and affirmed all five targets. Through the discussion it became clear that parents were developing their own thoughts about the targets; for example, they were suggesting potential ways the targets may be translated into practice. Parents identified three targets as a priority: these were targets One, Two and Three, concerned with the continued development of base provision, parental training and support for parents. Parents highlighted the continuing development of provision: *'you can't just stand still with it'* (Parent, Interview 7) and recognised the usefulness of liaising with other professionals and organisations, especially the National Autistic Society. It became apparent that parents felt that the base provision should be able to meet the particular needs of individual children. It should be flexible enough to allow for children to be taught within a class group of children of similar ability and need, who are broadly within the same Key Stage.

Parents were clear in their view that it was important for them to be trained in the basics of TEACCH[1] and SPELL[2], the two main approaches used in the bases. The importance of consistency in approaching children with autism is stressed in the work of Munro (2000). The value of being able to help their child by following through with similar strategies at home was repeatedly highlighted by parents, although they made an important point about the need to appreciate the differences between home and school settings when developing this training.

The value of collaboration between staff and themselves in developing and providing training was stressed by some parents who observed that: *'parents are the experts … everybody pulling together can move the school really forward'* (Parent, Interview 4). This view of parents as 'experts' is evident in the work of Wolfendale (1997) and stresses the need to plan and deliver training in a sensitive way. The

---

[1] TEACCH is a structured programme designed specifically as a community based intervention for children and adults with autism originating from North Carolina in the mid 1960s. The underlying principles of TEACCH include: improved adaptation through modifying the environment and individual skill improvement; parent collaboration; assessment for individualised treatment and structured teaching. All intervention is guided by cognitive and behaviour therapy.

[2] SPELL is an approach which developed from work carried out in schools and adult centres run by the National Autistic Society. This approach aims to reduce effects of impaired imagination, communication and social skills. The main principles of this approach are: structure of everything in the environment; positive attitudes; empathy; low arousal and the importance of linking with parents, other schools and organisations.

parents in this study further supported this when they highlighted the differences between parents: *'Some parents have totally different ideas and they're very delicate people to deal with'* (Parent, Interview 7).

It is clear that any developments in training would need to be cognisant of the experience, understanding and perspective of individual parents in order to develop sensitive and appropriate training and to understand where the issues and tensions may be. The timing of training sessions was debated and the importance of childcare being available in school to facilitate the attendance of both parents was emphasised.

In discussions about home–school contact parents repeatedly emphasised the importance to them of the daily home–school book. The range of information parents identified as important to be included in the home–school diary was: clear and simple details about the main activities of the day and their child's responses, especially any problems or distress; key words or symbols about the day's activities, to prompt communication at home between parent and child; and information to support target setting and progress review. The value attributed to this type of communication between home and school was illustrated by one parent: *'unless it's in the home–school diary, I mean you haven't got a clue of what they've been doing'* (Parent, Interview 5).

Generally, parents felt that their involvement in target setting, including Annual Review, was important. They felt that the Annual Review meetings were informal enough for parents to feel comfortable about giving their views. This is in contrast to the earlier research of Hughes and Carpenter (1991), which found that the group of parents involved in their research were negatively affected by the formality of the Annual Review meeting. It did become clear in the present research that there were some issues related to the Annual Review: one parent's comments illustrated a tension for parents in relation to target setting: *'You have an idea of what you'd like for your child's education but it's difficult to know exactly what you're aiming for'* (Parent, Interview 7).

It is clear then, that parents may well need support in being involved in the target setting process, and regular target setting meetings between teachers and parents were identified as being important. Presently these occur once a term and this appears to be about right: *'That's just right I would say ... one meeting per term'* (Parent, Interview 6).

All of the parents interviewed emphasised the need for informal support, whether from within the family or from outside. The role of the class teacher was highlighted as particularly significant and the personal touch was identified as a crucial factor in developing the relationship between a new parent and teacher: *'she telephoned every day ... and it was the best thing that anybody could have done'* (Parent, Interview 5). Pollard (1997) highlights that parents perceived the most important characteristic of a 'good school' as being the quality of the relationships between parents and teachers. The present research endorses this, especially in the early days of schooling. Parents suggested that it would be useful to have regular parents' group meetings to offer support to each other, but they also stressed that parents must want a support group in the first place, highlighting this as a critical factor in the success of such a group. They made several suggestions on how to develop this in the school. These include:

involving parents in the decision to develop a support group; the need for meetings to have a focus of interest to parents, in order to attract parental attendance; the need for a balance of staff and parent input to the meetings; the need for meetings to be focused on groups of parents of children with similar needs, to encourage greater empathy; and the need for appropriate childcare arrangements. These suggestions illustrate a clear example of how parents were actively engaging in the process of translating the targets into practice that had meaning for them.

Impact on school practice

This research has impacted greatly on school practice. It has influenced school development planning in different ways: firstly by providing specific focused targets (parental training) and secondly by informing and shaping other more general targets (home–school liaison and home learning). The school's autism department is in the process of developing policy documentation, and information from this research is informing and influencing this development. Two of the targets (One and Three) are to be more generally adopted within the aims and philosophy of the department. These relate to continuing development of the base provision and continuing development of parental involvement, from informal contact to target setting, progress and review. The present research is also impacting on other developments in the school. For example, the school has recently secured a study support grant for parents and staff to work collaboratively, in order to develop materials and activities to support home learning. There are consultations occurring with parents to seek their views on setting up a support group in school, including the recruitment of a parent volunteer to work alongside a member of staff as joint coordinator. The research has definitely been valuable by providing high quality information to inform school development planning. The school has expressed the view that it would be a worthwhile process to extend to parents of the general school population.

Reflections on methodology

The process of the research was very positive and constructive. The research team began with the belief that it is important that parents have an opportunity to become more actively involved in the school development planning process, and that this involvement may be enhanced through the adoption of a more qualitative process. At the end of the second stage of interviewing one parent encapsulated this when she said: '*It's not about just getting by, it's about moving on*' (Parent, Interview 6).

The qualitative paradigm for research offered the present study a process that gave parents an opportunity to express their views, and the school a strategy for listening and acting upon these views. Atkinson, Delamont and Hammersley (1993) state that this approach offers the opportunity to explore the present actors' perspectives and strategies in their own terms. This was done through the use of group interviewing where parents were offered an opportunity to express their feelings and aspirations, and school was supported in their process of analysing and responding to the views and aspirations that emerged from the interviews. The present study was set up to improve the strategies employed by school to involve parents in the school development planning process. The interview is a well-established process for gathering information in the qualitative paradigm of research. Patton (1990) tells us: 'The purpose of interviewing is to find out what is in someone else's mind … to access the perspective of the person being interviewed' (Patton 1990:278).

It was intended to use group interviews throughout to encourage parents to listen to the perspectives of each other and hopefully enhance their own understanding of the relevant issues. Lewis (1992) supports this reason for adopting group interviews through her work where she found that through the group dynamics all respondents improved their understanding of the main area of debate: in the case of the Lewis research the focus was severe learning difficulty. However, Cohen and Manion (1999) offer a cautionary note for the adoption of group interviewing: they believe that the 'group' may be a difficult arena for pursuing discussion of personal issues. At the second stage of research the present study did employ the individual interview strategy due to the difficulties parents encountered getting to the group interviews. It was felt that in this study the group interviews were more dynamic and generated a lot more discussion that was initiated and led by the parents.

This chosen process of involving parents was very time consuming. It took seven separate interview times to accommodate the small number of parents who wanted to be involved. As mentioned, in the second stage two interviews had to be conducted on an individual basis. The quality of discussion and involvement by parents in the interviews reflects the real value of this more qualitative approach. The interview sessions themselves proved to be a valuable learning ground. Parents listened and responded to each other in a lively, sympathetic and reciprocal way. The process of the interviews provided a vehicle for parents to express their views, concerns and aspirations and have some immediate feedback on these from a group of supportive and knowledgeable others. This is a good example of the two different but equally valuable roles of research: one of development, and one of knowledge building. Not only were parents contributing actively to the discourse of school evaluation and development, they were also learning from each other in the process. This dynamic interaction between parents in the two interviews that were held on an individual basis was felt to be clearly missing.

The decision to hold the first stage interviews with an impartial person was seen as positive by some of the parents: '*Sometimes it's best you talk to somebody independent. And you can talk and say well we would like this and we would like that*' (Parent, Interview 4). This would have been particularly important for some parents who may find it difficult to discuss issues that they perceive to be in the domain of the school and may have been influenced by the school representative being present. It was important to the researchers to encourage parents to talk freely without worrying they were discussing issues that they may have felt were the responsibility of the school. After the first transcriptions had been analysed, it was felt that it was important that the head teacher be involved in the second stage interviewing to emphasise the school's commitment and involvement in the research. It was the school that was taking the targets forward with the parents. It was interesting to note that the interviews at this stage were *very* affirmative of the school. Gray and Denicolo (1998) illustrate, with a cautionary tone, the influences and power base of the role of the researcher and chosen research method in the field of special needs education. They stress the need for active engagement of the target audience as one way of developing a more empathetic research paradigm. During the second stage of interviewing there was little 'new' information generated. There are a number of possible reasons for this: parents were happy with the targets and their level of involvement; the influence of the head teacher or the change in sample; or parents may have felt awkward responding to what other parents had said. Transcribing was very time consuming until the University supported the project and enabled professional transcription. The analysis of the data took time to ensure collaboration and moderation between school and the University. The process of developing accurate targets, which truly reflected parental discussions, proved to be a challenge. In a general sense targets came through clearly and strongly although there was diversity and differing nuances of feeling around individual parental thoughts. While the present research was designed actively to engage parents in the discourse of school development planning it did not have parents as co-researchers actively involved in the research team. The recent work of Wolfendale (1999) develops this and highlights the ethical issues of researching 'parents' views' as 'objects of research' and suggests a more collaborative framework where parents are seen as research partners. They become part of the research team, and, therefore, have more power to influence the research. Having a parent on the research team from the outset may help to develop a more collaborative model for research, which would enable parents to be more active throughout the process of research.

Conclusion

This piece of research has had significant impact on practice. Through it parents have discussed their aspirations and feelings and have directly influenced the school development planning process. Some of the targets appear to affirm the current practice of the school, and some call for more development, and some call for change on the part of the school. It is important for a school to receive affirmation of practice, but it is also important for a school to move forward in the development of provision and practice.

The research has also illustrated the complex nature of researching and analysing the views of parents and the need to develop research practice to recognise the valuable role of parents in the research team. This more qualitative involvement of parents through small group interviews complements the more usual quantitative style questionnaire format in the school development planning process. This is indeed an area that needs further research. This small piece of research has enabled some insight to be gained into this process to enable further development to take place. Significant insight was gained through this study and lessons have been learnt. These include:

- It is good to collaborate. The school and University working in partnership has been constructive and positive.
- There is a need to increase and develop the role of parents as co-researchers and to enable parents to be active participants involved in the whole cycle of research.
- It is valuable to offer an impartial listening ear in the first instance, but to involve school at an appropriate point.
- It is important to manage the number of interviews from a practical perspective.
- There is value in group interviews for research of this nature.

A final but significant recurring lesson is the continual need to reflect on the research process and the impact this has on practice.

References

Altrichter, H. (1993) 'The concept of quality in action research: giving practitioners a voice in educational research', in Schratz, M. (ed.) *Qualitative Voices in Educational Research*. London: Falmer Press.

Armstrong, D. (1995) *Power and Partnership in Education*. London: Routledge.

Atkinson, P., Delamont, S. and Hammersley, M. (1993) 'Qualitative research traditions', in Hammersley, M. (ed.) *Educational Research: Current Issues*. London: Open University Press.

Beveridge, S. (1997) 'Implementing partnerships with parents in school', in Wolfendale, S. (ed.) *Working with parents of SEN children after the Code of Practice*. London: David Fulton Publishers.

Bowers, T. and Wilkinson, D. (1998) 'The SEN Code of Practice: is it user-friendly?', *British Journal of Special Education* **25**(3), 119–25.

Carpenter, B. (ed.) (1997) *Families in Context. Emerging Trends in Family Support and Early Intervention*. London: David Fulton Publishers.

Cohen, L. and Manion, L. (1999) *Research Methods in Education*. London: Routledge.

Connor, M. (1999) 'Children on the autistic spectrum: guidelines for mainstream practice', *Support for learning* **14**(2), 80–6.

Department for Education and Employment (DfEE) (1994) *Code of Practice on the Identification and Assessment of Special Educational Needs*. London: DfEE.

Department for Education and Employment (DfEE) (1997a) *Excellence for All Children*. London: DfEE.

Department for Education and Employment (DfEE) (1997b) *Excellence in Schools*. London: DfEE.

Department for Education and Employment (DfEE) (1998) *Action Plan for Special Educational Needs*. London: DfEE.

Dunkeford, B. (1997) *The Whole School Audit. Development Planning in the Primary School*. London: David Fulton Publishers.

Evans, L. (1998) 'An untapped resource', *Special Children* **113**, September.

Farrell, P (1997) *Teaching pupils with learning difficulties: strategies and solutions*. London: Cassell.

Gray, D. E. and Denicolo, P. (1998) 'Research in special needs education: objectivity or ideology?', *British Journal of Special Education* **25**(3), 140–5.

Happe, F. G. E. (1995) 'The role of age and verbal ability in the theory of mind task performance of subjects with autism', *Child Development* **99**, 843–55.

Hughes, N. and Carpenter, B. (1991) 'Annual Reviews: an active partnership', in Ashdown, R., Carpenter, B. and Bovair, K. (eds) *The Curriculum Challenge*. London: Falmer Press.

Inclusion for children with autism: The TEACCH position. 8 October 1998. http://www.unc.edu/depts/teacch/inclus.htm

Jordan, R. (1999) *Autistic Spectrum Disorders*. London: David Fulton Publishers.

Lewis, A. (1992) 'Group interviews as a research tool', *British Educational Research Journal* **18**(4), 413–21.

Mesibov, G. (ed.) *Diagnosis and Assessment in Autism*. New York: Plenum Press.

Munro, N. (2000) 'Education, education, education', in Nye, A. (ed.) *The Autism Handbook*. London: National Autistic Society.

National Autistic Society (1995) *Could this be Autism?* London: National Autistic Society.

Nickles, C. (1995) *Autism Focus on*. London: National Autistic Society.

Park, K. (1997) 'How do objects become objects of reference?', *British Journal of Special Education* **24**(3), 108–14.

Patton, M. Q. (1990) *Qualitative Evaluation and Research Methods*. London: Sage.

Pierce, P., Glad, K. and Schreibman, L. (1997) 'Social perception in children with autism', *Journal of Autism and Developmental Disorders* **27**, 265–82.

Pollard, A. (1997) *Reflective Teaching in the Primary School*, 3rd edn. London: Cassell.

Prevezer, W. (1990) 'Strategies for tuning into autism', *Therapy Weekly*, 19 October.

Seach, D. (1998) *Autistic Spectrum Disorder: Positive Approaches for Teaching Children with Autistic Spectrum Disorder*. Stafford: NASEN.

Ward, D. (1998a) 'Quest for a remedy', in Home News, *Guardian*, 14 February.

Ward, D. (1998b) 'Council under fire on autism', in Home News, *Guardian*, 14 February.

Wolfendale, S. (1997) *Working with parents of SEN children after the Code of Practice*. London: David Fulton Publishers.

Wolfendale, S. (1999) 'Parents as partners, in research and evaluation methodological issues and solutions', *British Journal of Special Education* **26**(3), 164–70.

Wright, J. (1999) 'Placating "peasants" ', *Special Children* **123**, October.

CHAPTER 13

Questionnaires

Effective use of questionnaires in research is predicated upon careful deliberation about conceptual aims, the information that is required to fulfil these aims, the resources available, the population sample, type of questionnaire, questionnaire construction, the administration of the questionnaire and analysis of data collected. The nature of the research question, the identified data required to answer the question and the resources available will generally determine the type of questionnaire that the researcher will employ.

The researcher can use a postal or self-completion questionnaire, a telephone survey or a face-to-face interview schedule. The postal questionnaire is a relatively cheap method of data collection, allows for a wide geographical spread and anonymity, but it also has several disadvantages. The researcher operates at a distance from the respondents, the opportunity to correct any misunderstandings are reduced, the questionnaire could be completed by someone other than the targeted recipient and unless there is an incentive to complete and return the questionnaire a low response rate can occur. The latter problem can be offset by the researcher actively being involved in the distribution and collection of the questionnaire. However, the researcher would have to consider the time impact of this strategy. Telephone surveys again offer the researcher a wide geographical spread of respondents and are time efficient. That said, there may be an in-built bias in the respondent sample in terms of the variables of gender, class and ethnicity and respondents may be unwilling to complete the telephone survey. In the face-to-face interview the researcher has a high degree of control and generally achieves a higher response rate but it is time expensive.

Having chosen the type of questionnaire the researcher then has to consider the types of questions to be used and their wording. Questionnaires tend to be a mixture of factual and opinion questions, and open and closed questions. In constructing questions the researcher needs to be conscious of bias, of not using language which will lead the respondent towards an answer or language which is technical and whose meaning all respondents will not understand. If the data collected is to be comparable the researcher needs to be confident that each respondent will interpret each question in a similar way. Brown and Dowling (1998) illustrate the difficulties associated with achieving this objective by exploring the problems of using a questionnaire distributed to school students to investigate the incidence of bullying. The question 'how many times have you been bullied this month?' can elicit a range of responses determined by what the respondents consider bullying to be – a single incidence of name calling or physical intimidation over an extended time frame. If the researcher includes a definition of bullying in the questionnaire they will present an objectively defined meaning of what it is to be bullied, but will no longer be gathering data on the extent to which school students subjectively feel that they are being bullied. Alternatively, the researcher can accept the definition that each respondent offers of bullying and thereby focus the research on what bullying means to each individual. As Brown and Dowling conclude: 'the decision to either include a definition of a key term or not ... fundamentally affects the nature of the study.' The decision is not a technical issue, but relates to the theoretical framework from which the research is derived (Brown and Dowling 1998:67).

May (1997) offers detailed guidance on the procedures in questionnaire construction. The following list of 'avoids' is adapted from his guide:

- Avoid questions that are too general.
- Avoid complicated language.
- Avoid using prejudicial language.
- Avoid ambiguity or imprecision.
- Avoid the use of vague terms.
- Avoid leading questions.
- Avoid hypothetical questions.
- Avoid the use of too many questions couched in negative terms.
- Avoid the use of insensitive personal questions.
- Avoid the use of too many open-ended questions.
- Avoid having too many questions.

The researcher also needs to consider the sequence of questions, their coding, the clarity of all instructions, and the actual 'look' of the questionnaire. A questionnaire should be as user-friendly as possible. Denscombe (1998) suggests a design which is 'easy on the eye' (to encourage a more positive attitude to filling it in) and is highly functional, this would include the use of single-sided coloured paper, page numbering, and effective spacing and an easily readable size of print (Denscombe 1998:96–7). If the data being collected is relatively simple it is possible to pre-code responses on the questionnaire to ease analysis.

Where the research project demands data on the opinions, attitudes and beliefs of a sample population the researcher might employ a scale for the measurement of attitudes. The most widely used scale is that devised by Likert. The Likert scale is made up of a number of positive and negative statements relating to the attitude being measured and the respondent is asked to indicate, using for example a 1 to 5 numerical scale, the extent to which they agree or disagree with each statement. The statements included must have face validity. In the analysis of responses numerical values are given to each statement, they are totalled and comparisons are then made between respondents. Oppenheim (1992) and Robson (1993) offer detailed guidance for constructing a Likert scale. Fowler (1995) gives details of other scaling methods.

When using a questionnaire it is always advisable to carry out a pilot study with a sample of respondents who match the profile of the sample in the substantive research project. A pilot study allows questionnaire items, their sequence and the format of the questionnaire to be trialled and modifications made on the basis of feedback. Where the researcher is actively involved in administering the questionnaire it is valuable that field notes are kept about the observed dynamics of the process.

As questionnaires are often designed to collect discrete items of information, to look at the relationships between variables (for example, gender, ethnicity and truancy) and usually involve larger numbers of respondents than other research methods they lend themselves to quantitative forms of analysis. Such analysis will of necessity involve the researcher in the use of statistics. For example, the researcher might use descriptive statistics to identify variable frequencies, averages or ranges in the data extracted from questionnaires, or they might explore simple interrelationships between pairs of variables, or they could employ multivariate analysis to study the linkages between more than two variables. If interrelationships between variables are explored it is important for the researcher to recognise that causality does not necessarily follow. Statistical relations between variables can be a matter of chance. Having to use statistics in order to extract answers for a research project is potentially intimidating for the researcher, but teacher–researchers will generally be engaged in small scale research which will usually only involve the use of descriptive statistics or the exploration of simple interrelationships. Further, as Pugh (1990) has written, statistics:

> are only numbers: they are constructed, as words are in ethnography; and they reflect their construction even if outsiders do not know enough about the context of their production to recognise this. Equally it is important not to be frightened by statistics, to let them intimidate you, or naively believe that 'statistics = bad'. Counting is an everyday action basic to many activities. Statistics need to be demystified.

Guidance on statistical analysis of data and the use of computer packages can be found in a range of texts: see, for example, Marsh (1988), Sprent (1988), Rose and Sullivan (1996).

Florian and Rouse's use of questionnaires

Florian and Rouse (Chaper 14) used questionnaires as a central research tool in their social survey. This approach to data collection was effectively combined with observation (see Chapter 4), interviews (see Chapter 12) and the use of teacher journals (see Chapter 7) in order to gain a picture of how inclusive education was being managed in a small sample of secondary schools. Questionnaires are seldom easy to construct and often subject to a low return rate. However, Florian and Rouse were able to overcome this latter difficulty by incorporation of the questionnaire administration within staff development activities in the sample schools. This ensured a good return and also placed a high importance upon the questionnaire, which was seen as being endorsed by school management and an integral part of school development.

Questionnaires can provide the researcher with both qualitative and quantitative data. Florian and Rouse obtained both in their survey and demonstrate a range of approaches to data analysis. Their sample was of sufficient size to justify the use of a standard statistical procedure (chi square analysis) to define differences between subjects taught by teachers and the strategies used to promote the inclusion of pupils with special educational needs. Such procedures are useful to the researcher in providing information through a test of the significance of the differences between individuals or groups in a sample. However, the test alone is of limited value unless care is taken in the management of the analysis of the results obtained. Florian and Rouse used the statistical data from their research as the basis for focused discussion and in order to develop further tools which enabled them to gain qualitative information which may ultimately inform classroom practice. Robson (1993) emphasises the value of multiple technique approaches to gathering survey information in order to permit triangulation. The use of questionnaires alone is seldom a satisfactory approach to educational research: Florian and Rouse are able to draw conclusions from their work because of the care which they take in combining the use of questionnaires with other related approaches. In their conclusion they point out that their own survey may well be of use in encouraging other teacher researchers to investigate similar areas in order to gain a better understanding of practices which influence inclusion. They provide important guidelines with regards to both the methods which may be deployed in such a study, and the ethical considerations which need to be followed.

Examples of other research in special education using questionnaires

'Irish children and adults with Down's Syndrome and their families'.

Egan, M. (1997), *Reach Journal of Special Needs Education in Ireland* **10**(2), 79–89.

'Multidisciplinary support and the management of children with specific writing difficulties'.

Lie, K. G., O'Hare, A. and Denwood, S. (2000), *British Journal of Special Education* **27**(2), 93–9.

'Parents' views of the efficacy of conductive education in Sweden'.

Lind, L. (2000), *European Journal of Special Needs Education* **15**(1), 42–54.

References and guide to further reading

Brown, A. and Dowling, P. (1998) *Doing Research/Reading Research.* London: Falmer Press.

Denscombe, M. (1998) *The Good Research Guide.* Buckingham: Open University Press.

Dillon, J. T. (1990) *The Practice of Interviewing.* London: Routledge.

Eichler, M. (1991) *Non-Sexist Research Methods: A Practical Guide.* New York: Routledge.

Fowler, F. (1995) *Improving Survey Questions: Design and Evaluation.* London: Sage.

Gilbert, N. (ed.) *Researching Social Life.* London: Sage.

Lloyd-Brown, F., Amos, J. R. and Mink, O. G. (1975) *Statistical Concepts: A Basic Program,* 2nd edn. New York: Harper and Row.

Marsh, C. (1988) *Exploring Data: An Introduction to Data Analysis for Social Scientists.* Cambridge: Polity.

May, T. (1997) *Social Research. Issues, Methods and Process,* 2nd edn. Buckingham: Open University Press.

Miles, M. B. and Huberman, A. M. (1994) *Qualitative Data Analysis: An Expanded Sourcebook.* London: Sage.

Oppenheim, A. N. (1992) *Questionnaire Design, Interviewing and Attitude Measurement.* London: Pinter.

Pugh, A. (1990) 'My statistics and feminism – a true story', in Stanley, L. (ed.) *Feminist Praxis: Research, Theory and Epistemology in Feminist Sociology.* London: Routledge.

Robson, C. (1993) *Real World Research: A Resource for Social Scientists and Practitioner-Researchers.* Oxford: Blackwell.

Rose, D. and Sullivan, O. (1996) *Introducing Data Analysis for Social Scientists,* 2nd edn. Buckingham: Open University Press.

Rowntree, D. (1981) *Statistics without Tears.* Harmondsworth: Penguin.

Sprent, P. (1988) *Understanding Data.* Harmondsworth: Penguin.

CHAPTER 14

Inclusive practice in secondary schools

Lani Florian and Martyn Rouse

Introduction

One of the aims of inclusive education is to improve the learning outcomes for children with special educational needs who otherwise would be educated separately. At present there appears to be some general agreement across the strands of the inclusion literature about the potential efficacy of a number of teaching and organisational strategies thought to promote inclusive practice. However, relatively little is known about the ways in which these and other techniques work (or do not work) in the context of a national curriculum and the demand for higher standards in classrooms which include pupils with a wide range of learning needs. Furthermore, there has been little consideration in the literature about whether such strategies are equally appropriate across all phases of education and in all subjects of the curriculum.

The limited research that has been carried out on effective teaching in inclusive classrooms tends to focus on the primary years. In an extensive review of the research on inclusive practice, McGregor and Vogelsberg (1998) reported only seven studies specifically focused on secondary school practice. Clearly there is a need to investigate what is happening in secondary schools that are committed to the development of inclusive practice.

This chapter describes a research project designed to investigate what happens in secondary schools when subject specialist teachers attempt to create the conditions for inclusive learning in their classrooms. The aim of the research was to find out what teachers know about inclusive practice and to describe the classroom strategies and techniques currently being utilised in secondary schools that have a long-standing commitment to developing inclusive practice. The research was designed to examine the extent to which classroom practice in the various subjects of the curriculum was consistent with that which is promoted as effective by the literature on inclusion. It also sought to identify any other strategies that were being used which seem successful in extending inclusive practice. We were also interested in the ways in which there might be differences between teachers of various subjects and the extent to which there might be an 'inclusive pedagogy' that incorporates aspects of special and mainstream teaching approaches.

Design and procedures

Over the past four years, a network of secondary schools from around England has been meeting termly in order to share experiences and ideas about how they can develop more inclusive practice. Though the schools vary in terms of size, location and the type of community served, the members of the network all share a philosophical commitment to inclusive education. The activities of the network, known as UDIS (Understanding the Development of Inclusive Schools) are supported by a small grant from the DfEE.

In June 1998, the UDIS network was briefed about a project intended to investigate effective classroom practice in inclusive education. Following this, four member schools volunteered to participate, beginning in September 1998. All were comprehensive, two 11–16, the other two 11–18, schools. Two were multicultural comprehensives situated in Greater London. One school was located in the Home Counties and the fourth was in a northern city. The participating schools had between 1,100 and 1,800 pupils on roll. All of the schools were additionally resourced to meet pupils' special educational needs through a variety of funding mechanisms. Three of the schools had current or historical links with special schools or units. In all cases these facilities have been incorporated as departments within the school. All of the schools had learning support teams or departments with responsibility for promoting equal opportunity and access to the curriculum, and all of the schools provided services to pupils with a wide range of disabilities and learning difficulties on all stages of the Code of Practice. The special educational needs of pupils included physical disabilities (i.e. muscular dystrophy, spina bifida), emotional and behavioural difficulties, severe learning difficulties (including autism, Down's syndrome), dyslexia and other literacy problems, speech and language difficulties, and moderate learning difficulties. By selecting schools with a long-standing commitment to inclusive practice we were able to have some degree of control over other important intervening variables such as school ethos and teacher attitude, as ethos and attitude were assumed to be positive in schools with a commitment to increasing capacity to include more diverse groups of pupils.

Meetings were held at each school with senior management teams at the start of the 1998–9 school year to brief them about the research and to negotiate access to the school as a variety of methods were to be used to collect data for the project, including:

- a survey of teachers designed to ascertain the extent to which they are familiar with, and use the strategies and techniques that are thought to promote inclusive practice;
- classroom observations to investigate what teachers from various subject areas actually do to include all learners in the lesson;
- 'Inclusion journals' kept by volunteer teachers for a period of five weeks; and
- follow-up interviews with those teachers who kept journals and had been observed.

A questionnaire was developed as a result of feedback from teachers and senior managers in the schools. It was designed to examine possible relationships between subject taught and teaching strategy used. We were interested in the extent to which a strategy that was seen as useful and appropriate to teachers of one subject was also seen as useful and appropriate to teachers of other subjects. We were also interested in discovering if the use of particular strategies might be associated with any other variables such as the number of years teaching, participation in INSET or aspects of initial teacher training. The schools incorporated the administration of the questionnaire into planned staff development activities. This gave the research high status within the school and helped to achieve a high return rate.

A qualitative dimension was added to the study design in order to capture the kind of contextual information not permitted by survey research. We sought nominations from senior staff and the SENCO at each school to identify two subject-specialist teachers we could invite to participate in the qualitative aspect of the study. The teachers they identified were those they considered skilled in including pupils with SEN in their classes. We were interested in getting as wide a range of subject area teachers of different year groups as possible. During the course of the project, one teacher was replaced due to illness, increasing the number of teachers observed by one. The following subjects were represented: English (n=3), humanities, maths, science (n=2), geography, and modern foreign language.

Each teacher was observed for the equivalent of two full teaching days (across several days) and this was set up in a way that allowed for follow-up interviews to be held as soon after the observation as possible, often the next period. This enabled the interviews to focus on what had been observed in the classroom. A total of 48 observations and 24 interviews were conducted. Table 14.1 provides the number of observation periods and interviews per teacher.

Teacher	Subject	Observations	Interviews
JG	English	5	3
LP	English	4	2
ML	English	2	1
SM	Humanities	7	4
BM	Maths	6	2
LR	Science	8	4
AM	Geography	5	4
MS	Modern Foreign Language	8	4
CM	Science	3	1
	Totals	(48)	(25)

Table 14.1 Number of observation periods and interviews per teacher

Participating teachers also kept 'Inclusion journals' for a period of five weeks between the October half-term and the Christmas break. This was intended to provide data about the ways in which the teachers reflect upon their practice. The journal guidelines asked the teachers to make one entry each day, paying particular attention to their own thoughts and feelings about their commitment to inclusive practice, how subject area knowledge informs their teaching, how they account for individual differences, and what works particularly with respect to the way in which their department approaches the National Curriculum and preparation for the GCSE examination. Six of the eight teachers observed submitted journals at the end of the term.

Questionnaire

The questionnaire was divided into four parts. Section 1 asked questions about the teacher, such as the number of years teaching, subject taught, and the extent of any recent SEN training.

Section 2 contained a list of 44 teaching strategies mentioned in the literature as helpful in promoting inclusive practice (see Table 14.3). These were derived from a review of the literature carried out by Scott *et al.* (1998). We organised the strategies under the following broad headings: differentiation strategies; cooperative learning strategies; classroom management strategies and social skills. Teachers were asked to rate their familiarity with these strategies on a scale of 1 (very familiar) to 3 (not familiar).

In Section 3 the list of strategies was repeated and teachers were asked to rate the strategy as appropriate or inappropriate to the teaching of their subject. If they thought the strategy was appropriate they were asked to indicate if it was a teaching technique that they typically used or something additional that was used specifically to ensure the inclusion of pupils with special educational needs. If they thought the strategy was inappropriate they were asked if this was because it was unhelpful or too difficult to manage.

In Section 4, teachers were asked to list the three or four strategies they have found to be most effective in including pupils with SEN in the classes they teach, as well as to list any strategies they used which were not included in the questionnaire. A final item simply asked for any other comments. A glossary defining ambiguous terms was appended to the questionnaire.

Questionnaires were distributed to teachers in the four participating schools. In three of the schools they were given out on staff development days in the Autumn term. Overall, 66 per cent of teachers turned in the questionnaire. In total, questionnaires were completed by 268 teachers (45 per cent male and 55 per cent female) representing most subjects of the secondary curriculum. The number of years teaching ranged from newly qualified teachers to 40 years, 23 per cent had been teaching five years or less, 25 per cent teaching between five and 15 years and 52 per cent having more than 15 years' teaching experience. Teachers who taught more than one subject were coded by their main subject, for example if a teacher reported teaching geography and business studies they were coded as a geography teacher. The number of teachers by subject can be found in Table 14.2.

Subject	Number of teachers	Per cent
English	43	16
Maths	40	15
Science	38	14
History/Humanities	25	9
Geography	16	6
Technology	24	9
Modern Foreign Language	30	11
P.E.	20	8
Art	14	5
Music	2	0.7
Business	4	2
IT	2	0.7
SEN	6	2
RE	3	1

Table 14.2 Number of teachers by subject

Results

Teacher familiarity with and use of strategies

The design of the questionnaire permitted 15 different responses for each of the 44 teaching strategies: however, a number of these categories were combined to simplify data analysis. Of particular interest was the level of reported use of the various strategies listed on the questionnaire. Table 14.3 lists the percentage of teachers claiming to use each of the strategies typically (i.e. for all pupils), or additionally (i.e. for pupils with special educational needs). With few exceptions, teachers overwhelmingly reported they were familiar with and used all of the strategies listed in the questionnaire. The most frequent response was that the teacher was very familiar with the strategy and used it typically (i.e. with all pupils). Only two strategies (consult with pupil on preferred learning style, and the use of learning support assistants for 1:1 teaching) were identified as additionally used (i.e. for pupils with SEN), and teachers were evenly divided as to the use of team teaching as a typical or additional strategy. The percentage of teachers reporting that they were either somewhat or very familiar with and used various strategies ranged from nearly half (45 per cent for use computer-assisted instruction), to 96 per cent. Because a number of teachers who noted in written comments that they did not differentiate between teaching strategy and whether a pupil had a special educational need, these categories were combined to give an overall impression of familiarity and use for each strategy. Table 14.3 gives a summary of responses for each strategy.

Variable	Per cent familiar who use strategy
Give supplemental instructions (12)	96
Use of praise (45)	96
Vary teaching style (13)	96
Alter instruction (14)	95
Break down activities into smaller steps (19)	95
Modify seat planning (47)	94
Adjust performance expectations (8)	93
Frequent monitoring and feedback (46)	93
Shorten assignments (6)	93
Adapt the curriculum (5)	92
Adjust lesson pace (15)	92
Use alternative papers, worksheets (7)	91
Allow additional time to complete assignments (22)	91
General help from learning support assistants (33)	91
Adapt assignments (17)	90
Modify lesson objectives (16)	90
Review prior learning (39)	89
Use of visual cues around the room (44)	89
Teaching of specific or specialist vocabulary (40)	87
Learning support assistants for 1:1 teaching (32)	87
Offer choice of material (9)	86
Peer collaboration (28)	86
Vary group composition for different kinds of activities (43)	86
Teach study skills (37)	85
Use supplementary aids (calculators, enlarged text, tape recorders, etc.) (18)	85
Base evaluation on the amount of individual improvement (24)	84
Explicitly teach social and group skills (48)	80
Provide abridged/modified texts (20)	78
Teach self-management skills (36)	77
Demonstrate problem-solving strategies (34)	77
Use shorter and more frequent methods of assessing performance (23)	77
Team teaching (30)	71
Co-teaching (31)	68
Peer tutoring (29)	68
Use of mnemonic devices (35)	68
Teach meta-cognitive strategies (e.g. reflection on learning) (42)	64
Use of scaffolding (38)	56
Use of drama or role play (25)	55
Jigsawing (27)	52
Offer choice of task (11)	51
Consult with pupils on preferred learning styles (10)	51
Allow alternative responses (e.g. tape recorder answers) (26)	50
Use of advanced organisers (41)	46
Use computer-assisted instruction (21)	45

Table 14.3 Summary of responses for each strategy

Such a skewed distribution of scores would suggest either a very good match between teacher familiarity with and use of strategy and inclusive practice, or considerable response bias associated with teachers wanting to present themselves favourably. Indeed, 96/95 per cent of teachers reported that they were very familiar or somewhat familiar with using praise, giving supplemental instructions, altering instruction, and breaking down activities into smaller steps. At least half of all teachers rated all but two strategies as something they were at least familiar with, if not something they routinely used. Such high levels of familiarity with and use of strategies suggest these results may be inflated, a common problem with self-reporting techniques and one we followed up during the observations of classroom practice.

When the variability in teachers' use of strategies was examined, an interesting picture began to emerge. Although 'very familiar' and 'typically used' was the single most frequent response for almost every variable, the actual numbers of teachers who said this ranged from 16 to 89 per cent, suggesting that teachers are not quite as familiar with or actually using the strategies as often as it would appear when categories of familiarity and use are combined. In other words, the variability between teachers' responses suggests differences in the extent of this familiarity and the usefulness depending on the strategy. Although 90 per cent of teachers reported being familiar with and using the strategy of 'basing evaluation on the amount of individual improvement', only 45 per cent said they were very familiar with this strategy and typically used it. Three-quarters of teachers said they were very familiar with co-teaching but only 25 per cent used this typically. Relatively few teachers reported that strategies with which they were familiar were unhelpful or too difficult to manage. When teachers were unfamiliar with strategies they were more likely to rate them as unhelpful to inclusion or too difficult to manage.

These data were then cross tabulated with other variables (subject taught, gender, length of service and recent training for special educational needs). This permitted us to identify and correct anomalies in the data prior to performing further statistical analysis and to begin to look for any relationships or differences between the variables.

Separate chi square analyses were performed to investigate differences between subject-area teachers and their reported use of teaching strategies. As expected, the strategies that appeared to be used most frequently (see Table 14.3) show no significant difference between subjects. However, there were numerous interesting and statistically significant differences between teachers of different subjects and their use of particular strategies. For example, English teachers were more likely than maths teachers to use the following strategies:

- provide abridged/modified texts;
- use of drama or role play;
- allow alternative responses;
- jigsawing;
- peer collaboration;
- peer tutoring;

- use of scaffolding; and
- explicitly teaching social and group skills.

Maths teachers were more likely than English teachers to make use of mnemonic devices.

There were also differences between English and modern foreign language teachers' with English teachers more likely to use the following five strategies: consulting with pupils on preferred learning style, jigsawing, peer tutoring, use of scaffolding and teaching meta-cognitive strategies.

Differences were also found between maths and science teachers. Maths teachers were more likely than science teachers to use mnemonic devices while science teachers were more likely to use drama or role play, jigsawing, and peer collaboration. There were no differences between history and geography teachers in their reported use of any of the strategies.

When asked about strategies which were not included in the questionnaire, teachers' responses fell into three categories: affective strategies, conferring with others, and more detailed and specific versions of the listed strategies. Affective strategies included such things as using humour as a teaching strategy, and providing discrete support to pupils so they will not feel singled out. Teachers most frequently mentioned the importance of developing pupils' self-esteem and sense of belonging by establishing relationships with pupils outside of class, being involved with pupils on an extracurricular basis, offering supplementary sessions at mutually convenient times, running homework clubs, mentoring, and offering what one teacher called the 'careful mix of praise and criticism'.

The open-ended comments sections of the questionnaire enabled us to identify intervening variables which aided the interpretation of the data: one was that teachers commented that the use of some strategies was resource dependent (e.g. use of computer-assisted instruction), while others depend on administrative arrangements and support (e.g. 'team teaching and co-teaching are difficult to organise but they work'). Some teachers went out of their way to comment that they made no distinction between pupils with SEN and others when it comes to teaching strategy although others made very specific comments about how they included pupils with SEN (i.e. 'give the pupil a responsibility vital to the lesson') suggesting that the teachers individualised on the basis of their knowledge about individuals rather than whether a pupil had a special educational need in a formal sense.

In response to a question about the nature and extent of any specialised training in special educational needs (i.e. seminar, INSET, course or combination), 78 per cent of teachers reported that they had received nothing within the past five years. Teacher responses varied somewhat by subject, with English and maths teachers more likely than teachers of other subjects to have had some kind of additional training. Although we speculated that there might be differences between male and female teachers in the reported use of various strategies and that experience and/or training may also be a factor, no statistically significant differences were found between these variables.

Observations, interviews and journals

We organised classroom observations so that we observed whole-class teaching but then structured follow-up interviews to explore how the teachers were responding to individual pupils who were experiencing learning difficulties as well as specific information about the nature of those difficulties. The resulting field notes were then reviewed to identify strategies the teachers were using. This was accomplished by searching for evidence of strategy utilisation (what was observed or became apparent during discussion) matched to the questionnaire data (see Table 14.4), or emerging from the dialogue between the teacher and the interviewer. An example of this procedure is provided in the following transcript excerpt from the observation of a Year 9 English class:

> Period 2. (10.15–11.05 a.m.) Twenty students arrive and take seats in pairs or trios. Judy passes out a script – one per table and I notice that a man is seated at one of the tables. Judy explains to the class that the task is to act out part of the script (based on the novel the class is reading) developed by one of their classmates when they were asked to do this activity the preceding week. Judy then rearranges the pupils into groups of four to make sure each part can be played. She tells the class to rehearse the script as if preparing to perform as she intends to call on Andrew's group and one other. She notes that one of the characters does not have a large speaking part. She and the other adult in the class move around the room supporting the small groups of pupils.
>
> At 10.40 Judy calls the whole class together and reviews the scene: How are each of the characters feeling? Why? The class discusses this. Judy moves around the room, gently touching one boy on the shoulder as a way of gaining his attention. She calls on John's group: 'Spotlight's on you!' and the pupils perform the script to the delight of their classmates. When they are finished Judy asks what was good about the performance and the class engages in a critique. Andrew's group performs next. Their scene begins before the previous one and then repeats it. During the ensuing critique Judy notes that a strong point is that because the scene starts before the others it sets context.
>
> Judy has the pupils rearrange the tables back to how they were at the beginning of the lesson. She tells the group there are 10 minutes left and she wants to 'look at someone else's work and to recap Chapter 5 ... Last week I gave you the option of writing a script or writing an article for a newspaper. Brian finished an article so I'd like to ask the group to read his article and answer what was good about it. What makes it like a real newspaper article and what is needed to make it better?' The pupils read in pairs and threes. (They are now seated in their original configuration.) Judy leads a whole-group discussion and the class concludes that the layout, font, and headline are strong points but that the use of language (i.e. use of words like 'alleged') though strong in the beginning was not sustained throughout the piece of writing.

	Eng JG n=5	Eng LP n=4	Eng ML n=2	Hum SM n=7	Mat BM n=6	Sci LR n=8	Geo AM n=5	Mfl MS n=8	Sci CM n=3
Adapt the curriculum (5)			X				X	X	X
Shorten assignments (6)									
Use alternative papers, worksheets (7)	X	X			X		X		
Adjust performance expectations (8)		X	X	X	X	X			
Offer choice of material (9)	X				X				
Consult with pupils on preferred learning styles (10)									
Offer choice of task (11)	X			X		X	X		
Give supplemental instructions (12)			X		X				
Vary teaching style (13)									
Alter instruction (14)					X				
Adjust lesson pace (15)						X			
Modify lesson objectives (16)									
Adapt assignments (17)	X			X			X		
Use supplementary aids (calculators, enlarged texts, tape recorders, etc) (18)	X	X			X				X
Break down activities into smaller steps (19)					X				
Provide abridged/modified texts (20)									X
Use computer-assisted instruction (21)		X		X					
Allow additional time to complete assignments (22)									
Use shorter and more frequent methods of assessing performance (23)									
Base evaluation on the amount of individual improvement (24)		X	X	X		X			
Use of drama or role play (25)	X	X							
Allow alternative responses (e.g. tape recorder answers) (26)	X	X							X
Jigsawing (27)	X	X		X			X		
Peer collaboration (28)	X	X	X				X		
Peer tutoring (29)		X	X			X			
Team teaching (30)	X								
Co-teaching (31)		X							
Use of learning support assistants for 1:1 teaching (32)		X	X	X	X	X	X	X	X
General help from learning support assistants (33)	X	X		X	X			X	X
Demonstrate problem-solving strategies (34)	X	X		X	X	X	X	X	X
Use of mnemonic devices (35)							X		X
Teach self management skills (36)									
Teach study skills (37)	X	X							X
Use of scaffolding (38)	X			X	X				X
Review prior learning (39)	X		X	X	X	X	X	X	X
Teaching of specific or specialist vocabulary (40)	X	X						X	
Use of advanced organisers (41)	X	X				X			
Teach meta-cognitive strategies (e.g. reflection on learning) (42)	X			X	X		X		
Vary group composition for different kinds of activities (43)	X	X		X	X			X	
Use of visual clues around the room (44)		X				X	X	X	
Use of praise (45)	X	X		X	X			X	
Frequent monitoring and feedback (46)	X	X	X	X	X	X			
Modify seating plan (47)	X								
Explicitly teach social and group skills (48)	X	X		X					

Table 14.4 Observations

Key: Eng – English, Hum – Humanities, Mat – Maths, Sci – Science, Geo – Geography, Mfl – Modern foreign language

For the last minute of class everyone lists three things that happened in Chapter 5 of the book.

During the post observation interview Judy discloses that the group includes Michael, a non reader. The other adult in the room was the Head of the Drama Department who supports the class two periods per week. Judy tells me she has decided to let pupils read at their own pace, something she had expressed reservation about in an earlier conversation. Her classroom grouping strategy is to form mixed ability groups and to reassign them every half-term. The previous week she had chosen a scene from S.E. Hinton's novel *The Outsiders* for the pupils to script because 'it was dramatic, short, could be performed on stage and each group member could participate'. Scripting this scene was one of two activities offered to the class that period. The other activity involved writing a newspaper article about the same scene from the novel. During this period pupils worked in the IT room on the script or newspaper article. Michael was given a sheet with vocabulary words from the novel to write out. During the observation, Judy structured the lesson in such a way that the script and newspaper article developed by the pupils who were further ahead in the novel were used to engage all the pupils in the class.

From the observation it is possible to note the use of a number of strategies listed on the questionnaire such as: use of drama or role play, offering choice of task, using alternative worksheets, adaptation of assignment, and peer collaboration. The interview and a reading of the teacher's journal revealed her use of additional strategies as well as information about the school policy of teachers providing learning support for each other (as opposed to using learning support assistants).

This procedure for analysing field notes was repeated for the remaining observations and interviews and these are summarised in Table 14.4. The procedure enabled us to confirm the teachers' self-reports on the use of strategies from the questionnaire (Table 14.4).

Discussion

The teachers we observed were skilled in whole-class teaching, presenting one lesson but offering a choice of tasks and varying expectations with respect to individual pupils as is traditionally understood and promoted as good practice. What enables these teachers to include pupils with a wide range of learning abilities seems to be the way in which they embed a responsiveness to individual need within the process of whole-class teaching, a finding consistent with other studies on inclusive practice (e.g. Jordan and Stanovich 1998). In addition, there was an awareness that certain strategies may be associated with particular kinds of special educational need. As a result, circulating information about individual special educational needs and disabilities was seen as very important. All the schools in this study had devised mechanisms for doing this. Although teachers spoke and wrote about their concerns relating to their own capacity with respect to mixed ability teaching, they viewed the learning support departments in their respective schools as sources of knowledge and support for teaching and learning.

We found no apparent difference between schools with respect to teachers' knowledge about practice although teachers in schools with more experience in mixed ability teaching made more suggestions about what works. That they may not be able to engage in a practice is different from not knowing how to do it, and some teachers made this comment when filling out the questionnaire. Organisational arrangements and resource constraints were more likely to determine whether certain strategies were used. For example, it would not be possible to make use of information and communication technology in a school where the hardware was not available.

The differences we found between subjects in the use of the various strategies could be a function of any number of factors including the nature and status of the knowledge in a particular subject domain and whether the teachers perceive learning their subject being related to prior learning. Maths and modern foreign languages tend to be seen as sequential while the humanities and English much less so (Hallam and Ireson 1999). The training of teachers is organised on a subject basis and most secondary schools are organised into subject departments which have different histories, varying degrees of autonomy and different priorities. All these factors produce a range of subject and department 'cultures' that may have an impact upon teachers' practice and their views about what works in promoting inclusion.

Conclusion

This study combined quantitative and qualitative methods in an attempt to determine what is known about inclusive practice in four English secondary schools and to identify the strategies associated with implementing inclusive education policies across the subject areas of the National Curriculum. Differences were found between teachers of different subjects in the use of certain strategies and these differences should be explored in a series of follow-up studies to see if they are found in other schools and in a larger sample of teachers.

Although we have begun to identify some of the factors that appear to have an impact upon teachers' use of strategies thought to promote inclusive practice, more questions were raised than are answered. In particular the following questions require further detailed investigation:

- What factors are associated with the differences between the various subjects and the ways in which strategies are used?
- Are there differences in the use of the strategies between schools?
- How do various streaming and grouping arrangements affect practice?
- To what extent does the nature of the support and advice offered to subject teachers affect their practice?

- How does the deployment and role of classroom assistants impact upon practice?
- What are the implications for future practice in teacher education and support?

These questions may provide fertile ground for further investigation by the school based researcher, particularly where issues are linked to school or departmental priority development areas. Many schools are currently reviewing aspects of teaching and learning and the special needs department has an important role to play in improving the learning experiences for all children. Single school studies of issues such as support in the classroom, deployment of additional adults, pupil groupings, peer support and the use of information technology are all topics of potential relevance for whole-school development.

SENCOs and other teachers who have special needs responsibilities within schools have many opportunities for working closely with colleagues. They have unrivalled access to practice in their schools. In the research outlined above, we used the results of a survey to provide a framework for a series of observations of practice. Interviews with the teachers took place a soon as possible after the observations. Because the interviews concentrated on aspects of practice that had been observed, we were able to be focused in our discussions and produce data from the interviews that related to the survey and the observations.

A class teacher contemplating a similar study within a school must keep in mind that there are ethical issues that have to be considered before undertaking such research with colleagues and access should always be negotiated. Successful research requires the systematic collection and careful analysis of data if it is to inform practice. Yet, if school based research is to develop practice within a school, it should be research that is *with* colleagues, not research that is *on* them.

References and further reading

Ainscow, M. (ed.) (1991) *Effective schools for all.* London: David Fulton Publishers.

Ainscow, M. (1997) 'Towards inclusive schooling', *British Journal of Special Education* 24(1), 3–6.

Ainscow, M. (1999) *Understanding the development of inclusive schools.* London: Falmer Press.

Babbage, R., Byers, R. and Redding, H. (1999) *Approaches to teaching and learning: Including pupils with learning difficulties.* London: David Fulton Publishers.

Booth, T. and Ainscow, M. (eds) (1998) *From Them to Us: an international study of inclusion in education.* London: Routledge.

Chang, H. (1984) *Adolescent life and ethos: an ethnography of a U.S. High School.* London: Falmer Press.

Clark, C. *et al.* (1999) 'Inclusive education and schools as organisations', *International Journal of Inclusive Education* 3(1), 37–51.

Creemers, B. (1996) 'The goal of school effectiveness and school improvement', in Reynolds, D. *et al.* (eds) *Making good schools: Linking school effectiveness and school improvement.* London: Routledge.

Forest, M. and Pearpoint, J. (1992) 'Putting all kids on the MAP', *Educational Leadership* **50**(2), 26–31.

Giangreco, M. F. (1997) 'Key lessons learned about inclusive education: summary of the 1996 Schonell Memorial Lecture', *International Journal of Disability, Development and Education* **44**(3), 194–206.

Hallam, S. and Ireson, J. (1999) 'Pedagogy in the secondary school', in Mortimore, P. (ed.) *Understanding pedagogy and its impact on learning*. London: Paul Chapman.

Hart, S. (1996) *Beyond Special Needs: enhancing children's learning through innovative thinking*. London: Paul Chapman.

Jordan, A. and Stanovich, P. (1998) 'Exemplary teaching in inclusive classrooms'. Paper presented at the Annual Meeting of the American Educational Research Association, San Diego, California, April.

Jordan, L. and Goodey, C. (1996) *Human rights and school change: The Newham story*. Bristol: Centre for Studies in Inclusive Education.

Jorgensen, C. M. (1998) *Restructuring High Schools for All Students: taking inclusion to the next level*. Baltimore: Paul H. Brookes.

Lipsky, D. K. and Gartner, A. (1997) *Inclusion and School Reform: transforming America's classrooms*. Baltimore: Paul H. Brookes.

Martin, J., Jorgensen, C. M. and Klein, J. (1998) 'The promise of friendship for students with disabilities', in Jorgensen, C. *Restructuring High Schools for All Students: taking inclusion to the next level*. Baltimore: Paul H. Brookes.

McDonnell, L., McLaughlin, M. and Morison, P. (eds) (1997) *Educating one and all: Students with disabilities and standards-based reform*. Washington, DC: National Academy Press.

McGregor, G. and Vogelsberg, R. T. (1998) *Inclusive Schooling Practices: Pedagogical and Research Foundations*. Baltimore: Paul H. Brookes.

Rouse, M. and Florian, L. (1996) 'Effective inclusive schools: A study in two countries', *Cambridge Journal of Education* **26**(1), 71–85.

Rouse, M. and Florian, L. (1997) 'Inclusive education in the marketplace', *International Journal of Inclusive Education* **1**(4), 323–36.

Scott, B. J., Vitale, M. R. and Marsten, W. G. (1998) 'Implementing instructional adaptations for students with disabilities in inclusive classrooms: a literature review', *Remedial and Special Education* **19**(2), 106–19.

Sebba, J. and Sachdev, D. (1997) *What Works in Inclusive Education?* Ilford, Essex: Barnardo's.

Skrtic, T. (1998) 'The organisational context of special education', in Meyen, E. L. and Skrtic, T. M. (eds) *Exceptional children and youth: An introduction*. Denver: Love.

Thousand, J. S. and Villa, R. A. (1991) 'Accommodating for greater student variance', in Ainscow, M. (ed.) *Effective Schools for All*. London: David Fulton Publishers.

Villa, R. A. *et al.* (eds) (1992) *Restructuring for caring and effective education: an administrative guide to creating heterogeneous schools*. Baltimore: Paul H. Brookes.

CHAPTER 15

Life stories

> I was about 31 when I went to Whyteleafe House. I've been out of St Lawrence's 16 years now. I asked to leave. My friend, Eva, she wrote and asked. She said I might be able to cope a bit. She got in touch with the social worker what used to be in the hospital ... I never saw children, only children in wheelchairs and what-have-you, not children running about and doing all the things they're doing. So really the children fascinated me ....

The above words are taken from Mabel Cooper's life story, constructed from tape recorded interviews (Cooper 1997:30). As a child she lived first in a children's home and later in a long stay hospital. Recounting life stories is a social process. Life stories are generally 'told' and told to someone else. For Atkinson that someone else has two main roles: to 'facilitate the telling of the story and to listen attentively to its telling (to be its 'audience'); and later, to be its compiler and its writer (though not its owner)' (Atkinson *et al.* 1997:7). Life stories involve the researcher in biographical and family history research.

Miller (2000) has advocated the collection of life stories in social research because they offer a perspective that is 'holistic'. Life story data ranges across time. The respondent who tells her story does so in the present, but the events recounted range over the past. Life story research is therefore appropriate if the researcher wishes to explore the effects of change over time, or how particular events have impinged on an individual, or how certain individuals have followed their life course. The researcher's role is to facilitate the respondent's recall, to help her make linkages between different types of events in her life story and segments of her life. The life story is also about the interplay between personal and the public history, between the individual as a social actor and the social structure. To tell one's life story, as Miller writes:

> means telling about the constraints and opportunities that were available in the past and how one dealt with these – circumventing (or being thwarted by) obstacles, taking advantage of (or missing) opportunities. (Miller 2000:75)

In collecting a life story the unstructured interview is frequently used because of its potential to allow the participant to talk about events in terms of his own frames of reference, to use his own language of description, to give meaning to his life experiences in his own terms. Thus, for some writers the collector of life stories should of necessity in an interview maintain a low profile, keeping their interventions to a minimum. The probing questions usually associated with the unstructured interview (see above) are therefore kept in check (Miller 2000). To help respondents make connections between past events and their life experiences some researchers (Walmsley 1995, Lawn and Grosvenor 2001) have used photographs and other material traces of the past as triggers. Walmsley, in her life story research, has also used diagrammatic representations, a 'life map' and a 'network diagram', as research tools both to make sense of her data and to advance the collection of further data from her respondents, who all had learning disabilities.

In using life stories as a research method and analysing the data collected Miller has usefully identified three basic approaches: realist, neo-positivist and narrative. The realist approach is inductive. Information collected through life story research is used 'to construct general principles concerning social phenomena'. Information is collected from a cross-section of informants to provide a basis upon which to generalise. The neo-positivist approach is concerned with testing theoretical concerns against observed or reported phenomena. In the narrative approach 'understanding the individual's unique and changing perception' takes precedence over questions of fact. The present acts as a lens through which both the past and the future are seen. The three approaches can overlap in practice (Miller 2000:10–14).

In education the use of life story or the biographical approach in research is focused predominantly on the life stories of teachers and issues around professional development (Ball and Goodson 1985, Woods 1987, 1993, Louden 1991, Goodson 1990, 1991). Hitchcock and Hughes (1995) have argued for life story research to be broadened and to focus on both teachers' and pupils' life stories as a means of relating individual experience to the wider school, community or societal context. They suggest six themes for exploration in pupils' life stories: experience of previous schools, views of subjects, attitudes to gender issues, 'disaffected' pupils, special needs, and experience of ethnicity (Hitchcock and Hughes 1995:202). A focus upon researching the life stories of people with learning difficulties is a relatively recent phenomenon. Walmsley (1995), Booth and Booth (1996), Atkinson *et al.* (1997), Rolph (1998) and Brigham (1998) have all engaged with life history research with participants who have learning difficulties. Self-advocacy has also led to a growing interest among people with learning difficulties in reclaiming their histories (Barron 1996, Cooper 1997, Lewis 1997).

Life story research engages with issues of motivation, with the construction of social identity and the making of meaning. Its use of the life history approach in research has been criticised because the texts produced are highly personalised, the data subjective and because of its limiting reliance upon single informants. However, 'life history work produces detailed personal subjective accounts because that is what it precisely aims to do' (Hitchcock and Hughes 1995:208). Rather than focus on the reliability and validity of the data produced (although through triangulation with other testimonies and documentary sources this is possible) the researcher should be concerned with exploring and analysing issues of authenticity, interpretation and the social production of meaning.

Life story research has the potential to raise many ethical dilemmas for the researcher (Measor and Sykes 1990, Jones 1998). There has to be understanding and agreement about confidentiality and ownership. Informants are involved in a process of sharing their lives and as a consequence have a right to determine what happens to that story once it is told. Such meaningful involvement in the research process becomes particularly acute when the respondent has learning difficulties. Issues of informed consent, anonymity, privacy, power and control, inclusion and exclusion are challenges which the researcher has to confront, but there are no easy answers to the ethical dilemmas associated with researching 'lost voices' (Walmsley 1995, Brigham 1998, Rolph 1998). That said, life story research is extremely valuable for gathering social data, for bringing the diversity of individual and group experience to the surface. Life story research is also important to the informant whose voice is being heard perhaps for the first time. Recounting a life can contribute to a sense of identity, as Mabel Cooper commented on her own 'ghosted' autobiography:

> It is an achievement with me being in St Lawrence's for so many years, and not knowing anything else but St Lawrence's. I thought it would be nice to let people know what it was like, and to let people know how difficult it was for someone with a learning disability, and who was stuck away because of that. I thought that people outside should know these things because they're not aware of it at the moment and I think it would be nice. (quoted in Atkinson *et al.* 1997:9)

More than this, the production of life stories like that of Mabel Cooper , can also challenge stereotypes and offer other perspectives on the construction of reality.

The chapter by Christina Tilstone which follows is different to earlier paired chapters in that it does not report details of a particular research study, rather it offers an account of some of the issues relating to using life story approaches with people and young children with learning difficulties. The use of life story is relatively new as a research approach in this context and is very much linked to the emergence of the advocacy movement. Tilstone, through case study examples, shows that individuals with learning difficulties have much to tell us about their lives and are able and willing to take control of the research process. She also describes a range of techniques for life history research which do not depend upon the ability to communicate through speech.

Examples of other research in special education using life stories

'Pupils tell their stories'.
Cooper, P. (1993), in *Effective Schools for Disaffected Students*. London: Routledge.
'Ann – the challenge of a difficult to reach five year old'.
Hawkins, R. (1998), in Hewett, D. (ed.) *Challenging Behaviour.* London: David Fulton Publishers.
'Another world: experiences of residential special schooling'.
Humphries, S. and Gordon, P. (1995), in Potts, P., Armstrong, F. and Masterton, M. (eds) *Equality and Diversity in Education: Learning, Teaching and Managing in Schools.* London: Routledge.

References and guide to further reading

Atkinson, R. (1998) *The Life Story Interview*. Vol. 44, *Qualitative Research Methods*. Thousand Oaks, CA: Sage.

Atkinson, D., Jackson, M. and Walmsley, J. (1997) 'Introduction: methods and themes', in Atkinson, D. *et al.* (eds) *Forgotten Lives. Exploring the History of Learning Disability*. Kidderminster: BILD.

Ball, S. J. and Goodson, I. F. (eds) (1985) *Teachers' Lives and Careers*. Lewes: Falmer Press.

Barron, A. (1996) *A Price to be Born*. Harrowgate: Mencap.

Booth, T. and Booth, W. (1996) 'Sounds of still voices', in Barton, L. (ed.) *Disability and Society*. London: Longman.

Brigham, L. (1998) 'Representing the lives of women with learning difficulties: ethical dilemmas in the research process', *British Journal of Learning Disabilities* **26**, 146–50.

Cooper, M. (1997) 'Mabel Cooper's life story', in Atkinson, D. *et al.* (eds) *Forgotten Lives. Exploring the History of Learning Disability*. Kidderminster: BILD.

Goodson, I. F. (ed.) (1990) *Studying Teachers' Lives*. London: Routledge.

Goodson, I. F. (1991) 'Sponsoring the teacher's voice: teachers' lives and teacher development', *Cambridge Journal of Education* **21**(1), 35–45.

Hitchcock, G. and Hughes, D. (1995) *Research and the Teacher: A Qualitative Introduction to School-Based Research*, 2nd edn. London: Routledge.

Jones, D. W. (1998) 'Distressing histories and unhappy interviewing', *Oral History* **26**(2), 34–48.

Lawn, M. and Grosvenor, I. (2001) '"When in doubt preserve": exploring the traces of teaching and material culture in English schools', *History of Education*, Spring (forthcoming).

Lewis, R. (1997) *Living in Hospital and in the Community*. Brighton: Pavilion Publishing.

Loudon, W. (1991) *Understanding Teaching: Continuity and Change in Teachers' Knowledge*. London: Cassell.

Measor, L. and Sykes, P. J. (1990) 'Ethics and methodology in life history', in Goodson, I. F. (ed.) *Studying Teachers' Lives*. London: Routledge.

Miller, R. L. (2000) Researching Life Stories and Family Histories. London: Sage.

Rolph, S. (1998) 'Ethical dilemmas: oral history work with people with learning difficulties' *Oral History* **26**(2), 65–72.

Simeoni, D. and Diani, M. (1995) 'The sociostylistics of life histories: taking Jenny at her word(s)', *Current Sociology* **43**(2/3), 27–39.

Walmsley, J. (1995) 'Life history interviews with people with learning disabilities', *Oral History* **23**(1), 71–9.

Woods, P. (1987) 'Life histories and teacher knowledge', in Smyth, J. (ed.) *Educating Teachers: Changing the Nature of Pedagogical Knowledge*. Lewes: Falmer Press.

Woods, P. (1993) 'Managing marginality: teacher development through grounded life history', *British Educational Research Journal* **19**(5), 447–65.

CHAPTER 16

Research with people with learning difficulties: challenges and dilemmas

Christina Tilstone

Introduction

There is a growing body of knowledge which shows that people with learning difficulties have much to contribute to research into the discourse of disability and special educational needs. They have a great deal to tell about their lives and their autobiographical accounts provide compelling insights into their experiences and opinions. Goodley (2000), writing in association with researchers with learning difficulties, comments that the common belief that people with learning difficulties are unable to talk about their experiences has now been discredited, and their narrative inquiries allow us to understand the histories of people whose voices have been 'lost' in the past. Through a greater understanding of the ideas and views which they choose to present it is likely that there will be sharper insights into the meaning of disability. Although adults with learning difficulties are beginning to find a voice it is taking children much longer to learn that their ideas are important and that they too can become 'empowered agents of social change' (Mittler 1996).

This chapter takes the work of adult researchers with learning difficulties as a starting point and attempts to explore a number of practical techniques which may be employed to break down some of the barriers when there may be differences in the perceptions and methods of communication of these researchers. The profiles of Mabel and Laurie, both of whom are considered to have severe difficulties in learning, illustrate the *differences* in skills, knowledge and understanding of those so labelled. Mabel has speech whereas Laurie uses non-verbal means of communication. Adults and children like Laurie, whose difficulties are complex, are often at early stages of development and the different techniques used to encourage Mabel and Laurie to tell their stories are described in some detail. For Laurie a multi-method approach, based on innovative work on gathering the views of young infants and/or pre-verbal children (the Mosaic approach), is presented as a way of involving him in researching his own important experiences.

What is the nature of learning difficulties?

Mabel

Ian Grosvenor in his introduction to this chapter provided some fascinating information about Mabel Cooper. Mabel was born in 1945, and under the regulations of the 1944 Education Act was labelled 'educationally subnormal'. At the age of seven she was sent to a residential institution which used a dependent model of care (Atkinson *et al.* 1997). She was excluded from the education system and, like many thousands of others who were considered to be 'ineducable', became the responsibility of the Health service. Children like Mabel did not become part of the Education service until the passing of the Education (Handicapped) Children Act in 1970, and consequently did not have a legal right to education until 1971. Mabel has written prolifically about her life, and her stories provide dramatic insights into her early experiences (Cooper 1997, 2000, Atkinson and Cooper 2000). From Mabel's accounts of her problems in learning it seems that there were no organic or neurological disorders which may have contributed to her difficulties but, in the segregated environment of the hospital, learning experiences were minimalised and expectations of her achievements were greatly reduced. Such a restricted learning context and non-responsive environment will have undoubtedly contributed to Mabel's learning difficulties (Tilstone *et al.* 2000). Mabel received a medical model of care in which her difficulties were located 'within her', and the power to define, control and treat her was seen as a medical phenomenon (Oliver 1996). When Mabel was young, children with learning disabilities were presented as 'tragic' because it was considered that they were unable to conform to normality (Shakespeare and Watson 1998); a situation which is beginning to disappear in the twenty-first century.

Laurie

Laurie is seven and is considered to have profound and multiple learning difficulties. A near drowning accident at the age of eighteen months, in which he was thought for some time to be dead, resulted in cerebral palsy (athetosis) and considerable damage to the brain. He is a wheelchair user and can sit upright if supported at the hips in a specially adapted chair. The involuntary writhing movements of the athetosis are difficult to control and therefore he is not able to pick up, or hold objects without help. He needs assistance with all aspects of personal care and he communicates by idiosyncratic non-verbal means. He has good eye contact and will smile when he wants something and pout when he does not. He is extremely sociable, and enjoys the presence of adults and peers. He has a good memory for familiar faces but in general all cognitive skills, knowledge and understanding are at an early level of development. Clearly the techniques employed to enable him to comment on his life will be very different to those used to encourage Mabel to tell her story.

Since Mabel was born a new understanding of differences and disability has emerged through a consideration, by people with disabilities themselves, of the social structures which maintain obstacles to learning opportunities (Barnes 1991, Morris 1991, Oliver 1990, Shakespeare 1996). The 'social model of disability' identifies such barriers as inaccessible physical environments; discriminatory employment or welfare policies; segregated education or transport; negative stereotypes; prejudiced attitudes; or restricted social relationships as the main contributors to difficulties in learning (Shakespeare and Watson 1998). Although the social model has been criticised for the non-acceptance of organic difficulties (for example, birth damage, resulting in brain damage, a genetic disorder, or the lived experiences of those with progressive diseases; see Pinder 1995, 1996, 1997, Shakespeare and Watson 1997), in Mabel's case it is more than likely that her limiting early environment is causally linked to her learning difficulties.

Autobiographies and biographies

In the past the lives and opinions of those with learning difficulties were represented through the biographical accounts of others either acting *for* them or *against* them (Ryan and Thomas 1987). Atkinson and Walmsley (1999) provide an example of how biographical notes were used as propaganda by the National Association for the Care and Control of the Feeble Minded, an organisation which supported institutional care:

> Hr, a little feeble minded girl. Turned into the streets by her father. Found by the School Attendance Officer and placed in safe keeping. Was actually starving and filthy – verminous. Horribly disfigured by burns. Her feeble-minded brother had put her on the fire and kept her there. (Quoted in Jones 1972:196–7).

As Atkinson and Walmsley point out both children were said to be feeble minded; the girl is portrayed as an innocent victim; the brother as a sadist. The authors make the point that 'there is a mixture of "acting on behalf of" and "acting against" in this biography' (Atkinson and Walmsley 1999:205).

Many researchers who are themselves disabled, for example Oliver and Shakespeare, have been unhappy about the exclusion of those with disabilities and/or learning disabilities from the research agenda and have been exploring strategies which are both emancipatory (seeking positive societal change) and empowering (seeking positive individual change) (Kitchin 2000). They are critical of the fact that those with disabilities have, until recently, been the *objects* of research by the non-disabled. It is likely that non-disabled researchers are caring individuals, but they are part of a society which, over a long period, has institutionalised, sterilised, stigmatised and excluded those with learning difficulties. Jackson (2000) makes the point that the policies which set those with difficulties or disabilities apart from society were not imposed by people with learning difficulties themselves, but by people acting on their behalf. Children, particularly those with learning difficulties, have been cast in the role of *subjects* of research rather than active participants. The changes to the National Curriculum, the recognition of key skills across the curriculum and new research into children's learning styles and strategies are providing the foundation for children to become their own advocates in the learning process (DfEE and QCA 1999a, 1999b, Riding and Rayner 1998).

People with learning difficulties have a shared history which needs to be documented and written by members of a social network, although academics, practitioners and others may be able to offer different perspectives and approaches.

The importance of self-advocacy

The growth of the self-advocacy movement has meant that people with learning difficulties have challenged the negative attitudes which have become their legacy and are raising pertinent issues on which they are now crusading; see Hersov (1996) and Whittaker (1996) for comprehensive accounts of the *People First* movement. The consequent rise of emancipatory research brought about by the self-advocacy movement has meant that people with learning difficulties are making increasing demands to be included in the research process. With minimal support they are not only researching the past, but are also articulating what life is like for them in the present.

The structures are in place for children with learning difficulties to make similar demands. The Code of Practice and new structures embedded in the National Curriculum require pupils to take an active part in planning, developing and evaluating their learning experiences (DFE and Welsh Office 1994, DfEE and QCA 1999a, 1999b). Pupils as partners is the focus of a chapter in the consultation document on the new Code of Practice which emphasises the importance of gaining information on the *lived experiences* of children at school (DfEE 2000).

Trevor, Pauline, Brian, Jackie, Robert and Douglas, six people with learning difficulties, left school some time ago and therefore have not had the benefit of these structures. Nevertheless through a nurse facilitator, members of the group have been researching into their own 'lived experiences'. The items which they chose for a poster (see Figure 16.1) presented at a conference are the ones they want others to know about.

In this example the six researchers not only contributed to the research process, but controlled it and presented their findings to people with and without learning difficulties. At one level their approach is *emanicipatory* research, which ensures that the findings are not only a tool for improving the lives of the disabled but that the researchers themselves are accountable to others with learning difficulties (Zarb 1992).

How We Live

We are Trevor, Pauline, Brian, Jackie, Robert and Douglas. We live in a large town. We meet every week and we talk about things – anything we choose. Our conversation is recorded so that we don't forget what we have said. We have talked about all sorts of things so that we can tell you how we live.

We share our home, our bills and our cars. Some of us go to work, some go to college. Some of us go to day care or the women's group. We meet our friends often. We invite them to parties, barbecues, and take-aways. Our friends stay overnight. We visit friends. We follow the news and football. We do housework. We watch TV. We go bowling. We go swimming. We like the cinema and videos. We plan our holidays. We furnish our homes. We shop. We cook for ourselves and for our friends. We wash and iron our clothes. We have a door key. We put money in our savings account. We love our gardens. We choose our things.

Our nurses and staff assist us, they find out what we like. We like to exercise regularly. We like good food and healthy foods like fruit and vegetables. We like where we live. We don't like strict people who boss us around. We don't like to complain even if we can. We have our private thoughts. We live with people we like. We don't like living with people who upset us. When our friends die we go to their funerals, we miss them (from Richardson 2000).

Figure 16.1 The Poster

Facilitating research

At another level their research was made possible by a facilitator and therefore has a number of characteristics which are part of *participatory* research, whose principles Cocks and Cockram define as:

- a problem identified by disabled people, who together with non disabled researchers, bring it to the attention of the disabled;
- disabled people and researchers working together to achieve a collective analysis of the research problem;
- disabled people, researchers and other experts, form alliances which are 'under the control' of, and primarily in the interests of, disabled people. (Adapted from Cocks and Cockram 1995:32)

The facilitator wished to learn about what people with disabilities, who are living in the community with nursing support, have to say about their lives and experiences. The techniques employed to enable them and other relatively articulate people with learning difficulties to tell their own narratives depend upon research into interviewing techniques which are now being recognised and documented (Atkinson and Walmesley 1999). The facilitator is, in a sense an interpreter, who must be constantly aware that his or her perceptions and biases can influence the work. The following questions are ones which need to be constantly at the forefront of all interviews:

- Who initiated each aspect of the story?
- Who owns the story?
- How was the dialogue developed?
- What checks and balances were put into place to ensure that the interpretation was the one that the person with learning difficulties wished to present?

These questions relate to the way in which questions are framed, and the style of the facilitator. As Swain *et al.* (1998:26), point out, 'acceptance of participants as worthwhile, unique and valued beings seems an unquestionable principle', but what is ultimately reported often relies on the discretion and interpretation of the facilitator.

Some of the challenges

Open-ended questioning is a common technique used to encourage people with learning difficulties to express their opinions, but the statements recorded need to be constantly checked to ensure that meaning has not been altered and misinterpreted. The nurse facilitator, who supported Trevor, Pauline, Brian, Jackie, Robert and Douglas, constantly repeated (over a number of sessions) their exact phrases to them in order to ensure that the points he had 'heard' were correct. The status of the facilitator may encourage those with learning difficulties to express views which it is thought that he or she would want to hear. In this case the statements of the group could be linked to other evidence to ensure that members were not trying to please him. At all times leading questions were avoided, he regarded nothing as trivial, and took time to negotiate meanings.

Time (but in a very different sense to that of 'giving time') is one of the challenges that Booth and Booth (1996) recognise for the facilitator who is working with adults and children with more severe difficulties in learning, including limited language skills. Although the writers recognise that participatory research is time consuming, they also found that people and children whose skills, understanding and knowledge are at early stages of development (as Laurie's are) often confuse time sequences and settings. Therefore the ordering of their past, as Mabel was able to do, even if it is only the ordering of events which happened a few minutes ago, is not possible. More valuable is the discovery of the 'here and now' (i.e. what is meaningful and important at this point in time). Such meaningful events are likely to shift and change as the skills and views, of the child or adult, develop. The knowledge gained is not unquestionable, but it is respected and there is the possibility that it will have been raised to such a level that it forms the core of subsequent discoveries (Clark and Moss 2001).

It is likely that open-ended questioning is not possible when working with children like Laurie. In order to elicit a response he will need specific questions which allow him to produce his clear, but limited, non-verbal responses. His 'voice' is unique and therefore working with those with complex needs will require a different set of 'listening' skills.

Listening skills

Researchers working with very young children have developed a framework for listening, which has applications for work with children with complex needs (Clark and Moss 2001). The framework, called the Mosaic approach, has six elements:

- multi-method (recognises the different 'voices' or languages of children);
- participatory (treats children as experts and agents in their own lives);
- reflexive (includes children, practitioners and parents in reflecting on meanings and therefore attempts to obtain as true an interpretation as possible);
- adaptable (can be applied in a variety of situations);
- focused on children's 'lived experiences' (can be used for a variety of purposes including looking at lives being lived rather than on the knowledge gained by the person with learning difficulties or on the care he or she receives);
- embedded in practice (a framework for listening which has potential to be both used as an evaluative tool and to become embedded into practice) (adapted from Clark and Moss 2001:5).

The framework draws on the research on participatory rural appraisal which is used in development work to empower poor communities to have a 'voice' in the changes made in their own communities. The techniques do not rely on the written word and both the children, and the adults working with them, are regarded as co-constructors of meaning. The framework has two stages:

1. children and adults gather documentation
2. they piece together information for dialogue reflection and interpretation.

The two stages are interrelated and therefore the practical implications will be explored together.

Co-constructing meaning

Observation

Observation carried out by an adult is one of the key aspects of gathering information in the Mosaic approach. Clark and Moss (2001) point out, however, that observation only gives one perspective on children's lives, that of the observer, and must be checked out with other sources of information. Tilstone (1998), in discussing observation and children with learning difficulties, states that the personal theories of professionals on what children are experiencing are often built upon very little evidence and result in snapshots or 'implicit theories' of what the child likes to do or what life is like for him or her. There is, in her view, a need for 'explicit theorising' which employs systematic observation as a method of enquiry and heightens awareness, formulates ideas and tests beliefs and assumptions. Being systematic means using the snapshots (the implicit theories) as the starting point for gathering data leading to the collection of more substantial evidence, the testing of ideas and the search for better understanding. Gathering substantial evidence can be carried out through more in-depth observation to build up a strong impression of the likes, needs or wants of an adult or child with learning difficulties.

Observations of Laurie over a long period, for example, showed that he was particularly responsive to music: he would smile broadly, move his head towards the source of sound, and giggle when musical instruments were played. He pouted when a musical activity came to an end and refused to make eye contact. An observer could be fairly confident that he liked music and that it was an important activity in his life.

Such information gained can be discussed with adults and children with learning difficulties who have some verbal skills. The Mosaic approach regards child conferencing (i.e. talking to young children about what adults have observed using a variety of means) as an important part of participatory research. Lewis (1991) adopts the term *adult-child conferencing* to describe the reciprocal nature of a sharing procedure in which an adult and a pupil exchange information on the learning involved in a specific activity. Although not directly connected with life stories she provides some common sense, but easily overlooked, pointers on the setting up and implementation of conferences. Two are:

- conferences cannot be hurried and therefore adequate time needs to be set aside;
- tape recorders can be used to record the discussion and to provide a permanent record.

Co-constructing meaning through other methods

As with audio recording, video recording can also provide a permanent record of important data which can either be discussed in the conferences mentioned above, or the reactions of child and adults with limited skills noted when the recordings are played to them in order to further test the accuracy of the theories put forward.

McLarty and Gibson (2000) use video in a different way. Their work focuses on the value of video footage in emancipatory research with young people with complex needs who have not achieved a recognised method of communication at the end of their secondary education. The recordings capture individual modes of non-verbal communication in order to develop individual 'video dictionaries'. Such 'dictionaries' are designed to continue to encourage positive communication between those with learning difficulties, their carers and educators and the wider community.

> Fitton (1994) takes a related approach in compiling a 'care book' for her daughter Kathy who was a young adult with profound and multiple learning difficulties. The book was built upon detailed observations and recordings of indication of how she liked to spend her time and what made her happy and comfortable. Fitton attempted to 'speak' for her daughter and to enable others to interpret Kathy's needs more accurately. (Tilstone and Barry 1998)

Grove and Park (1996) use a similar approach in constructing 'life quilts' for people with severe and profound learning difficulties. Building on the ideas of the community tradition of quilting, a patchwork of important items and events is created using objects of reference, tangible reminders, symbols, pictures and sensory cues to create a visual picture. Working with children who are more cognitively able, the Mosaic approach recommends that children take their own photographs of events and important physical locations in order to 'map' their experiences (Clark and Moss 2001). Children as young as two or three years took photographs, or instructed adults to take photographs, of friends, favourite play equipment, hidden spaces, trees, key workers and furniture which all helped to 'map' their views of their preschool experiences. The children led tours of their environments which provided information on their local knowledge. Such 'transect' walks are used in Participatory Rural Appraisal to gather detailed information about an environment from the people who live there (Hart 1997). The tours in the Mosaic approach can be seen as a walking documentary controlled by the children.

Similar work was undertaken by Taylor (1998) in the production of personal history books of people with complex needs using information technology. Workbooks which chronicle a person's life history have also been developed by the National Association of Bereavement Services (NABS 1996). Initially produced to commemorate the life of a friend of a person with learning difficulties, with contributions from family friends and professionals, pictures, drawings or photographs were used to tell the life story of an individual with limited communication skills.

Sanderson *et al.* (1997) used a combination of Fitton's approach and that of NABS in their work on lifestyle planning in order to discover a person's desired lifestyle and preferences. Mortimer (2000a, 2000b), however, takes a more direct approach to participation with children who can follow a simple story. In her work on encouraging children to voice their opinions on their own assessment of their special educational needs, and on their transition into new educational settings, she encourages those with some communication skills to identify the challenges they present to professionals in order to build up a picture of themselves as individuals and to identify their likes and dislikes. Role play has also been used in a number of situations to encourage children to relate their own narratives, particularly in public law proceedings (Clark and Sinclair 1999).

Conclusions

People and young children with learning difficulties have much to tell us about their lives and are able and willing to take control of the research process. Many of the techniques described do not depend upon the ability to communicate through speech, but explore a range of innovations which allow children and adults with learning difficulties to express what is, or has been, important to them. Such ideas should be seen as a starting point for the exploration of flexible methods designed to allow a wide range of views to contribute to the research agenda.

References and further reading

Atkinson, D. and Cooper, M. (2000) 'Parallel lives', in Brigham, L. *et al.* (eds) *Crossing Boundaries: Change and Continuity in the History of Learning Difficulties.* Kidderminster: BILD.

Atkinson, D. and Walmsley, J. (1999) 'Using autobiographical approaches with people with learning difficulties', *Disability and Society* **14**(2), 203–16.

Atkinson, D., Jackson, M. and Walmsley, J. (eds) (1997) *Forgotten Lives: Exploring the History of Learning Disabilities.* Kidderminster: BILD.

Barnes, C. (1991) *Disabled People in Britain and Discrimination.* London: Hurst & Co.

Booth, T. and Booth, W. (1996) 'Sounds of silence: narrative research with inarticulate subjects', *Disability and Society* **11**(1), 55–69.

Clark, A. and Moss, P. (2001) *Listening to Young Children: The Mosaic Approach.* London: National Children's Bureau Enterprises.

Clark, A. and Sinclair, R. (1999) *The Child in Focus: the Evolving Role of the Guardian Ad Litem.* London: National Children's Bureau.

Cocks, E. and Cockram, J. (1995) 'The participatory research paradigm and intellectual disability', *Mental Handicap Research* **8**, 25–37.

Cooper, M. (1997) 'Mabel Cooper's life story', in Atkinson, D., Jackson, M. and Walmsley, J. (eds) *Forgotten Lives: Exploring the History of Learning Disabilities.* Kidderminster: BILD.

Cooper, M. (2000) 'My quest to find out', in Atkinson, D. *et al.* (eds) *Good Times; Bad Times: Women with Learning Difficulties Telling their Stories.* Kidderminster: BILD.

Department For Education (DFE) (WO) (1994) *Code of Practice on the Identification and Assessment of Special Educational Needs*. London: DFE.

Department for Education and Employment (2000) (DfEE) *SEN Code of Practice on the Identification and Assessment of Pupils with Special Educational Needs* (consultation document). London: DfEE.

Department for Education and Employment (DfEE) and Qualifcations and Curriculum Authority (QCA) (1999a) *The National Curriculum Handbook for Primary Teachers in England*. London: HMSO.

Department for Education and Employment (DfEE) and Qualifcations and Curriculum Authority (QCA) (1999b) *The National Curriculum Handbook for Secondary Teachers in England*. London: HMSO.

Fitton, P. (1994) *Listen to Me: Communicating the Needs of People with Profound Intellectual and Multiple Disabilities*. London: Jessica Kingsley.

Goodley, D. with Downer, J., Burke, P., Kershaw, J., Page, L. and Souza, A. (2000) 'Collecting the life stories of self-advocates: crossing the boundary between researcher and researched', in Brigham, L. *et al.* (eds) *Crossing Boundaries: Change and Continuity in the History of Learning Difficulties*. Kidderminster: BILD.

Grove, N. and Park, K. (1996) '"Life Quilts" for people with severe and profound learning difficulties: a venture into the unknown', *PMLD Link* **24**.

Hart, R. (1997) *Children's Participation*. London: UNICEF and Earthspan.

Hersov, J. (1996) 'The rise of self-advocacy in Britain', in Dybwad, G. and Bersanti Jr., H. (eds) *Self-advocacy by People with Disabilities*. Cambridge, MA: Brooks.

Jackson, M. (2000) 'Introduction', in Brigham, L. *et al.* (eds) *Crossing Boundaries: Change and Continuity in the History of Learning Difficulties*. Kidderminster: BILD.

Jones, K. (1972) *A History of the Mental Health Services*. London: Routledge and Kegan Paul.

Kitchin, R. (2000) 'The researched opinions on research: disabled people and disability research', *Disability and Society* **15**(1), 25–47.

Lewis, A. (1991) *Primary Special Needs and the National Curriculum*. London: Routledge.

McLarty, M. and Gibson, J. W. (2000) 'Using video techniques in emancipatory research', *European Journal of Special Needs Education* **15**(2), 138–48.

Mittler, P. (1996) 'Preparing for self-advocacy', in Carpenter, B., Ashdown, R. and Bovair, K. (eds) *Enabling Access: Effective Teaching and Learning for Pupils with Learning Difficulties*. London: David Fulton Publishers.

Morris, J. (1991) *Pride Against Prejudice*. London: The Women's Press.

Mortimer, H. (2000a) *Taking Part: Helping Young Children Take Part in a Statutory Assessment of their Special Educational Needs*. Lichfield: QEd Publications.

Mortimer, H. (2000b) *Starting Out*. Lichfield: QEd Publications.

National Association of Bereavement Services (NABS) (1996) *My Story: a Celebration of My Life*. London: NABS.

Oliver, M. (1990) *The Politics of Disablement*. Basingstoke: Macmillan.

Oliver, M. (1992) 'Changing the social relations of research production', *Disability Handicap and Society* 7, 101–14.

Oliver, M. (1996) *Understanding Disability: From Theory to Practice*. Basingstoke: Macmillan.

Pinder, R. (1995) 'Bringing back the body without the blame? The experience of ill and disabled people at work', *Sociology of Health and Illness* 17, 605–31.

Pinder, R. (1996) 'Sick-but-fit or fit-but-sick? Ambiguity and identity in the workplace', in Barnes, C. and Mercer, G. *Exploring the Divide: Illness and Disability*. Leeds: The Disability Press.

Pinder, R. (1997) 'A reply to Tom Shakespeare and Nicholas Watson', *Disability and Society* **12**(2), 301–5.

Richardson, M. (2000) 'How we live: participatory research with six people with learning difficulties'. Unpublished PhD thesis, The University of Sheffield.

Riding, R. and Rayner, S. (1998) *Cognitive Styles and Learning Strategies*. London: David Fulton Publishers.

Ryan, J. with Thomas, F. (1987) *The Politics of Mental Handicap*, revised edn. London: Free Association Books.

Sanderson, H. *et al.* (1997) *People, Plans and Possibilities – Exploring Person Centred Planning*. Edinburgh: Scottish Human Services Publications.

Shakespeare, T. (1996) 'Disability, identity and difference', in Barnes, C. and Mercer, G. (eds) *Exploring the Divide: Illness and Disability*. Leeds: The Disability Press.

Shakespeare, T. and Watson, N. (1997) 'Defending the social model', *Disability and Society* **12**(2), 293–300.

Shakespeare, T. and Watson, N. (1998) 'Theoretical perspectives on research with disabled children', in Robinson, R. and Stalker, K. (eds) *Growing Up With Disability*. London: Jessica Kingsley.

Swain, J., Heyman, B. and Gilman, M. (1998) 'Public research, private concerns: ethical issues in the use of open-ended interviews with people who have learning disabilities', *Disability and Society* **13**(1), 5–19.

Taylor, J. (1998) 'Technology for living and learning', in Lacey, P. and Ouvry, C. (eds) *People with Profound and Multiple Learning Difficulties: a Collaborative Approach to Meeting Complex Needs*. London: David Fulton Publishers.

Tilstone, C. (ed.) (1998) Observing Teaching and Learning: Principles and Practice. London David Fulton Publishers.

Tilstone, C. and Barry, C. (1998) 'Advocacy and empowerment: what does it mean for pupils and people with PMLD?', in Lacey, P. and Ouvry, C. (eds) *People with Profound and Multiple Learning Difficulties: A Collaborative Approach to Meeting Complex Needs*. London: David Fulton Publishers.

Tilstone, C. *et al.* (2000) *Pupils with Learning Difficulties in Mainstream Schools*. London: David Fulton Publishers.

Whittaker, A. (1996) 'The fight for self-advocacy', in Mittler, P. and Sinason, V. (eds) *Changing Policy and Practice for People with Learning Difficulties*. London: Cassell.

Zarb, G. (1992) 'On the road to Damascus; first steps towards changing the relationships of disability research production', *Disability Handicap and Society* 7, 125–38.

CHAPTER 17

Special needs and the educational researcher: moving ahead

Richard Rose and Ian Grosvenor

What is it that motivates teachers to conduct research? There are common factors in the research described within this book which can assist us in understanding why individuals and groups of teachers come together to undertake school based enquiry. Each of the chapters describes a journey followed by inquisitive teachers and researchers who set out in the hope that they might improve the lot of the teachers and pupils at the heart of their studies. They started from the premise that formalised investigation could increase their understanding of a phenomena, or provide insights into the ways in which a problem might be addressed. The research questions which inspired their studies were not significantly different from those which confront most teachers in their day to day management of classrooms and pupils. Perhaps the most significant difference between the writers in this book and many other teachers is that they were motivated to build an investigation around their areas of concern. This is not to suggest that other teachers are simply content to let such issues pass them by, but it may be symptomatic of the view which persists that research is within the domain of the 'academic', rather than an essential feature of the armoury of the class teacher.

In our opening chapter we argued that educational research should have a role in improving our understanding of processes, practices and organisations associated with teaching and learning. We further suggested that much research, particularly that which is small in scale, will not necessarily provide an answer to the wider issues researched, and that it may indeed raise new questions based upon the findings of the enquiry. For some critics of educational research the lack of concrete conclusions emanating from classroom research has been portrayed as a weakness. The notion of research as hypothesis generation has been devalued as so much academic navel gazing, the results of which have minimal impact upon classroom practice or the raising of educational standards. Speaking in the House of Lords on the issue of the future funding of educational research, Lord Skidelsky stated:

> I have had occasion to study professionally much of the research that has taken place and I have also had experiences in my own university. Many of the fruits of that research I would describe as uncontrolled growth of theory, an excessive

> emphasis on what is called the context in which teaching takes place, which is code for class, gender and ethnic issues, and an extreme paucity of testable hypotheses about what works and does not work. (Hansard 1993: Columns 882–883)

This negative view of the value of much educational research, in common with other opinions examined in Chapter 1 of this book, suggests that a research focus determined by classroom teachers and researchers who consider socio-political and economic issues, may be of less significance than that which endorses a current political agenda such as raising standards or promoting a specific teaching methodology. While we would concur with the notion that national educational priorities should provide the focus for large scale research which can inform policy, we would suggest that research conducted in a single school may have a significant impact upon practice within that institution. The research described in this book demonstrates how small scale projects can have a positive bearing upon the management of individuals or groups of pupils, and in bringing about change for the benefits of whole school communities. Such benefits should not be underestimated in their potential to change practice and increase understanding.

Clearly there are issues surrounding the dangers of generalisation of small scale research findings. The many variables which impact upon schools are such that it is seldom possible to take the findings of research from one establishment and apply these directly or without modification in another. Teachers reading research need to consider their own teaching situation and to interpret findings in relation to their own context. Yet this may be equally true of larger government funded research which leads to the implementation of national policy. Edwards (2000) recognises this dilemma when he writes:

> Generalising beyond the settings investigated depends on identifying necessary or favourable conditions for something to work elsewhere. But although this requires some consistency in relevant findings, 'the facts' are unlikely to point only in one direction. Sherlock Holmes' warning that 'the temptation to form premature theories upon insufficient evidence is the bane of our profession', can apply to researchers eager to get their findings noticed, but the temptation appears more often to afflict policy makers whose usual disregard of research is interrupted by drawing conveniently selective conclusions from what it has 'shown'. For example, an Ofsted report on *Setting in Primary Schools* (1999) attributed 'spectacular improvements' in mathematics to that form of pupil grouping. The evidence for the assertion was promptly described by the head of the National Numeracy Programme as 'flimsy and inconclusive', and the fact of improved standards as open to very different explanations. (Edwards 2000:302)

In raising this issue Edwards recognises a dilemma which has confronted teachers of pupils with special educational needs over many years. Educational policy and its ensuing procedures, such as the National Curriculum and National Literacy Strategy, have often been implemented with minimal consideration of how this may be accessed or adapted for pupils with special educational needs, leaving teachers to experiment, adapt and modify in order to provide pupils with their entitlement. It has, on occasions been small scale research which has considered issues of access to such requirements which has enabled pupils to participate in national programmes (Lewis 1999, Lingard 2000). Indeed, it may be argued that the term 'special educational needs' itself is problematic (Norwich 1996). Approaches and adaptations which have proved successful with one group of pupils, such as those described as having severe learning difficulties, may be less appropriate for teachers working with others who have, for example, autistic spectrum disorders. This alone provides justification for research, which concentrates its attention upon discrete populations or single schools.

Writing about research in the area of learning disabilities, Goodey (1999:40) suggests that 'like it or not, research is participation in social change and in mutual reflexive exploration'. He sees the relationship between research and power as one in need of careful management if we are to do justice to those whom we study. We must examine our motives for getting involved in research, and must exercise caution in representing those at the centre of our enquiries. In the case of pupils with special educational needs, some of whom may have difficulties in expressing their own opinions, the care which we exercise in both conducting and reporting research must be transparent, and open to scrutiny. Researchers in the field of special education, suggests Goodey, have a responsibility to help policy-makers to understand, trust and learn from the subjects of our research. This being the case, can we afford to leave such research to those whose contact with pupils with special educational needs may be at a distance? It is precisely because of their commitment to pupils with special educational needs that teachers are well placed to conduct research into the ways in which they learn. It is equally because as teachers of pupils with special needs we have become aware of how little we know that we should engage in such research in order to increase our understanding and knowledge.

Statements such as that made by Skidelsky display an arrogance in suggesting that issues such as class, gender and ethnicity should not be at the core of the educational research agenda, when in fact these may have a significant bearing upon the ability of pupils to access learning. Similarly, suggestions that the growth of theory has been perpetuated by researchers belies the fact that so much legislation which has influenced classroom practice has been introduced with very little foundation upon an empirical base. The role of the classroom researcher has in many instances been one of exploring the means by which pupils can be provided with access to learning within the context of poorly constructed legislation and ill thought out schemes. For the teacher of pupils with special educational needs, investigation of alternative teaching methodologies, exploration of adapted resources and reconfiguration of materials has become a feature of day to day classroom management. Discussions about what works in the classroom, with which pupils and using which approaches, have become part of everyday life for the teacher who is concerned to achieve success with pupils who face major challenges with learning. It is these same teachers who are, as Stenhouse (1981) suggested, surrounded by rich opportunities to conduct classroom based research.

Unless teachers of pupils with special educational needs become more actively engaged with a culture of research, policy will continue to be developed upon the basis of ill formed theory and be implemented by those who have an inadequate understanding of the specific needs of pupils. It is critical that teachers become more active in developing an enquiry based profession, and equally necessary that those colleagues working in higher education who may have developed an expertise in conducting research develop a partnership with classroom based practitioners. Only through such collaboration will we gain a clearer understanding of how the needs of all pupils may be more effectively addressed.

What are the issues in need of enquiry?

The identification of priorities for small scale classroom based research must remain the prerogative of the teacher. Effective research will continue to be dependent upon teachers identifying key questions and working with colleagues to develop the appropriate approaches for their investigation. However, it is possible to identify within the debates which are current within education a number of issues which may provide a focus for immediate enquiry. Wedell (1985:23) identified six priority areas for special education research, each of which has received some attention in the intervening years. His six areas of need were described as:

1. The evaluation of intervention approaches.
2. The methodology for evaluating intervention.
3. Within the area of descriptive research, emphasis should be placed on the study of functional impairment rather than diagnostic categories of children with special needs.
4. The process of innovation.
5. The methods of disseminating research information.
6. The preparation of critical summaries of existing relevant research, particularly in areas which extend across disciplines.

Each of these six areas remains in need of the consideration of the researcher, and indeed some have been discussed within this book. Inevitably, as education continues to move on apace, other priorities have surfaced and are now demanding the attentions of the special needs researcher.

The 1990s saw an expansion in the use of a range of teaching approaches and methods designed specifically to address the needs of identified groups of pupils. Some of these approaches such as those designed to meet the needs of pupils with autistic spectrum disorders, multi-sensory impairments, profound and multiple learning difficulties or challenging behaviours have been criticised for perpetuating deficit models and for a lack of an empirical foundation upon which to justify their application. Teachers will often provide anecdotal evidence with regards to the efficacy of particular approaches, either applauding their successes or lamenting the failure of a system to meet the needs of the pupils in their class. In talking to such teachers it is often apparent that a specific approach may work in one class but not in another, or with a particular individual pupil while failing with others. The numbers of variables in special education and among a population described as having special educational needs is considerable, and this in itself presents a challenge to the researcher.

It is certainly true to say that many of the approaches which have been adopted specifically to address the special needs of pupils which are in common use in today's classrooms are being implemented upon the basis of a woefully inadequate research base. There is an urgent need for teachers to provide a more critical review of the value of these approaches, to ask when they work? who with? and why? Such questions will only be answered through systematic research which identifies critical issues, establishes a detailed evidence base and maintains records which can be evaluated by other colleagues. In order to achieve this, however, it is necessary to ensure that teachers are encouraged to connect with the established research community. Those with experience in research must take steps to involve teacher colleagues at all stages of the research process. Teachers working with pupils with special educational needs will be able to identify issues which demand enquiry and may well be able to provide direction for the researcher. The researcher in turn should be able to work in collaboration with teachers in order to develop a project which has both sound methodology and the assurance of an ethical framework. The DfEE in recognising the value of such partnerships has instigated its 'best practice' research programme which has encouraged teachers and researchers to form an alliance in developing school focused research projects. However, it should not be assumed that such partnerships will be achieved without a shift of attitudes on the parts of both researchers and teachers, and without the encouragement of policy-makers at both national and local level. Gore (1995) has urged all parties with a vested interest in education to appreciate the differing talents and skills which they can bring to research. In particular she places an emphasis upon the democratic imperative within the term partnership, stressing that projects must be 'owned' and accessible to every member of the team. This theme is developed further by Grundy (1998) who recognises that there are cultural and structural impediments to partnership which result from the differing pressures upon, for instance, schools and universities, differing perceptions of role between teachers and researchers and probably different priorities in terms of the ways that classrooms are viewed and interpreted. Clearly the achievement of research partnerships will not be easy and will demand that each member of such a group spends time understanding the perspectives and opinions of the others in a research team. Grundy makes the important observation that the differences between research partners can be as much a strength as an impediment. Opportunities to share and debate differing perspectives can sharpen the framing of research questions and enable members of a team to learn from each other. She also suggests that this will only be achieved when we start to develop research communities where teachers and researchers come together regularly and build a basis of trust, rather than relying upon progress through one-off projects.

When considering the research agenda, attention might well be afforded to those strategies recently introduced to schools to address standards in literacy and numeracy. The special education press has included a number of papers which have discussed implementation with pupils with special educational needs (Dehany 2000, Adhami 2001), but as yet there is little by the way of critical analysis to either demonstrate the impact of the strategies upon specific groups of pupils, or to demonstrate the effectiveness of adaptations put in place to assist teachers in addressing these pupils. Teachers are at the centre of these initiatives and provide the best opportunities for the development of systematic enquiry. It is unlikely that a true picture of the impact of these strategies will emerge in the short term, and it will again be necessary to examine them within the context of other changes within schools. The very fact that teachers are finding it necessary to make adaptations to the numeracy and literacy strategy in order to provide access for pupils with special educational needs (Byers 1999, Pietrowski and Reason 2000) suggests that there is a need to research the effectiveness of such changes as are being made, and to evaluate the overall efficacy of the strategies as presented.

Of all the issues confronting education today it is that of inclusion which is leading to the most heated of debates. Much of the discussion of inclusion has been based upon theoretical models whose roots lie within socio-political and humanistic philosophy. Such discourse has served a valuable purpose in focusing attention upon the rights of all pupils, including those with special educational needs. In recent years there has been a call to move the inclusion debate forward upon the basis of a more critical analysis of what works in the classroom. Dyson (1999) in a thoughtful appraisal of the current debate has called for a move away from a concentration upon ethics and rights, and to focus efforts upon an understanding of the efficacy of inclusive practice. Hornby (1999) in questioning our understanding of the processes of inclusion urges us to undertake a more detailed analysis of the benefits of inclusion and the challenges which may confront its achievement. Both of these writers are putting forward an agenda, which if left to administrators and theorists, may result in policy which becomes at best ineffective, and at worst unmanageable in the classroom. Teachers are at the centre of this debate, and are furthermore the professionals who will be charged with the implementation of policy resulting from the deliberations surrounding inclusion. Here again is an ideal opportunity for classroom based enquiry into the approaches which are currently being deployed to meet special needs in a variety of contexts.

Wilson (2000:298) in a scathing attack upon what he has described as a largely vacuous and mistaken proposition for the development of inclusive schools believes that because of the many variables which will inevitably impact upon study in this area it will be extremely difficult to construct valid research. He does, however, suggest that empirical on-the-ground study may provide some evidence with regards to the efficacy of specific kinds of inclusion and may provide a more informed discussion about beneficial or non-beneficial practices. The establishment of the type of empirical base which Wilson is seeking will demand research which has direct access to schools and a methodology which can address the many variables which will almost certainly be present. The current demand for greater inclusion is such that the importance of research to inform policy and practice must not be ignored.

The suggestions provided here identify only a few of the potential areas in need of further systematic investigation. Teachers working in special education have always shown themselves to be both innovatory and reflective with regards to their own practice. To apply these attributes further in the development of research skills which will further inform and advance the education of all pupils, including those with special educational needs, remains as a challenge for both teachers and those who have traditionally worked within spheres of research. In moving forward in our understanding of how best to address the needs of all pupils we must resist the temptation to simply adopt the latest theories and ideas until such time as we have put these to the test through a systematic and well founded process of enquiry.

At the outset of this book we suggested that while some of the criticisms of educational research may be justified the remedy to identified problems lies in a realignment of the research agenda and greater ownership by a partnership of teachers and researchers. We further commented that research independence was an essential factor in encouraging debate and improving our understanding of influences upon teaching and learning. Throughout the process of compiling this book we have been heartened by the willingness of teachers to engage in discourse based upon a desire to understand and use research to promote improvements in practice. Research is essentially about knowledge, understanding and learning and essentially it must therefore be at the core of educational activity. As Isaiah Berlin reminds us:

> The goals and motives that guide human action must be looked at in the light of all that we know and understand, their roots and growth, their essence and above all their validity, must be critically examined with every intellectual resource that we have. (Berlin 1998:2)

End note

In editing this book we have been privileged to work alongside teachers and researchers from many schools, universities and other institutions. We have gained much from this dialogue and hope that others may wish to make contact with us to contribute to the continuing debate and discussion of teacher research in special education.

References and further reading

Adhami, M. (2001) 'Responsive questioning in a mixed ability group', *Support for Learning* **16**(1), 28–34.

Berlin, I. (1998) 'The pursuit of the ideal', in Berlin, I. *The Proper Study of Mankind*. London: Pimlico.

Byers, R. (1999) 'The National Literacy Strategy and pupils with special educational needs', *British Journal of Special Education* **26**(1), 8–11.

Dehany, R. (2000) 'Literacy hour and the literal thinker: the inclusion of children with semantic-pragmatic language difficulties in the literacy hour', *Support for Learning* **15**(1), 36–40.

Dyson, A. (1999) 'Inclusion or inclusions: theories and discourses in inclusive education', in Daniels, H. and Garner, P. (eds) *World Yearbook of Education: Inclusive Education*. London: Kogan Page.

Edwards, T. (2000) '"All the evidence shows...": reasonable expectations of educational research', *Oxford Review of Education* **26**(3 and 4), 300–11.

Goodey, C. (1999) 'Learning disabilities: the researcher's voyage to planet Earth', in Hood, S., Mayall, B. and Oliver, S. (eds) *Critical Issues in Social Research*. Buckingham: Open University Press.

Gore, J. (1995) *Emerging Issues in Teacher Education*. Perth, Western Australia: Murdoch University.

Grundy, S. (1998) 'Research partnerships: principles and possibilities', in Atweh, B., Kemmis, S. and Weeks, P. (eds) *Action Research in Practice*. London: Routledge.

Hansard (1993) Columns 882–883, 7 December, Speech in House of Lords – Lord Skidelsky. London: HMSO.

Hornby, G. (1999) 'Inclusion or delusion: can one size fit all?', *Support for Learning* **14**(4), 152–7.

Lewis, J. (1999) 'Teacher research and literacy support', *Support for Learning* **14**(3), 135–43.

Lingard, T. (2000) 'Is the National Literacy Strategy raising the achievement of lower attainers?' *British Journal of Special Education* **27**(3), 117–23.

Moore, M., Beazley, S. and Maelzer, J. (1998) *Researching Disability Issues*. Buckingham: Open University Press.

Norwich, B. (1996) 'Special needs education or education for all? Connective specialisation and ideological impurity', *British Journal of Special Education* **23**(3), 100–104.

Pietrowski, J. and Reason, R. (2000) 'The National Literacy Strategy and dyslexia: a comparison of teaching methods and materials', *Support for Learning* **15**(2), 51–7.

Stenhouse, L. (1981) 'What counts as research?', *British Journal of Educational Studies* **29**(2), 103–14.

Wedell, K. (1985) 'Future directions for research on children's educational needs', *British Journal of Special Education* **12**(1), 22–6.

Wilson, J. (2000) 'Doing justice to inclusion', *European Journal of Special Needs Education* **15**(3), 297–304.

Author index

Subject index